AESCHYLUS

THE COMPLETE PLAYS
VOLUME II

FOUR PLAYS

AESCHYLUS

THE COMPLETE PLAYS
VOLUME II

FOUR PLAYS

PERSIANS
SEVEN AGAINST THEBES
SUPPLIANTS
PROMETHEUS BOUND

Translated by Carl R. Mueller
Preface by Hugh Denard

GREAT TRANSLATIONS SERIES

A Smith and Kraus Book

A Smith and Kraus Book
Published by Smith and Kraus, Inc.
177 Lyme Road, Hanover, NH 03755
www.smithkraus.com

First Edition: November 2002
10 9 8 7 6 5 4 3 2 1
Manufactured in the United States of America

Cover and Text Design by Julia Hill Gignoux, Freedom Hill Design
Cover art: The Battle of Gods and Giants. North frieze of the Siphnian
Treasure House. c. 525 B.C.E. Delphi Museum, Delphi.

The Library of Congress Cataloging-In-Publication Data
Aeschylus
[Works. English. 2002]
Aeschylus : the complete plays / translated by Carl R. Mueller ; preface by Hugh
Denard. —1st ed.
p. cm. — (Great translations series)
Includes bibliographical references.
ISBN 1-57525-312-7 (v.1) — ISBN 1-57525-313-5 (v.2)
1. Aeschylus—Translations into English. 2. Mythology, Greek —Drama. I.
Mueller, Carl Richard. II. Title. III. Great translations for actors series.
PA3827.A2 M84 2002
882'.01—dc21
2002070807

In Memory of
JAN KOTT
1914 – 2001

CONTENTS

PREFACE

The Tragedy of Others

By Hugh Denard

What you are about to read are the first surviving plays in the Western tradition. As I write, the earliest of them, the *Persians*, is approaching its two-thousand-five-hundredth birthday. Their age might lead us to expect them to seem rather "simple" or naïve, but nothing could be further from the truth. These plays were produced within one of the most sophisticated and creative cultures that the world has yet seen, and by one of its greatest playwrights. The *Persians* was written over sixty years after a prize for tragedy was first awarded in Athens, and we can probably assume that tragedy had been a vibrant part of Athenian culture for quite some time before the prize ceremony was invented. This means that the tragedies translated here emanated from a highly developed theatrical tradition. It was a tradition characterized by innovation; by the time of Aeschylus, tragic form was strong and supple enough to allow itself continually to be reinvented as technological, philosophical, ideological, and economic transformations rippled through Athens in the course of the fifth century B.C.E.

These political and cultural revolutions in Athens laid the foundation for many aspects of how we think about, represent, and structure our world today. But we should not underestimate the vastness of the temporal distance separating us from Aeschylus and Athens. Immense imaginative energy is required on our part to translate these bare ink marks on the page into vivid, spectacular, formalized, theatrical performances of music, poetry, and dance. Greek tragedy traces its roots back to communal rituals of worship grounded in sacrifice, hymn, and dance. Like other overtly conventional art forms such as opera and ballet, tragedy was designed to liberate, rather than act as a pallid substitute for, the audience's creative and critical faculties. If we read these plays as if they were crude attempts at naturalistic drama we are going to be frustrated, disappointed, and probably bored.

Genre is not the only marker of difference that lies between us and antiquity. It takes considerable time and effort to wrest from the traces of the past some sense of the shape of Athenian society—the belief systems and cultural practices that circulated within it; the political, legal, military, and competitive structures through which it shaped itself; and the historical moment out of which these plays emerged. So widely do ancient and modern societies diverge that when we read these plays we can be confident that our initial, intuitive interpretation of what they are "about" and what they "mean" will fall far wide of the mark. The more persuaded we are by our "gut feeling," the more likely it is that this feeling corresponds to some need or desire of our own, rather than to a connection that closer, historically informed examination will bear out. (Often this takes the form of a romantic desire, rooted in deeper cultural needs, to find that the Greeks are "just like us after all.") In short, the attempt to read these plays is fraught with difficulty.

This is perhaps their greatest gift to us. When meaning is deferred by strangeness, we are challenged to reconsider the way in which we make sense of the world. These translations by Carl Mueller, dramatic analogues for the ancient plays, evoke something of the vitality and immediacy of the Greek dramas. Critically, and greatly to their credit, they do not attempt to eradicate the difficulty that they present to modern readers.

For different reasons, tragedy was also difficult for the Athenians: Its difficulty was inseparable from theatre's role as an extension of the state. Tragedy's (ideal) spectators were the citizens of Athens—that is to say, the adult, freeborn males who directly voted in assembly or juries on every major decision taken by the city-state. (The "representational democracies" of the West today are pale shadows of the executive power held by the humblest Athenian citizen, although we have at least succeeded in widening the suffrage base somewhat.) Tragedy was one of the means through which Athenian citizens acquired the capacity and desire to reflect critically upon the world around them and their own roles within it. Tragedy was required to weld the disparate interests and understandings of a dispersed populace into a single, cohesive citizen body capable of understanding the implications of the decisions that lay before it, and of taking responsibility for exercising power. Tragedy offered its spectators exemplary conflicts that brought into sharp relief issues of importance to the citizen body before it.

The spectators were shaken and stirred by some of the dramas, although they had to be disciplined by "beaters" into paying attention to others. Elements in a production, such as the expression of pro-Athenian sentiment, or innovative staging techniques, might contribute to the play's success as a contribution to the great festival celebrations of Athens. But the popularity and success of a tetralogy (three tragedies and a satyr play) was judged in quite different terms to those that would apply to most theatrical productions today. The spectators' criteria for evaluating the theatrical experience did not include how "entertaining" it was, in any modern use of the term, but rather whether it was a sufficiently lavish and excellent production to be worthy of the festival and its patron god, Dionysos; whether it offered acceptable and useful wisdom to the city; or whether it exercised a strong emotional effect upon the spectators. Tragedy subjected ideas and beliefs to the test of communal response; the spectators' collective expressions of approval and disapproval during performances were a core part of the meaning of the tragedies. Voting with their hisses, applause, derisive laughter, tears, cries, and silence, the city used the theatrical event to construct a consensus of values among its citizens. The playwright was a teacher—a city sage.

If this ancient drama is another world to us, it was also a drama of "Others" to the Athenians. Whereas the public life of the city was exclusively concerned with the voicing of Athenian citizens' interests, tragedy symbolically gave voice to those normally excluded from formal, public utterance: women, slaves, children, non-Greek and non-Athenians. I say "symbolically" because these marginalized, conquered, oppressed figures were exclusively the theatrical and rhetorical creations of male, citizen playwrights and performers. We can be sure that these representations of Others had much less to do with the reality of being a female, slave, child, or foreigner to Greece or Athens, than with serving the interests of Athenian citizens (the fictionalized homecoming of Xerxês in *Persians* is a case in point). We can also be sure that primary among those interests would have been the need to reaffirm the marginal or subordinate position of these Others. Control over how non-citizens were represented to the city was itself the fundamental means through which citizen superiority was symbolically reproduced.

These dramatic representations of Others contributed to the "self-fashioning" of Athenian citizens in two apparently contradictory ways. On the one hand, the Other presented to the citizen spectator an image of all that he was not (to be)—i.e., Athenian men were enabled more clearly to define themselves by setting themselves *in opposition to* the Other. If, for instance, the Persian courtiers in the *Persians* are effete and slavish, the implication is that Athenian citizens are "manly" and slaves to no man. Yet, the plays also invited their spectators imaginatively to participate in the predicament of the besieged, suppliant, and enslaved Other. Just eight years after the Persian army had sacked the Akropolis and made widows of Athenian wives, Aeschylus invited his Athenian spectators to imagine the suffering of their enemies in terms that do not always invite jubilation: "And marriage-beds, / empty of lusty men, / are wet with the tears of gentle Persian girls, / each grieving softly for her mate, / the warrior mate she joyfully sped on his way, / grieving with aching love and desire for her man." If the emotional impact of tragedy depended upon its spectators' readiness to sympathize with the Others that it represented, in this case, the citizen spectator enlarged his mastery of the world by extending his capacity to imagine reality from other perspectives—i.e., to redefine himself *by identifying with* the Other.

Acting, too, was a citizen duty that involved turning oneself into a sign of Otherness. Many of the spectators would have performed in the dramatic festivals at some time, and most would have known some of the performers. Comic playwrights in Athens parodied the sympathetic association between citizen and Other that tragedy induces: in Aristophanes' *Thesmophoriazusae*, the tragedian Agathon is displayed costumed as a tragic heroine whose part he is composing. The importance to the Greek sense of theatre of an affective association between character and citizen was so strong that Plato concluded that by acting or watching the roles of bad characters, citizens might become like them in real life.[1]

Whether by opposition or identification, tragedy enabled its citizen spectators to see themselves in the light of the Other. But more importantly, by revealing identity as something that could be constituted, even symbolically, by signs, tragedy revealed to its spectators that they could also invent and reinvent themselves: a potent message for a sovereign city seeking to control its own destiny.

The Athenian citizen's imaginative engagement with Others—this disruptive, generative dialectic of association and differentiation—also offers a possible paradigm for our own encounter with Greek tragedy. To the contemporary West, tragedy is at once Other and Own, past and present, familiar and strange, connected and disconnected. We can situate our own responses to Greek tragedy between the counterpoised forces of association and estrangement in a way that is reminiscent of Athenian self-definition through tragic Others. But before we allow this resemblance to envelop us in a dream of "authentic" connection with the past, tragedy's fictionalization of Others reminds us that our readings of tragedy are also overwhelmingly conditioned by our own needs and desires. It is by preserving this sense of ourselves as creators of meaning that we acquire the capacity to remold ourselves through Greek tragedy. Encountering tragedy as Other may also permit us to see ourselves and the world that we inhabit as Other, and to pit those disruptive perceptions against the ready-made meanings through which everyday life strives to inoculate us against consciousness.

Hugh Denard
School of Theatre Studies
University of Warwick
Coventry, United Kingdom

---

[1] In more recent times, during his incarceration by the Apartheid regime in South Africa, Nelson Mandela played the role of the tyrant, Kreon, in a prison production of Sophokles' *Antigone*. President Mandela later recounted how this experience gave him insights into the perspective of white South Africans upon which he later drew in the negotiations that finally led to the fall of Apartheid and to the introduction of democratic elections.

Aeschylus and the Athenian Theater of His Time

I

Aeschylus was born most likely in 525 B.C.E. and died in the year 456. Although we are not certain, his birthplace was probably Eleusis, up the coast of Greece, not far from Athens, the same Eleusis that was the seat of the Eleusinian Mysteries, making it one of Attica's most sacred spots and Athens' most famous deme. We also know that Aeschylus was born of an aristocratic family and that at the age of forty-five he fought in one of the decisive battles of the Persian Wars, the Battle of Marathon, in 490—that conflict between the Athenians and the Persians. In 480 he either fought in or was an eyewitness to the final defeat of Persia at Salamis, an island off the western coast of Attica. His description of that battle in *Persians* is the only firsthand account that survives of the historical event that freed the Athenian state to pursue its own agenda and become one of the cultural pinnacles in the history of Western civilization.

Aeschylus' first tragic production was in 499, and his first victory with a tragedy came in 484. Thereafter it is not unlikely that he was almost always victorious in the tragic competition at the City (or Great) Dionysia, the annual Athenian religious festival that centered around the presentation of tragedy and eventually comedy, as well as other musical and choreographic events. In any case, he won a total of thirteen first prizes. His first extant play, *Persians,* was written in 472 and enjoyed so great a success that he was invited to restage it in Syracuse at the invitation of the Sicilian dynast Hieron, and also to write for him his *Women of Aitna* in celebration of the founding of that city. *Seven Against Thebes,* Aeschylus' second extant play, was first produced in Athens in 467 and was followed in 463 by the Danaïd-tetralogy of which the extant *Suppliants* is a part and which won first prize over Sophokles. Aeschylus' final production during his lifetime, *Oresteia,* was first produced at Athens in 458, a tetralogy with which he honored his beloved Athens and its bold experiment in democracy. This behind him, he again visited Sicily, where he died at Gela in 456. It will likely never be known, but it's possible that it was in Sicily that he wrote *Promêtheus Bound,* the play that was produced posthumously by his son Euphorion.

The extent of Aeschylus' work is not certain, but it is likely to have been somewhere between seventy and ninety plays. The seven that have survived the twenty-five-hundred years since their creation come to us not as originals but in the form of medieval copies. We do know, however, that a good number of his productions were tetralogies, three tragedies united by a single theme and followed by a satyr play that dealt comically with the same material. Just how many such tetralogies he composed is unknown, though there is certainty regarding at least four: the *Oresteia,* the Theban-tetralogy, the Danaïd-tetralogy, and *Lycurgia.* Only *Oresteia* survives, though only as a trilogy (the satyr play having been lost), and one play each from the Theban and Danaïd tetralogies, with none from *Lycurgia.* But it is also possible to reconstruct from the names of the plays that have been lost at least seven additional tetralogies.

The *Vita,* the ancient source that records the life of Aeschylus, notes that his epitaph makes no mention of his art, but—as Sommerstein notes in *The Oxford Classical Dictionary*—refers "only to his prowess displayed at Marathon; this estimate of what was most important in Aeschylus' life—to have been a loyal and courageous citizen of a free Athens—can hardly be that of the Geloans and will reflect his own death-bed wishes . . . or those of his family."

II

One of the fascinating questions in regard to Aeschylus and his work is what was his theater like? The fact is we know virtually nothing about it, as little as we know about the origin of Athenian tragedy. What we do know is that the first performances of Athenian tragedy in the mid-sixth century took place in the Agora, the Athenian marketplace—a place of general assembly—and that spectators sat on wooden bleachers. Then, around 500, the theatrical performance site was moved to the Sacred Precinct of Dionysos on the south side of the Akropolis. At first spectators may have sat on the natural slope of the hill to watch the performance, an arrangement most likely superceded by wooden bleachers introduced for greater audience comfort—but even this is guesswork, logical as it sounds. From here (or perhaps even before we arrive here) the general public image of the Athenian Theater of Dionysos makes a great and very wrongheaded leap some one hundred and fifty years into the future to the middle of the fourth century and the most esthetically harmonious of all Greek theaters, that at Epidauros. There we have a stone skênê building to serve as backing for the action, a building with from one to three doors and fronted by a line of pillars, the proskênion; possibly there is a second story to the skênê building and a logeion—the skênê's roof for the appearance of gods and even mortals. We then perhaps see a raised terrace or low stage area in front of the skênê where some if not most of the action takes place. Then, in front of all that, the most crucial element of all, a perfectly round and very large orchestra made of pounded earth and circled in stone. And, not least, the vast reaches of a stone auditorium, in Greek the theatron. Certain as that structure may still be at Epidauros, it has no precedent in Athens until the 330s when stoa, skênê, and auditorium were finally finished in stone. There is evidence, however, that the oldest stone skênê in Athens dates from sometime between 421 and 415. We know that for some years prior to that the skênê was made of wood, torn down at the end of each festival and rebuilt (perhaps newly designed) the next year. Just when, however, that wooden skênê was first introduced is a mystery that may never find an answer, if for no other reason than the fragility of such a structure and/or the fact that it was regularly demolished at the close of each festival.

About the only thing that is certain in all this speculation is that the earliest extant plays of the Athenian Theater of Dionysos are those of Aeschylus and that they require no skênê building, suggesting that none existed. The earliest play, *Persians,* in 472, requires only a raised mound to serve as the grave or tomb of Dareios, whereas *Seven Against Thebes* needs only a representation of statues and altars of gods, and *Suppliants* requires much the same, except in place of statues of gods are symbolic representations of them. It is frequently believed that a raised area was required for *Suppliants,* an area that would serve as a place of sanctuary on which the symbols were placed and to which the Chorus retired for safety. This, however, is dubious inasmuch as the Chorus could not with any great facility perform its choreographed dance on such a platform, and therefore we are left again with a large playing area on a single level as the most logical possibility. It is not until *Oresteia* in 458 that an extant play of Aeschylus calls for a skênê with at least one and perhaps more doors, and in front of that skênê it is possible that there was a raised acting area, perhaps the first. But it is only in the late fifth and early fourth centuries that there is evidence in the form of vase paintings of a low, raised platform for the performance of tragedy, a platform raised about a meter (roughly forty inches) and mounted via a flight of steps in the center, steps suggesting that action was not confined to the platform but spilled out into the orchestra. This, of course, still tells us nothing about the positioning of theatrical action in the earlier period from the late sixth to well into the fifth century, nor is it conclusive evidence that such a raised level actually existed in Athens in the fifth century. Nothing short of archeological evidence could do that, and of that there is none. From a purely practical standpoint it must be asked what if anything would have been served by such a raised level, especially considering that the action of the play was looked down upon by a steeply raked auditorium of spectators, and that even the first row of seats, the thrones for priests and dignitaries, was itself raised above the ground-level playing area.

But there is another issue involved here that goes well beyond a question of sight lines, and that is the nature of Aeschylus' plays. They don't lend themselves to a separation between character and chorus, for the simple reason that it is precisely the relationship between them that is at the heart of the plays—they are inextricably bound up. Eteoklês in *Seven Against Thebes* is who and what he is by virtue of his relationship with the people of his polis, his city; it is how they treat each other that determines the sort of hero that Eteoklês is, and that relationship has inevitably to be at close quarters. To see Eteoklês on a raised platform speaking like any orator to the city, or castigating the chorus from there, is unheard of if one has any real understanding of the nature of Aeschylus' play. The same is true of Klytaimnêstra and Agamemnon in *Oresteia*. For Agamemnon to enter at ground level and confront Klytaimnêstra situated an entire meter above him on a platform is to say in semiotic terms that Klytaimnêstra needs elevation to register (maintain, generate) power: It weakens rather than strengthens her. Let them meet at ground level and our sight tells us without recourse to words that they are equals and that Klytaimnêstra knows it even if Agamemnon doesn't. Tigers don't stalk their prey from a distance.

It is also not known what the original shape of the early Athenian orchestra might have been, that area where the Chorus sang and danced elaborate choreographies. There are examples of smaller, outlying Attic theaters of the later fifth century, whose orchestras were other than circular. Both Thorikos and Trachones had tiny provincial deme-theaters in which the audience was seated on wooden benches in a rectangular arrangement in close proximity to the acting area, which, as well, may have been loosely rectangular, or, even more likely, trapezoidal, with only two sides being parallel. It is possible that the early shape of the theater at Athens was the same, with the exception that it would have been on a much grander scale. Where does all this lead? Not much of anywhere except more speculation. Some scholars maintain, for example, that there is no evidence for a circular orchestra in Athens before the 330s, whereas others argue that the choreography performed by the Chorus required a circular area and thus there must have been one from the start. Who knows?

III

There are several conventions of classical Athenian tragedy that must be considered, namely masks, the chorus, music, and dance.

Whatever the layout of the early Athenian Theater of Dionysos, it is a fair guess that in order to accommodate the numbers of male citizens of that thriving metropolis and many from its outlying demes, not to mention important foreign visitors, the structure could not have been less than sizable. Size brought with it distance from the theatrical event as the eventual auditorium at Athens in the 330s still demonstrates, rising as it does to touch the fortified walls of the Akropolis some hundreds of feet away. The capacity of the theater has been judged to be somewhere between fifteen and twenty thousand.

Whether distance served as an incentive to the use of masks (some have speculated that they served as a megaphone to project the voice to the farthest rows) is not known, nor is it the most salient reason for the use of the mask, for there are others. There is ample evidence, for example, that in Greece the use of the mask in cult ceremonies was widespread. Adolescent rites of passage, puberty rites, known from Sparta, made use of masks of considerable grotesqueness; and the cult of Dêmêtêr and Dêspoina at Lycosura is known for its use of animal masks. Then, of course, there is the mask used closer to home, in the cult of Dionysos, from which the mask in Greek tragedy most likely derives. Whether amplification had any part in the use of masks on the Athenian stage, they at least gave a greater presence to the actor wearing one, for they were large enough to cover the entire head. Made generally of linen, the fifth-century mask represented types rather than individuals. Perhaps the most compelling reason for them is the need for two and later three actors to act out all of the speaking roles.

The rationale might also have been one of economy. Considering that tragedy was a masked entertainment, it was only practical to confine the number of speaking parts in any one scene to three actors, the reason most likely being, as Easterling suggests, to enable the audience to tell "where the voice is coming from," inasmuch as facial movements were obscured by masks. This practical limitation, however, permitted an actor to be double- and perhaps even triple-cast, a practice much used and most often, one must assume, to very good effect. In any case, even though the primary reason for only three actors was very likely a financial consideration, to have a single actor play, for example, the roles of Klytaimnêstra, Êlektra, and Athêna in *Oresteia;* or, in the same play, the roles of Agamemnon and Orestês; or in Euripides' *Bakkhai* Pentheus and his mother Agavê, and in Sophokles' *Women of Trachis* the roles of Dêianeira and Heraklês—each of which possibilities offers resonances that are far-reaching and highly intriguing. One must also not forget that masks were helpful in disguising the male actor who traditionally assumed female roles, women being excluded from theatrical performance. As for the numbers of non-speaking actors on stage there was no limit and exciting stage effects with scores of "extras" would not have been unusual.

IV

Of all the elements of theatrical practice the importance of the Chorus cannot be overestimated. In Athens especially there was a long tradition (even before tragedy) of and emphasis on the competition of dithyramb choruses that consisted of both song and dance. Even in the days of tragedy, there were separate competitions devoted to the dithyramb in which each of the ten demes of Athens participated. In Aeschylus' day the tragic Chorus numbered twelve, then Sophokles added three more for a total of fifteen. In his *Tragedy in Athens* David Wiles gives a brilliant and convincing exposition of the degree to which the tragic Chorus participated in the theatrical event. He posits (with help from other scholars) that not only was the choreographed movement of the Chorus not in straight lines or highly formalized, as previously thought, but that it was often particularly active. When, for example, the Chorus of Young Theban Women in *Seven Against Thebes* makes its first entrance, it is anything but sedate, it is disordered in the extreme (choreographed disorder, to be sure), but their terror of the encroaching war outside their city gates is such that it prompts the agitated reentry of Eteoklês who deals harshly with them for their civic disturbance. In Sophokles' *Oedipus at Kolonos* there is a similar entry by the Chorus of Old Men who dart wildly about the orchestra in search of the intruder into the Sacred Grove.

Wiles makes a most insightful deduction when he posits that the subject of each choral ode is acted out by the Chorus in choreographed dance. Even more startling, that during long narrative speeches, such as the Persian Herald's speech in *Persians,* in which he describes the defeat of the Persian forces in the naval battle at Salamis, the Chorus was actively acting out a choreography that visually complemented the verbal narration. The brilliance of this deduction is staggering in indicating the participation of the Chorus in Athenian tragedy: They were seldom inactive, and not only did they wear the persona of their first function as Old Men of Kolonos or Young Theban Women, but they served also as an abstract or distanced body that acted out the subject of others' narration of which in no event could they have had any foreknowledge. It helps to understand why when Athenians attended the theater at festival times they spoke of going to the "choreography" rather than to the play.

V

Of music in Archaic and Classical Greece we know very little. Some music scores survive, but they are largely fragmentary and date from the Hellenistic period or later. Although the Greeks were knowledgeable about a great many musical instruments, especially from their eastern neighbors, they adopted only two main sorts: stringed instrument (lyre) and wind instrument or pipe (*aulos*), not a flute but sounded with a reed (single and double). In tragedy of the fifth century the double-pipe *aulos* was the instrument of choice to accompany the musical sections of the dramatic action.

The musical element in the performance of fifth century tragedy was of primary importance, and its similarity to modern opera is not unnoticed. Every one of the extant tragedies has built into it a number of choral sections (usually five) that cover generally short passages of time and in which the singing and dancing Chorus holds the center of attention in the orchestra. In addition, there are sections in which song is exchanged between characters, as well as an alternation between spoken dialogue and recitative or song, the latter often between a character or characters and the Chorus. As Easterling rightly points out, these sections exist in the same time frame as the scenes of exclusively spoken dialogue. The rationale behind this practice being "to intensify emotion or to give a scene a ritual dimension, as in a shared lament or song of celebration." To what extent music was employed in performance is not known, but it is intriguing to speculate that its role was enormous and went far beyond those sections of the plays that call unequivocally for music.

VI

What we know about the production of tragedy in Greece is almost totally confined to Attica, though other areas were also active producers. In any event, from the close of the sixth and throughout the fifth century, tragedy was primarily performed as part of the Great or City Dionysia in Athens, though tragedy was also a part of the Rural Dionysia during the winter months when access to Athens was inhibited because of weather. But tragedy was not the sole reason for these festivals. They also scheduled processions, sacrifices in the theater, libations, the parade of war orphans, and the performance of dithyramb and comedy. As summary, the final day was devoted to a review of the conduct of the festival and to the awarding of prizes.

Three tragedians competed with three plays each plus a satyr play, all chosen by the archon, a state official who also appointed the three *chorêgoi* who undertook the expense of equipping and training the choruses, the actors and playwrights being paid for by the state. One judge from each of the ten tribes or demes of Athens was chosen to determine the winners of the competition, and the winning playwright was crowned with a wreath of ivy in the theater. Till about the middle of the fifth century, the three tragedies of each day's performance comprised a trilogy; eventually each of the three plays had a different subject and were independent of one another, but always there was a satyr play.

And then there was Dionysos.

VII

Dionysos. What had the theater to do with Dionysos, and Dionysos with the theater? How did the two become one and mutually express one another as an indigenous Athenian institution? What is it that is quintessentially associated with Dionysos that makes him the appropriate representative of the art of drama, and in particular of tragedy?

Some scholars believe that, since the subject of the dithyramb chorus was Dionysos, tragedy, developing out of the dithyramb (as Aristotle conjectured), simply took with it its subject. Now, of course, we are less than certain of that succession, especially when one considers, as Herington puts it, the "catholicity of the art form" of tragedy in the subjects it treats; for, though Dionysos plays a significant part as a subject, he has considerable competition. Or is it his Otherness that makes him tragedy's apt representative, his transformative aspect (both animate and inanimate), or simply his inability to be pinned down as being either this or that? Some would say that his cult ritual, which existed long before tragedy, possessed aspects that made it prototypical of drama: the use of masks for disguise, ecstatic possession and the capacity to assume alternate personalities, mystic initiation. Then there is wine, discovered by Dionysos, and the wildness of nature, the power of his ambivalent sexuality, his association with dance in partnership with satyrs and maenads. These are only a few of the possibilities that may have led to this inexhaustible god's association with drama. Which it was, of course, we will never know; but a fair guess might be that each of these attributes, and perhaps others, had its share.

One thing, however, is certain, that in the early period of tragedy, from the late sixth and well into the fifth century, tragedy was associated with the satyr play, that light send-up of a classical mythological subject. What's more, once tragedy emerged, the same playwrights who wrote the tragedies also wrote the satyr play that culminated the day's dramatic event.

Easterling finds that all three of these forms (dithyramb, satyr play, and tragedy) share one thing: song and dance, and, as she says,

> among them it was satyr play that was the most obviously Dionysiac element, since the chorus of satyrs, far more than any other choral group, was explicitly and by definition part of the god's entourage, and satyrs of various types, as we have known from vase-paintings, had been associated with Dionysus well before the dramatic festivals were established.

The question remains: What made Dionysos the god uniquely suited to drama? Authentic, testable proof from the time of its formation doesn't exist and we have only the extant plays (a small remnant of the total production of those years) to look to for possibilities.

Perhaps one of the most salient reasons for Dionysos as god of theater is the mask, for at its core it is the very essence of the Dionysiac, which, ultimately, is escape. But who would think of Greek tragedy as escapist fare, the means of leaving reality behind? And yet, is it so impossible that tragedy's removal from real life gave the same satisfaction, then as now, albeit of a different kind? Greek tragedy, after all, is filled with Alienation devises. Just as the Elizabethan playgoer didn't in the street speak the language of Shakespeare's stage, the diction, the vocabulary, the very syntax of Attic tragedy (not to mention the emotional manipulation possible through various skillfully applied metric systems) was even more removed from the daily patter of the Athenian Agora.

And as far as the mask and its Dionysiac potentialities, it permits an actor to take on not just one but as many roles as needed in the course of the tragic trilogy and its culminating satyr play. In the early days of tragedy there was one actor, then Aeschylus added a second, and Sophokles a third. No matter how many actors (one or three), he/they were required to play as many speaking roles as the play called for, each time changing his mask to assume another character. Since only males were permitted to act, a male would as easily perform a female as a male role. Pentheus, for example, in Euripides, also plays his mother Agavê who at the end enters carrying her son's severed head. In other cases an actor could play four or even five roles. Furthermore, each of the four choruses in a tetralogy would assume another, separate, identity, finally and inevitably ending up as a band of cavorting and lascivious satyrs. Then, of course, there is the distancing of the music as well as the elaborate choreography of the chorus.

So fictive is this convention of masks in the Attic theater that it is as iconoclastic in regard to everyday reality as is the Epic, anti-illusionist, theater of Brecht. No Athenian in that Theater of Dionysos could have failed finally to be aware of the game openly and unashamedly being played on him and he must have relished it, knowing by subtle means, by the timbre of a voice, by delivery, or some other telltale sign that Pentheus was now (in the terrible/wonderful deception that was theater) his mother carrying his own head. Which doesn't mean that theater couldn't also be the bearer of weighty messages, such as: As you sow, so also shall you reap—a lesson Pentheus learns too late. In any event, an illusion of reality was deliberately broken that said to that vast audience that this is not life as you know it, and, besides, there's always the down-and-dirty ribaldry of the satyr play to send you home laughing at its unmediated escapist function, just in case you fell into the trap of taking things a bit too seriously.

One other thing regarding the mask needs saying. As we know from Greek pottery (in particular large kraters for the storage of wine), in the cult rituals of Dionysos the god was frequently "present" in the form of a large suspended or supported mask, suggesting two intriguing possibilities: 1) that he served as an observer, and 2) that he observed the playing out in the ritual of many of his characteristics. It is fascinating to associate that spectatorship of the "ritual" Dionysos with the fact that at the beginning of every City Dionysia at Athens a large statue of Dionysos was placed dead center in the auditorium to oversee the day's theatrical representation of himself in the form of mask, transformation, disguise, ecstatic possession, dance (to name only a few), and, in the satyr play, debauchery, drunkenness, and general ribaldry.

And then there was sex.

VIII

The sexual import of Dionysos and his cult is quite beyond refutation. His most formidable aspect in absentia is the giant phallos, a sign of generation and fertility, a ritual instrument that was prominently displayed and carried through the streets in procession on various holidays, as well as ritually sequestered in a small, cradle-like enclosure and treated at women's festivals as the product of its fertility, a baby. In small, it was a piece of polished wood looking like nothing so much as a dildo.

As a subject for Attic tragedy sex cannot be denied; it appears so often as not only a motif, but as a catalytic motivational force in one play after another, so significant an element that Attic tragedy could scarcely do without it.

One has only to think of Phaidra and Hippolytos, of the Suppliants and their Egyptian suitors, Mêdeia and Jason, Laïos and Iokastê, Oedipus and Iokastê, Heraklês and Dêianeira, Pentheus and Dionysos. In each of these relationships sex is dark, disruptive, tragic, leading inevitably to the solution of all problems: Count no man happy till he is dead.

Dionysos and death? The Dionysos who gives wine, who causes milk to flow from the earth and honey to spout from his ritual thyrsos, who carouses with his satyrs and maenads in the mountains? The answer can only be yes, as much death as freedom, as much death as liberation, as escape, as dissolution, as sex itself—no infrequent carrier of the death motif as rapture in destruction. Death is, after all, the only total escape, the only true liberation from pain and distress and dishonor and fear, the only unalloyed pleasure that ultimately is nothing less than the paradoxical absence of that pleasure in Nothingness.

When we consider how often the death expedient is invoked in Athenian tragedy and how often it is the only answer to the dark plague of sex that enfolds these plays, we come to the realization that the Dionysos situated commandingly dead center in that Athenian theater that bears his name, watching himself onstage in every event that transpires on it, from the playful to the tragic. Dionysos is not only watching, not merely observing from his place of honor, but, like the gods in various of his plays, directing, manipulating the action and the fate of his characters—like Aphroditê and Artemis in *Hippolytos,* like Athêna in *Aias,* like Dionysos himself in *Bakkhai.* In the end, Dionysos is the god of the theater because Dionysos is Everything, All: light-dark, hot-cold, wet-dry, sound-silence, pleasure-pain, life-death. If he lures his Athenian audience unsuspectingly into his theater in order to escape "reality" by raising life to a level that exceeds, indeed transcends, reality, whether by means of language, or dimension, or poetry, or the deceptively *fictive* games he plays with masks and actors playing not only their own characters but others as well, he does so with a smile (he is, after all, known as the "smiling god," though at times demonically, eyes like spiraling pinwheels, tongue hanging lax from tightened lips), knowing what they don't know, that that really is life up there on his stage, a mirror of him, and as a mirror of him it is a mirror of all things, of his all-encompassing fertility (that also includes death), and as such there can be no question why he is the god of theater, but most specifically of tragedy, because in the end death is the only answer, and sex, life's greatest pleasure, becomes the catalyst that ultimately leads to death, which is the greatest pleasure of all, and has everything to do with Dionysos.

Carl R. Mueller
Department of Theater
School of Theater, Film, and Television
University of California, Los Angeles

The Plays

PERSIANS

I

Except for the comedies of Aristophanes, Aeschylus' *Persians* is the only surviving play of fifth-century Athens to borrow its subject matter from contemporary history, as opposed to the usual source, that "bible" of Greek life and religion that was Homer, as well as from the even greater corpus of Greek mythology. *Persians* was first produced at the Great (or City) Dionysia in Athens in 472 B.C.E, and it may have been meant to commemorate the Athenian victory over Persia at Salamis just eight years prior. That victory in 480 (along with victories at Plataia and Mykalê in 479) signaled for Athens an end to the Persian Wars.

That war is central in the history of Greece, and in particular in the history of Athens. The Persian Empire, under the leadership of Great King Dareios I, made its first concerted attempt to conquer mainland Greece in 490 with a naval invasion of the large Attic deme of Marathon on the northeastern coast of Attica, not far from Athens. That first incursion into mainland Greece came about as the result of the Athenian support lent to the Ionian Greeks settled along the western coast of Asia Minor. Early in the fifth century (in 499 to be exact) the Ionian Greeks—who since 546 had borne up under Persian rule and in the bargain had become a prosperous people—finally, because of increased taxation for imperialist expansion, revolted against the rule of mighty Persia. In sympathy with its Ionian brothers, Athens—though no longer a great power because of a decade of Spartan aggression against it— sent what ships it could, a mere twenty in all. As it happened, the Ionian Revolt of 499, led by the city of Miletos, was cruelly quashed by Dareios in 494; Miletos was sacked, and Persian rule firmly reestablished.

Persia, however, already held as subject considerable numbers of European Greeks in Macedonia and Thrace and realized that without control over all of Greece its conquests were not secure from further interference by independent European Greeks. This led to two decisive battles that changed the life and fortune not only of Persia, but of the Athenian state as well as all of Greece.

The first battle was in 490, at Marathon; the second in 480, at Salamis, an island in the Saronic Gulf off the western coast of Attica. The Battle of Marathon was fought between approximately 10,000 Greeks and possibly twice as many Persians, with the result that the resounding Athenian victory was won at the cost of 192 Athenian as opposed to 6,400 Persian lives. About the Battle of Salamis precious little is known, except that it was a naval battle in which, one night, on the basis of deliberately planted misinformation by Themistokles, the Athenian statesman and naval commander, the massive Persian fleet under Xerxês, son of Dareios, attempted to cut off the rumored escape route of the much smaller Athenian fleet. Aeschylus, who was an eyewitness to the scene, reports in his play that the Persian fleet numbered 1,207 ships and the Athenian a mere 310. That defeat, plus the final defeats in 479 at Plataia and Mykalê, sent Persia back to Asia Minor in total rout, and with it an end to the Persian threat. As a result of the victories at Salamis, Plataia, and Mykalê, Athens was propelled into a position of political, military, naval, and imperial power for most of the remainder of the fifth century. It is out of this milieu of prosperity that the Golden Age of Athens emerged. Democracy had already been established in the previous century, but now that citystate moved into other areas of excellence unparalleled in human endeavor. Through patronage of the arts it excelled as no civilization had before in philosophical inquiry, sculpture, architecture, poetry, science, medicine, mathematics—and, not least, in the development of Attic tragedy. This, then, is the background for Aeschylus' play *Persians*.

II

The scene is laid at Susa, the Persian capital, and its "action" consists of four major incidents: the anticipation of news of the Persian expedition's fate, the arrival of a Herald with news of the Persians' defeat at Salamis, the raising of the Ghost of Dareios who criticizes his son's intemperate action, and the appearance of King Xerxês, the expedition's leader, now ragged, humbled, and disgraced.

The play's dramaturgy has frequently been dismissed as uneventful and even as having no action, or at best very little—an attitude that will be seen not to be the case. And if the play fails to follow certain prescriptions laid down by Aristotle in his *Poetics* regarding tragedy, it must be remembered that Aristotle was as yet almost one hundred years unborn. The play's purpose has also frequently been questioned. It is said to have been part of a tetralogy whose parts together were titled *Phineos, Persians, Glaukos of Potniai,* and the satyr play *Prometheus the Fire-bringer.* Even if this is accurate, *Persians* fits into that structure very loosely, indeed. What is likely is that the playwright did not follow the tradition that he himself may have begun, and which he utilized in the *Oresteia,* namely to divide up a single story into three plays united by a thematic through-line and followed by a satyr play on the same subject. He had done so earlier in treating the story of Laïos and Oedipus, of which only *Seven Against Thebes* survives. The same is true of his Danaïd trilogy, the first play of which, *Suppliants,* is extant. In other words, *Persians* may have been written as an independent work that could stand alone as did the plays of Sophokles and Euripides.

About all we know from the written evidence is that *Persians* was composed at the suggestion of the twenty-year-old aristocratic statesman- and general-to-be, Pericles, as his first public act, and that he also served as the play's *choregos* or financial backer. Finally, we know that it won the first place for tragedy in 472. In any case, whether or not the second segment of a loosely connected tetralogy, *Persians* stands alone among the four single extant plays of Aeschylus (exclusive of the *Oresteia*) as an independent unit that makes a unified statement in and of itself. It is also the first extant play of Aeschylus as well as the first surviving Greek tragedy, and as such it must not be assumed that it was written by a novice playwright. Aeschylus' seven extant plays (out of a totality of between eighty and eighty-nine) were all composed during the last seventeen years of his life; and furthermore in 472, the year of *Persians'* first staging, he was in his early fifties. *Persians* is also, as said above, the only surviving tragedy of fifth-century Athens that is based on a recent historical occurrence, and this fact has divided critics into two camps.

One camp argues that the play is an unabashed self-congratulatory hymn of praise to the Athenian victory over the Persian barbarians, to the degree even, as C. J. Herington notes, "that the final scene is meant as open mockery of the defeated king." The other camp views it from the historical perspective, as if it were "a faithful dramatization of the historical event," and impugns Aeschylus for distorting the facts of history.

Perhaps the answer lies in the possibility that Aeschylus set out to accomplish in one play both of these designs, carefully, artfully balancing one view against the other, and refusing steadfastly to pander totally to either. Praise of the extraordinary Athenian victory at Salamis need not be blatant chauvinism or jingoistic. To make it such would have been unthinkable in so great a poet-playwright as Aeschylus. Praise for a deed bravely done against staggering odds need not inevitably be back-thumping jubilation and the waving of flags. The fact is there is not one line in *Persians* that falls into that category. Praise for Athens there is, of course, as we will see, but it is not the sort that brings smiles, but, rather, tears—of relief but also of pain at remembering the agony.

Another problem in evaluating *Persians* is the fact that Aeschylus was there, at Salamis, in 480, and either fought in the battle directly, as he had at Marathon, or was an eyewitness to it. Either way, his lengthy and brilliant evocation of that event in the Herald's speech (lines 417–867 in the Greek text) is one of the most precious of historical documents: It is the only surviving account of any aspect of the Persian Wars composed by someone who was actually there—and that is where the problem resides.

The question, then, is: What is history? And the answer can only be that what history is for the modern historian with all the tools and systems and methods of inquiry available and tested over the centuries is not what history was for Aeschylus in 472. History tells us that "history" as a meticulous gathering and sorting and evaluating of evidence from the past did not exist until Herodotos of Halicarnassos invented it in his *Histories*—a word which then meant not what it means to us but "research" or "inquiry." Herodotos, as it happens, is called the Father of History though that is not entirely certain. As Simon Hornblower reminds us: "the 'Jewish Succession Narrative' in the books of Samuel and Kings antedates every Greek claimant to be the first historian." He concludes that "direct Jewish influence on Greece is unlikely . . ." It is fair, then, to say that Herodotos invented it for the Greeks, but (having been born around 485) he did so at least a full generation after Aeschylus wrote *Persians,* and even so his methods are, by modern standards, highly suspect, his reliance frequently having been on dubious sources, on fading or inventive memory.

Now comes the question of the Greek tragedian's "right" to treat as subject matter contemporary historical events. There are at least two views on the issue. One is expressed by Michael Ewans, who asserts that for Aeschylus as well as for his audience in 472 "there was no firm dividing line between 'history' and 'myth.'" He goes on to say that the events in the Persian Wars were as readily at hand for use by him and others as tragic subject matter as were the distant histories of ancient Thebes and Argos that play so dominant a role in Greek tragedy. Furthermore, Aeschylus "had license to treat recent historical material with the same freedom as myth. As with myth, he was not able to change the basic features of the story, but he could select, compress, expand, and even distort all but the most central details in pursuit of his dramatic aims."

Herington, on the other hand, sees the matter somewhat differently. According to him: "It is a well-known—a crucial—feature of Greek art in all media, visual and verbal, that its regular subject matter was divine myth and heroic legend, not contemporary events or personalities." A different take altogether. But seductive when one considers his next point: "But the Persian Wars broke that taboo." What was it that brought about the change (albeit only in regard to the Persian Wars) to the exclusion of all other events? It is here that Ewans and Herington essentially agree, namely that the scope of the Persian Wars and the nature of the characters involved so totally eclipsed contemporary reality as to rival divine myth and heroic legend. Here is Ewans on the issue:

> The success of the Athenians in defeating first Dareios and then Xerxês against overwhelming odds provided Aischylos with a striking illustration of a recurrent motif in sixth- and fifth-century thought; the idea that excessive wealth and prosperity may invite the jealousy of the gods, and those who go beyond their natural limits may be struck down.

And here is Herington, though with an additional point of considerable importance:

> The Persian Wars must have seemed to fifth-century Greeks a perfect exemplification of the ancient law of *hybris-atê;* almost, one might dare to say, the incarnation of it, on the grandest conceivable scale. It is almost certainly for this reason that the Persian Wars, alone among the events of classical Greek history, were admitted into the repertoire of all the major arts. . . . The great contemporary choral poets had several poems on, or alluding to, the wars, and toward the end of the century the famous musician Timotheos wrote a long lyric on the subject, which is still partly extant; its title, like that of Aeschylus' play, is the *Persians.* Scenes of battle between Greeks and Persians are fairly common on Attic red-figure vase paintings, and occasionally even found their way into monumental paintings and sculptures. . . . It might even be argued that the overwhelming shock of the Persian Wars widened the very boundaries of Greek literature (and of our own) by creating historiography, in the unprecedented life-work of Herodotus. But however that may be, it must be clear from the evidence of lyric poetry, painting, sculpture, and the tragedies of Phrynichos that Aeschylus' choice of theme in the *Persians* is not an isolated phenomenon, nor a surprising one, for its time.

It can only be a guess, but what may have so captured the mind of the classical Greek in the very fabric of the Persian Wars may reside in what Herington calls the "ancient law of *hybris-atê*," which loosely means "pride and punishment." He continues:

> That swift expansion and abrupt disgrace of the Persian Empire, even when told as sober history, have already the quality of drama; it is not often that the raw material of historical events arrives in such aesthetically satisfying shape. This fact in itself might to some extent account for the appeal of the Persian Wars to the Greek artists of the fifth century. Far more important, however, must have been its moral-religious aspect. For the events of the Persian Wars conformed almost miraculously to the law of our mortal existence which the Greeks had understood since time immemorial: a law which had been respected implicitly by the unknown Bronze-Age creators of many a Greek myth, and which had been formulated explicitly by the archaic poets and thinkers. In its least refined form the law simply entails the visitation of God's ferocious punishment on anything that is unduly great, whether physical or mental.

It is a concept that even Herodotos applied in his *Histories.* In book seven of that work, during an imperial council session in which it is discussed whether to launch the Persian expedition, Herodotos has Artabanos, the uncle of Xerxês, advise his young nephew as follows:

> You know, my lord, that amongst living creatures it is the great ones that God smites with his thunder, out of envy of their pride. The little ones do not vex him. It is always the great buildings and the tall trees which are struck by lightning. It is God's way to bring the lofty low. Often a great army is destroyed by a little one, when God in his envy puts fear into the men's hearts, or sends a thunderstorm, and they are cut to pieces in a way they do not deserve. For God tolerates pride in none but Himself.

That Artabanos actually said such words is not terribly likely, but rather that it is an example of a speech made up by Greeks during the likely two or three generations since the Persian Wars, or by Herodotos himself. What is important is that it is the kind of thing that a Greek would have thought in retrospect of the great Persian catastrophe at Salamis, Plataia, and Mykalê. In any event, it is a sentiment expressed throughout Aeschylus' *Persians* as a kind of refrain or burden, a concept that all Greeks shared and one which more likely than not opened up the Persian Wars as subject matter for the arts in the fifth century.

In the Chorus' rousing opening hymn of praise for the expedition the possibility of defeat is always around the corner, and so, in the midst of extolling Persia's greatness, the old men, those wise lords of Susa and advisors to the king, almost imperceptibly merge into a darker mode, until finally what began as extravagant praise ends with the thought of the price that must be paid for too much pride, for too great daring in the eyes of god.

> Our ancient destiny is sent from god,
> god-ordained:
> to wage war,
> to tear down walls,
> to strike with thunderous cavalry charge
> and lay great cities low in the dust.
>
> But new knowledge now turns our eyes
> to the white-flecked sea when the stormwinds pound,
> and we tame its rage,
> and we straddle its back,
> and build a road bound tight with flax,
> and surge across to alien shores.
>
> But where is the man,
> where is he so keen
> as to cheat the snares of the gods with a leap?
> Calamity lures him,
> smiles,
> seduces him,
> into her net,
> and no escape.

Out of the divinely ordained Persian destiny to wage war and tear down walls, to the glorious construction of the bridge of boats that straddles the Hellespont, arises the idea that god punishes such extravagance. God's jealousy, his envy, is feared. Calamity lures man to his own destruction as payment for overreaching. Even the Herald speaks to Queen Atossa of the gods' jealousy of Xerxês' audacity: "Your son, at once, deceived by Greek treachery and the gods' jealousy . . .", he says; and a few lines later: "But little did he know the fate the gods had stored up."

When the Ghost of Dareios rises from his grave, he speaks in no uncertain terms of the stupidity of his son's flagrant defiance of the gods' law that keeps man in check and of the consequence if man fails to obey.

GHOST OF DAREIOS:
How swiftly god's oracles work!
How swiftly Zeus hurls it
    down upon my son! I had
hoped for more time,
    the distant future,
but when a man is a fool and loses control,
    the gods speed him on his way.
          A well of disaster
overflows for all I love.
And this was my son's doing,
    this his achievement, who in his
impetuous youth sought,
    like a slave, blindly, to
chain the sacred flowing Hellespont,
    god's holy spring, the Bosporos.
He made land of the sea,
    against all nature,
laying a great road for his great army.
How foolish to think he could master the
    gods, including Poseidon.
What was it but some disease that gripped his
          mind?
Now all I fought to win,
    the gold, the power,
are left to be plundered by anyone who wills.

And later, when foretelling the Persian defeat at Plataia, Dareios sees and describes the death and destruction that Xerxês' men will face, emphasizing again the rash and impetuous nature of his son's decision in undertaking the expedition:

There they sit by the Asopos
        whose welcome waters make
            rich the Boiotian plain,
                            waiting,
        waiting for the crown of misery to be
put in place, just payment for
        terrible pride and godless
                        arrogance.
They came to Greece and with no
        awe for the gods,
no shame, plundered images,
        torched temples, uprooted altars and
        pried up shrines, scattering them
            about in blind
                                confusion.
And so their suffering is no less
        evil than the evil suffering they
            caused.
And there will be more suffering.
Only the foundation of their
        evil is laid, the house is not yet
            built. So great will be the
bloody slaughter on Plataian
        land by the Dorian spear.
Piles of Persian corpses to
        generations hence will
        testify in silence to men's eyes
that mortal men should think only
            mortal thoughts.
Violence sown has reaped a harvest of
        ruin and bitter
                    tears.
Behold these things,
        behold these punishments,
        and as you do, remember
Athens, and remember
Greece, and never
        scorn the blessings heaven gives today
            while lusting for others

tomorrow, and so pour out a
          store of great
               prosperity.
Zeus watches, and
          Zeus is a stern chastiser of
          arrogant minds,
               nothing escapes him.

When he comes,
          when Xerxês comes,
counsel him in your
          wisdom; tell him in his
          foolishness to listen to you and
               stop offending god with
          overboastful rashness.

The terms of disapprobation could not be more harsh; they could as easily have come from the mouth of a Greek, which, of course, since ultimately
they came from Aeschylus, they did. They all add up to several lines uttered
by Atossa within seconds of her first entrance, lines not necessarily prophetic, but that grow out of knowledge of her son's true and ungovernable youthful nature. She expresses an idea that was current in sixth- and fifth-century
thought, and related to the *hybris-atê* notion mentioned above. As Ewans
expresses it: "the idea that excessive wealth and prosperity may invite the jealousy of the gods, and those who go beyond their natural limits may be struck
down." Atossa speaks:

          Care tears at my heart, anxiety
               that I will share with you, my friends,
          secret fears that grip me, from which I see no
                                        escape.
          Has our great wealth now tripped up prosperity
               and in a cloud of dust
               slammed it to the floor of the palaestra—
          the prosperity won by Dareios with a god's help?

The passage is a difficult one to interpret because of the opaque nature of its
expression in the original, but it appears to fit into what has already been discussed. The extraordinary wealth inherited by Xerxês from his father Dareios

has so deluded him with lust for more wealth and power that it may have doubled back and defeated itself. Out of wealth comes prosperity, but when an excess of wealth is sought, and acts are committed that exceed what man is allowed by the gods, then prosperity (that comes from wealth) is slammed, like a wrestler thrown and pinned to the floor, and destroyed.

This age-old Greek concept of *hybris-atê,* along with the larger-than-life designs and characters of the Persian Wars in which it was seen to be so essential a factor, is almost certainly what broke the (presumed) restriction on Greek tragedy as well as the other arts of treating contemporary historical events.

Why, then, does later Greek tragedy eschew recent history as subject matter? The question must be: Does it? And the answer is: yes and no. It does in the sense that literally identifiable events and characters, though they do not appear on stage, are alluded to by the tragic dramatists though never named. Oedipus, for example, standing in for Perikles, and plague-ridden Thebes for Athens under the plague in the time of Perikles, or a possible reference to the disastrous Sicilian Expedition (415–413) in the Peloponnesian Wars that Euripides may refer to in one of his later plays. Ancient stories were so manipulated by virtue of allowable alteration, that there is frequently little doubt about the allusion to contemporary events and people. For example, no contemporary Greek is named in the whole of *Persians,* and yet there is a central action on the evening preceding the Battle of Salamis on which everything depends. The unnamed Greek who deceptively delivers word to Xerxês that under cover of darkness the Greek fleet is set to flee the scene and escape the Persian threat—a bit of news in which Xerxês naively puts full trust (despite the fact that it comes from the enemy) and acts on, with the result that the Persian fleet is destroyed. That unnamed Greek on whom all hinges was Themistokles, and there cannot have been anyone among the many thousands in the Theater of Dionysos who did not pick up on the hint, who did not know that this was the man on whom the Athenian victory at Salamis depended, and who at the time of the play's first performance in 472 was in great trouble with the state, as well as a friend of the playwright.

Ewans adds insightfully that possibly another reason existed for later tragedy to avoid recent historical subject matter: Aeschylus, "chose to write about the fall of Persia because the vast power of Xerxês, his overreaching and consequent defeat, provided material analogous in scale and kind to the legendary events of myth, where other, less exalted moments in contemporary Greek politics did not." Another way of saying that the stuff of the Peloponnesian Wars that raged on and off again from 431 to 404 was pretty filthy and petty stuff when compared with Marathon and Salamis.

III

Aristotle in his *Poetics* (which was not to appear before the middle of the fourth century at best) has an interesting section in which he discusses history versus myth.

> From what has been said it is also clear that the poet's job is not to report what has happened but what is likely to happen: that is, what is capable of happening according to the rule of probability or necessity. Thus the difference between the historian and the poet is not in their utterances being in verse or prose (it would be quite possible for Herodotus' work to be translated into verse, and it would not be any the less a history with verse than it is without it); the difference lies in the fact that the historian speaks of what has happened, the poet of the kind of thing that *can* happen. Hence also poetry is a more philosophical and serious business than history; for poetry speaks more of universals, history of particulars. "Universal" in this case is what kind of person is likely to do or say certain kinds of things, according to probability or necessity; that is what poetry aims at, although it gives its persons particular names afterwards; while the "particular" is what Alcibiades did or what happened to him.

Realistically speaking, what Aeschylus does in *Persians* is quite in keeping with Aristotle's dictum when he says: "the historian speaks of what has happened, the poet of the kind of thing that *can* happen." In Aeschylus' case, he takes what *did* happen in history except that he treats history as if it were myth and applies to history all the stratagems that any tragedian would use in manipulating a mythic structure to make it conform to what he wants that structure to say. So to say that Aeschylus set out to write a historical tragedy rather than a straight history play, as is said by many, is not necessarily what appears to be true. A closer look at what Aeschylus has produced suggests, rather, that he set out to write a tragedy pure and simple, so great and so essential are his deviations from historical fact. The only reason for making such great deviations, which we will discuss, is to focus his plot in a way that the raw historical matter does not allow. History is an unruly master who spins his web not only loosely but at times haphazardly, so much so that incidentals are more likely than not to overwhelm the central event. Shakespeare knew this as did Schiller and every other major dramatist who has dealt with history with the intention of bringing it around to his intended theatrical view.

Let us begin gently with the poet in Aeschylus, rather than the historian.

Herington writes brilliantly of this aspect in regard to the justly famous Herald's speech describing the battle at Salamis:

> Aeschylus' painting of the event is mostly a matter of selected tones and colors rather than of sharp-edged lines. We are left with a vivid *impression* of what it was like to be at Salamis on that day. We re-experience the determination, almost elation, of the Greeks as the moment of crisis arrived, the shouting, the rhythmic crash of oars, the masses of warships locked together in the narrows, and perhaps above all the frightfulness of the contrast between the human work of butchery and the serene, sunlit natural background. . . . Thus Aeschylus' vision even of the shattering event in which he actually took part is to a great extent a poet's vision, not an objective historian's. But the greater part of the *Persians* concerns episodes and places which Aeschylus could not possibly have seen, and about which he could hardly have had much precise information. For affairs and personalities in the Persian capital at Susa, where his scene is set, and for the narrative of Xerxês' retreat through northern Greece, there was no way for a poet composing at Athens within eight years of the event to arrive at the objective historical particulars, even if it had occurred to him for one moment that such research was any part of a poet's trade. For we are, after all, dealing not merely with a poet, but with a classical Greek poet. And perhaps the most important single characteristic of the Greek poetic tradition within which Aeschylus worked, as opposed to poetry as it is usually understood in modern times, is this: the Greek poet consistently strove to set the transient doings of mortals against a permanent universe, a universe of ever-present death and ever-living gods. Unless so measured, the particular human act (whether a legendary event, or a contemporary victory at the Olympic Games, for instance) will scarcely be worth narrating, or even intelligible. Only the permanent will make sense of the ephemeral. So worked the mind of the Greek poet, whether epic, lyric, or tragic, from the earliest times into the late fifth century. . . . It is with this tradition firmly in mind, rather than in the expectation of a historical narrative, that we should probably do best to approach the *Persians*. On one side of us we shall see, as the poet had seen, an awe-inspiring series of purely human events; but on the other side, a no less awe-inspiring universe against whose laws those events can alone be fully understood. To relate those two is the poet's task, not factfinding.

What, then, is the nature of the changes made by Aeschylus in regard both to historical events and historical characters, and why were they made?

IV

The first and most obvious change is the decision to intensify the dramatic importance of the victory at Salamis to the demotion (at least for the time being) of that at Plataia, and the elimination entirely of Mykalê, several months later, for, devastating as the Salamis defeat was for the Persians, it was only at Plataia and Mykalê, half a year later, that the Persians and Xerxês were finally routed. In *Persians* Plataia is mentioned, but not where the historian would logically expect it and require it to be, in the Herald's speech, but much later in the play, in the speech delivered by the Ghost of Dareios in which he castigates his son Xerxês for his unconscionable recklessness and foretells the outcome of the Greek victory at Plataia over the select group of Persian warriors left behind by the Xerxês of Aeschylus' play. As of the play's dramatic time, Plataia has not even happened. What can have been behind Aeschylus' decision in making this alteration?

One salient reason might indeed have been chauvinistic. The fact is that the victory at Salamis was almost exclusively Athenian, whereas that at Plataia was largely Spartan, and Sparta and Athens as nations were no fast friends. The whole of the devastating twenty-seven-year-long Peloponnesian Wars, still forty-one years in the future, were fought between those two foes, leading to the defeat of Athens in 404. But Athenian relations with Sparta were scarcely better in the days of Salamis and the writing of *Persians,* or at any other time in Greek history.

Another reason for the displacement of Plataia, this time for reasons of dramaturgy, may have been the need to achieve with the Herald's Salaminian narration the greatest possible effect both on the audience and on the "Persians" on stage. To have dealt with Plataia in the Herald's narration would have achieved at least two unsalutary effects. It would have "crowded" the speech, making the Plataian defeat anticlimactic; and it would have deprived Aeschylus of one more terrible and effective stab to the collective Persian consciousness, not to say heart, by topping the utter devastation of the news of Salamis with news of an event still to come which even before it happens is known (via Dareios' foreknowledge) to be hopeless, thus rendering past, present, and future simultaneously a disaster. The First Old Man as Chorus Leader and the Chorus now knowing of their defeat at Salamis, but not yet of Plataia in the future, still hold out hope for a renewal of Persian might and spirit.

FIRST OLD MAN:

> What are we to do, lord Dareios?
> Where do your words point us?
>> To what good? Having suffered the worst,
> how may we, Persia's people,
>> win out to the best?

GHOST OF DAREIOS:

> You must never again campaign in
>> Greek territory; not even with a
>> larger Persian army.
> Greek soil is the Greek's staunchest
>>> ally.

FIRST OLD MAN:

> Ally? But how?

GHOST OF DAREIOS:

> It starves to death the invader with too many men.

FIRST OLD MAN:

> But we'll muster a fine force, carefully picked.

GHOST OF DAREIOS:

>> No,
> not even our ragged forces now in
> Greece will return home in safety.

FIRST OLD MAN:

>> What are you saying?
> Those Persians left behind
>> will never cross the straits from
>> Europe to Asia?

GHOST OF DAREIOS:

>> A few.
> Some few out of many thousands,
>> if one is to trust the gods'
>>> oracles.

Only look at how much they
        foretold has been fulfilled.
                Everything.
When Xerxês leaves his hand-picked
        troops behind, he's been
        persuaded by false hopes.
There they sit by the Asopos
        whose welcome waters make
                rich the Boiotian plain,
                        waiting,
                waiting for the crown of misery to be
put in place, just payment for
        terrible pride and godless
                arrogance.
They came to Greece and with no
        awe for the gods,
no shame, plundered images,
        torched temples, uprooted altars and
        pried up shrines, scattering them
                about in blind
                                confusion.
And so their suffering is no less
        evil than the evil suffering they
                caused.
And there will be more suffering.
Only the foundation of their
        evil is laid, the house is not yet
                built. So great will be the
bloody slaughter on Plataian
        land by the Dorian spear.
Piles of Persian corpses to
        generations hence will
                testify in silence to men's eyes
that mortal men should think only
                mortal thoughts.
Violence sown has reaped a harvest of
        ruin and bitter
                        tears.
Behold these things,

behold these punishments,
and as you do, remember
Athens, and remember
Greece, and never
scorn the blessings heaven gives today
while lusting for others
tomorrow, and so pour out a
store of great
prosperity.
Zeus watches, and
Zeus is a stern chastiser of
arrogant minds,
nothing escapes him.

Here, then, is the second devastating blow, from the mouth of their beloved former Great King Dareios, a final nail in the coffin of a nation that was once a fabled empire. As has been said, for this information to have come earlier, in the Herald's narration, would have been anticlimactic. Saving it for the Ghost of Dareios to reveal, and placing it in the near future, cuts off all remaining hope. Furthermore, if the play had followed the timetable of history, Salamis happening in the fall of 480 and Plataia and Mykalê in the summer of 479, with Xerxês not returning to Persia until a year after Salamis, those events would have been so spread out as to lose dramatic tension.

Even without the restructuring of history that Aeschylus does in altering the sequence of events dealt with above, the Persian Wars, as Herington has it, "saw history itself conforming to the terrifying moral patterns of Greek myth." Can we assume otherwise than that Aeschylus freely chose it as a subject that lent itself so compellingly to tragedy? His elder fellow tragedian Phrynichos in 476 had dealt with the same subject matter, the defeat of Xerxês at Salamis, under the title *Phoenician Women*. Historians call it a historical play, but it has as great a chance of being a full-fledged tragedy as Aeschylus' *Persians*. Unfortunately we know little of it besides the title and subject matter, as little as we know of his *The Sack of Miletos* performed at the City Dionysia in 493. That play also is not extant, though we know it dealt with Dareios' destruction of Miletos in 494, the city that began the Ionian Revolt in 499, and which precipitated the Persian Wars with the invasion of Marathon in 490. History or tragedy, we don't know, but what we do know is that Phrynichos was fined 1000 drachmas for having played too much on his Athenian audience's emotions, or, as Herodotos has it, "for reminding them of their own trouble" in the Ionian encounter to which Athens had sent aid as early as 499. Possibly by the time *Phoenician Women* came around he had learned to avoid engaging his audience's emotions too greatly for he won with that play the first prize at the Great Dionysia. Aeschylus may have learned the same, and his means of avoiding such a censure may have been to locate the action of *Persians* exclusively in the foreign and barbarian city of Susa, the Persian capital, and to banish from his stage every sign of a Greek character, as well as every Greek name. A cautionary move? Who knows. But a move in any event that he used brilliantly to his own dramatic ends.

V

Another point must be made. The scene of the raising of the Ghost of Dareios has frequently been cited as static and having no dramatic purpose, as stopping dead the little action the play is frequently, though wrongly, said to be plagued with. If for no other reason than the one dealt with above, the greater effectiveness of the Plataia information in the Dareios scene would justify the scene's inclusion. But there is one more significant reason for the scene, perhaps the most important of all, one that calls loudly for the alteration of historical fact: the characters of Dareios I and his son Xerxês. It is here that Aeschylus takes the greatest liberties with historical fact. But for good reason. He had a tragedy to write, a tragedy with a moral focus that even the unaltered historical facts strongly suggested, and yet, to achieve the greatest possible dramatic effect, those facts required alteration in order to focus as sharply as possible on the central hero, Xerxês. One of the best ways at the disposal of any playwright of any age, ancient or modern, is contrast in the form of a foil. Shakespeare does it in the creation of Fortinbras, Hamlet's polar opposite, a man who acts, who does, who wastes no time on moral considerations. Aeschylus, then, needed a figure of considerable authority, dead or alive, to serve the function of the play's moral center, and what better than the legendary, albeit dead, Great King Dareios who, moreover, is Xerxês' father. If for no other reason (and we have isolated several others above), this is a need in the play's dramatic structure that alone would justify the inclusion of the scene in which the Ghost of Dareios appears. But Aeschylus' problem as a playwright was that the historical Dareios himself had too many hybristic characteristics to serve as that moral center. He had, if not precisely to be whitewashed, then at least painted in lighter shades, whereas Xerxês required painting in darker shades than history ascribes, again for dramatic reasons.

Dareios, then, must be able to exclaim something resembling "Why was he not more like me?" or "How different he was from me!"

Aeschylus begins his transformation of Dareios almost immediately upon his arrival from the world of the dead. Present at his grave mound is the Chorus of Old Men, regents or lords of Persia, and honorable, devoted to their former Great King. They express their respect and tell him: "Majesty, the sight of you awes me! I shrink with awe from speaking with you! The old fear of the past is revived!" He enjoins them to speak freely, and to "spare the awe you had for me in days passed." But so great was their fear of their absolute monarch that they still hesitate. "Fear freezes me! How can I obey?" This retreat from elitism would most likely have resonated loudly with the audience of democratic Athens so resolutely opposed to tyranny and despots, which the historical Dareios most certainly was. It was Aeschylus' first step in making Dareios more human and more to be trusted.

Atossa, his wife, then tells him that Persia has been destroyed, and that it was "impetuous" Xerxês who was at fault. With this there begins the no uncertain castigation of Xerxês by the ghost of his dead father. "Stubborn fool," Dareios calls him, and asks:

> But how did so vast an army cross to Greece?
>
> ATOSSA:
> He yoked the Hellespont and made a road.
>
> GHOST OF DAREIOS:
> Closed the gap of mighty Bosporos?
>
> ATOSSA:
> Yes. But one of the gods must have helped.
>
> GHOST OF DAREIOS:
> Some powerful Spirit to relieve him of his wits!

Calling him "wretched fool," Dareios confirms for the Athenian audience what they already know, those thousands in the theater who fought at Salamis, and those Athenian citizens who were driven from their city and territory and twice endured the burning of Athens at the hands of the Persian army: That the fate of Xerxês was sealed by his hybristic, prideful action against not only Nature, in bridging the Hellespont, but against the gods themselves, and that it was the gods' envy that sealed his fate.

GHOST OF DAREIOS:
>How swiftly god's oracles work!
>How swiftly Zeus hurls it
>>down upon my son! I had
>hoped for more time,
>>the distant future,
>but when a man is a fool and loses control,
>>the gods speed him on his way.
>>>>A well of disaster
>overflows for all I love.
>And this was my son's doing,
>>this his achievement, who in his
>impetuous youth sought,
>>like a slave, blindly, to
>chain the sacred flowing Hellespont,
>>god's holy spring, the Bosporos.
>He made land of the sea,
>>against all nature,
>laying a great road for his great army.
>How foolish to think he could master the
>>gods, including Poseidon.
>What was it but some disease that gripped his
>>>>mind?

VI

This Dareios of Aeschylus' creation is one who vigorously defies historical fact regarding the real Dareios. Aeschylus' Dareios is shocked at the audacity of his impetuous son's daring to bridge the Hellespont with ships lashed together to form a thoroughfare for his vast army to cross from Asia to Europe. History, however, says otherwise. We learn from Books VII–IX of Herodotos that from the moment Dareios heard of the defeat of the Persian invasion at Marathon in 490 until his death in 486, he worked vigorously to organize a massive amphibious expedition against Greece. Furthermore, the historical Dareios had achieved much the same hybristic feat as Xerxês when he himself bridged the Thracian Bosporos at Chalkedon in his attempted invasion of Skythia in 514.

There then comes from Aeschylus' Dareios a curious statement that he gave advice to Xerxês:

Now it's young Xerxês rules.
　　　　Barely a man.
　　Inexperienced.
　　Impetuous boy. He thinks
　　　　as a young man
　　thinks, and forgets my
　　　　　　advice.

Neither in Herodotos nor in any other source is there indication of such an exchange. But regarding what Aeschylus' fabricated advice is there can be no doubt, because it is meant to accomplish two things in his dramatic plan. First, it is to improve the view of Dareios in Greek eyes; and second, to make Xerxês more culpable by forgetting/ignoring his father's "advice." And so, Dareios tells Xerxês that he is not to invade Greece. But, of course, Xerxês, as Aeschylus defines him, is impetuous, headstrong, and unruly, whereas Herodotos in Book VII writes that at first Xerxês had no interest in invading Greece and had to be coaxed by a politically motivated courtier. Here is Atossa's description of her extravagant son:

He kept bad company, our son,
　　wild, raging Xerxês, and learned his
　　lessons well from evil men.
He wasn't a man, they said, a courtyard
　　warrior, while you had fought and won vast
　　wealth and fame and left it to your sons.
But he, they said,
　　said it again and again,
did nothing to increase the prosperity you left him;
said it till he determined to prove his manhood and
　　launch this expedition against Greece.

In the last few lines of his final speech before returning to the Under-world, Aeschylus makes his Dareios be very clear about the difference between himself and his intemperate son when he speaks of the moral outrage Xerxês has perpetrated and the price he has had to pay: "just payment for terrible pride and godless arrogance," and that

they came to Greece and with no
　　awe for the gods,

no shame, plundered images,
>torched temples, uprooted altars and
>pried up shrines, scattering them
>>about in blind
>>>>confusion.
And so their suffering is no less
>evil than the evil suffering they
>>caused.

A universal view of things that recapitulates the *hybris-atê* design that the Greek world saw in the Persian Wars, and one that also takes us back to Aristotle's statement that "poetry speaks more of universals" than does mere history. It also reminds us of some of Dareios' first words in the play:

To be human is to suffer,
>nothing more.
Sufferings come.
Neither land nor sea is free of evil's sorrow.
And the longer men stretch out life
>the more evils come.

And he closes his scene with the moral statement "that mortal men should think only mortal thoughts."

VII

It is at this point, with the exit of the Ghost of Dareios, that the play begins its downward path to despair. Atossa, whose motherliness has been stressed throughout (her first concern upon entering is her son's fate, and it is about him she asks first of the Herald) leaves the stage in order to bring new clothes for her ragged son before he arrives, for to the Persian clothes ceremonially represent rank and with their loss comes its loss. We never see her again, but Aeschylus in stressing her profoundly motherly nature has successfully created a universal figure that cannot but have affected even the enemy Greek in Aeschylus' audience.

The ode sung by the Chorus of Old Men upon her exit recapitulates the greatness of Persia, of Dareios, and of Persia's people. Yet it is anything but jubilant. It evokes the past, all that is no more. It is all in the past tense. Nevertheless, it serves as a grand recapitulation of all that Aeschylus has stressed is great about his Dareios, ruler, lawgiver, conqueror of vast territories, leader of armies famous throughout the world. Dareios brought his men home time and again unscathed, undefeatable might—a ruler whose conquests never strayed beyond his western border, the River Halys. This is another editorial alteration of history, for there was Skythia, and Marathon, and another planned incursion into Greece. Nowhere is there mention that all that glory was won at the cost of absolute rule, loss of freedom, and tyranny.

How great,
how good was the life we lived,
the life of peace,
when our king of old,
our agèd ruler,
all-sufficing,
invincible and godlike,
who did us no harm,
Great King of Kings,
Dareios,
Lord Dareios,
ruled our land!
A country with armies famed in the world,
with laws strong as towered battlements,
a state well ordered,
and men returning,
unscarred, unscathed,
to happy homes.

And what cities he captured,
many, many,
and never left home,
never crossed the Halys!
Rivergod cities near Strymon's gulf,
hill-defended towns in Thrace,
knew him,
all knew him!
And cities with towers,
tower-walled cities,
cities outside the lake on the shore,
cities,

cities on the west coast of Hellespont,
and the Sea of Marmara
and the Thracian Bosporos!
And islands,
sea-washed,
islands near the headland:
Lesbos,
Samos where olives grow,
Chios and Paros,
Naxos,
Mykonos,
and Andros, nearest neighbor to Tênos!
Knew him,
all knew him,
knew Dareios as King!

And islands far out in the sea he ruled,
Lêmnos, Ikaria, Rhodos, Knidos,
and the cities of Kypros,
Paphos and Soloi and Salamis,
AIIII!
whose mother-city
now brings on our grief!
He ruled them,
ruled them all,
and all,
all knew him!

And Ionia he ruled,
Greek Ionia,
ruled in his wisdom,
cities teeming with men and many riches,
strength in men-at-arms,
undefeatable military might and many allies.
But now the gods turn all around,
we suffer defeat,
dreadful defeat,
defeat at sea,
the gods our enemies,
and we must endure.

It is a recapitulation of Persia's greatness that serves a decidedly dramatic intent, for as it concludes, the scene that has been prepared for from the first line of the play emerges on stage. Xerxês enters, his royal garments now ragged and torn, possibly seated in a curtained carriage that Herodotos says he used: but this time the curtain to give shade and privacy are as tattered and torn as he, drawn by near-naked men, remnant soldiers straggling behind. The contrast between the recapitulated past recalled by the grandly dressed Chorus of Old Men just seconds before and the sight of Great King Xerxês in ragged, humiliated defeat represents a theatrical coup. From this stunning entrance to the end of the play (166 lines in the Greek text), Aeschylus creates a scene of such theatrical effectiveness that it all but disappears on the printed page. In the first place, from here to the end everything is sung. The movement cannot but have been highly stylized in the choreography that Aeschylus was required to create for it. The multitude of stylized non-verbal exclamations of pain and despair: AIIII! OIOIIIIII! IO IO MOI MOIIIII! OTOTOTOTOI! among others, and then the music of the lyre and aulos—all conspire to create a scene of few words, but powerful in its visual and aural components: lamentations, cries of despair, and pain. It is packed with strange, alien Persian names: Pharandakes, Sousas, Pelagon, Agabatas, Pharnouchos, and Ariomardos. The scene is in fact a reversal on several levels of the play's initial scene, first with its choral litany of foreign (to Greek ears) names of men and places, praised in scene one, mourned here, then in the matter of clothing that plays so central a visual role in the drama. In the opening scene the opulently dressed Chorus of Old Men enters, joined later by the pomp and pageantry of Atossa's spectacular entrance in a chariot, accompanied by a splendid host of grandly costumed servants, attendants, and bodyguards. In this final scene the startling discontinuity between the still richly dressed Chorus and others who might be onstage, and the ragged, humiliated, and despairing Xerxês and his equally ragged men, is shattering. No words could have conveyed a more powerful statement. Musically, too, there is contrast, from proud, nationalistic, sung praise to a pandemonium of cries and lamentations accompanied by the shriek of the aulos. There is perhaps no scene so theatrically conceived in all Greek tragedy.

As the play nears its conclusion, the lines between Xerxês and the Chorus grow shorter and shorter, like hammer blows raining down on them from the heavens, until finally words all but fail and howls of agony and shame fill the scene. It is a fitting close, an apt final comment to a tragedy in which the universe is a cold and hostile place, the habitation of vengeful, envious gods whose mission is to maintain superiority over man at any cost, a universe rivaled only by the malignant universe of Sophoklean tragedy.

VIII

One thing more remains to be said. Nothing in what Xerxês says from his late entrance to his exit can be construed to be self-justification. His words are the pitiful lament of one who takes upon himself full responsibility for the disaster he has brought; he admits his tragic *hybris,* an admission required in the Greek tradition of the tragic hero.

> Behold me and weep,
> I am your
> > misery!
> The blight of my land,
> the ruin of my
> > family!

He then accepts his deserved retribution from the hands of envious gods:

> Sound your lament,
> your ragged-voiced
> > grief,
> for god now brings down
> his blast on my
> > head!

When we think back to that "ancient law of *hybris-atê,*" so powerful in the Greek consciousness, it is difficult to believe that Aeschylus' audience in that Theater of Dionysos at the foot of the Athenian Akropolis in 472—that audience that fought at Salamis and suffered the burning of Athens twice over—was not profoundly moved by the sight of the tragic working out of a destiny to which each of them was subject.

• • •

SEVEN AGAINST THEBES

I

Seven Against Thebes, which won for Aeschylus the first prize at the City Dionysia in 467 B.C.E., was conceived as part of a trilogy consisting of *Laïos, Oedipus,* and *Seven Against Thebes,* plus the satyr play *Sphinx.* Unfortunately, except for minor fragments of the other plays, only *Seven Against Thebes* survives. Unlike its predecessor, *Persians,* it is not an isolated drama, but part of what can only have been a tightly knit set of plays devoted to a single theme. As Winnington-Ingram has it: "In so far as we can discern a basic pattern in the play—and in the trilogy—it is the entanglement and disentanglement of house and city." The "house" is the legendary Theban dynasty, the House of Labdakos, that would be systematically destroyed over three generations.

From the beginning of the nineteenth century to the present, *Seven Against Thebes* has been a play with a heavy baggage of indifference to carry, or, as one classicist has put it, "indifference which has been deflected from time to time only into overt hostility and contempt"—and this for a number of reasons. Some decried it as not being up to the standards of Sophokles' *Oedipus Tyrannos.* Others fulminated against the mixed bag that Aeschylus delivered; as Michael Ewans puts it, his "fusion of the defense of Thebes with the curse of Oedipus and the Fury of the royal house [striking] many scholars as archaic, stylized and undramatic," not to mention ritualistic as well as boring. An odd series of attitudes for a play that was the culminating segment in a trilogy that won first prize. How does one explain such modern dismissal against the approbation of classical antiquity?

Since we have only *Seven Against Thebes* extant, we can scarcely with any certainty discuss the two lost plays of the trilogy. But as for *Seven Against Thebes,* it is a war play, and war was something that the classical Greek knew well and at firsthand. Scarcely a Greek youth of the Classical and Hellenistic periods but saw his share of battlefield conflict. Twice in the early fifth century, in 490 and 480, Athens had withstood invasion by Persia; and on the last occasion, the Battle of Salamis, the Athenians were obliged not merely to evacuate their territory but have their city burned and sacked. In Aeschylus' boyhood, Ewans continues:

> the city had also been racked by internal conflict leading up to the expulsion of the tyrants, and this was followed by Theban and Spartan attempts to meddle in the internal affairs of the newly formed democracy, and reimpose autocracy. After that there were political

manoeuvres, framed around the success and failure of military expeditions and the development of the Delian League, headed by Athens, initially to contain Persia; in Aischylos' last years these culminated in a major shift of foreign policy when Athens allied herself with Argos in 461. This led almost inevitably to the outbreak in 460 of the "First Peloponnesian War" between the new alliance and an anti-democratic Dorian coalition headed by the Spartans.

Though there is no solid evidence in the fifth century (as there is in the fourth) for the system of training boys of eighteen (*ephebes*) to become adult infantry soldiers (*hoplites*), there is little doubt that the adolescent Greek ephebe of the fifth century was at eighteen so trained. Fighting had been an essential of the Greek male from at least Homer onward. The willingness and capacity to defend *oikos,* home, and *polis,* city, constitute the standard by which the Greek male from prehistoric times was judged. One has only to consider the extent to which battlefield encounters and the minutiae of hand-to-hand combat are the subject of the *Iliad,* as well as the culminating violence of Odysseus' defense of his home against the suitors of Penelopê to know how native this ethic was to the Greek male.

Greek knows only one word for peace, and it occurs rarely in classical Greek literature; whereas for war and warfare there is a considerable vocabulary that clearly indicates the Greek concern with war in life as well as literature. Fully half of the extant Greek tragedies have war as their direct or indirect subject matter, and from the titles of hundreds of lost plays of the period it is possible to point to many more. Could a fifth century Athenian who endured the Persian Wars in 490 and 480, along with two burnings of Athens, have failed to respond sympathetically to those scenes in the *Iliad* that take place on the defensive walls of Troy? The answer almost certainly is no, even if it was the city of the Other, and the Enemy. Athenians knew from firsthand experience the fear and anxiety of having one's city destroyed. They also knew the bravery of the fighting men who defended it. In *Seven Against Thebes* they got both: a city in peril, as Athens had so recently been, and the heroic figure of a hoplite warrior. The fact that it was Thebes and not Athens, and Eteoklês as opposed to a Thêseus is immaterial. The same can be said of that audience in 472 that saw *Persians.* Trojan or Persian or Theban becomes an academic question when one has experienced a similar horror. Pathos is one of the strongest weapons of tragedy in its attempt to grasp an audience at its most vulnerable, and Aeschylus uses his theatrical and poetic genius to do so in *Seven Against Thebes.* If the play is so widely discounted in modern times, it may be that the wholesale destruction of great cities and the terror and anxiety that accompany it are not a part of the comfortable contemporary world. On those occasions when it is a part, that terror and anxiety are mitigated by distance and the minimizing effect of the television monitor reporting it—except, of course, for the citizens of great cities destroyed.

II
The cycle of prehistoric myths that concentrates on Thebes begins with its founding by Kadmos who slew a dragon, planted its teeth in the earth, from which rose a host of violent giants (Sown Men, as they were called), who immediately set to fighting each other until only five remained to become the founding families of Thebes. The cycle of Theban myths ends seven generations later with the capture of Thebes that is the subject of Aeschylus' play. The characters of this cycle most in favor with Greek tragedians of the classical period were Laïos, Oedipus, and his children: Antigonê, Ismenê, Eteoklês, and Polyneikês. Their stories were told many times over on the Athenian stage, each time with variations that could do almost anything but alter the myth's central core. How Aeschylus' treatment differed from other tellings in the first two lost segments of the trilogy is difficult to say, though there has been much speculation, and from certain allusions made in *Seven Against Thebes* some "facts" may be deduced with reasonable certainty. One of those has to do with the playing out of the curse put upon Laïos and his descendents for three generations.

Relatively late in *Seven Against Thebes*, in the second ode, we are informed by the Chorus that Laïos was guilty of a crime, sin, or disobedience (παρβασια is a difficult word to translate). It is so brief a reference as to suggest that much was made of it earlier in the trilogy, in the *Laïos* surely, and perhaps even in the *Oedipus*, so that now, toward the end of the final play, it only requires brief mention in the attempt to summarize the trilogy's theme. The Chorus sings:

> I tell of a crime of long ago,
> one swift in retribution,
> yet with us still,
> to the third generation,
> when Laïos defied Apollo
> who three times told him at Delphi,
> at Earth's navel,
> if he chose to save his city,
> he must live his life childless.

But Laïos listened to the folly of his own counsel
and sowed his own disaster,
Oedipus, son,
Oedipus, father-killer,
who sowed the sacred soil where he was sown,
and harvested a bloody crop;
Oedipus,
son of parents caught up in frenzy.

According to Thalmann in his study of *Seven Against Thebes*, the word παρβασια "implies a violation of divinely sanctioned limits on human conduct." He questions whether Laïos' refusal to take Apollo's advice warrants being called a crime or sin, and he states that the curse that plagued Laïos and his descendents for three generations is not likely to have come from that source. His reason being that punishment for failing to follow oracular advice was not common. A command not to have children and so secure the continued safety of Thebes is one thing, advice (or foretelling) another. Thalmann questions, therefore, whether the crime of Laïos might not have been something else entirely. In response, he finds a single story that relates a crime by Laïos in which his deed is of that nature. According to it, Laïos as a young man was in exile from Thebes and took refuge in the house of Pelops. He subsequently abducted and raped Pelops' son Chrysippos, who, in some versions, commits suicide out of shame. Pelops then curses Laïos and his descendents through the third generation for one or perhaps both of two reasons. For the death of Chrysippos and/or for violating the guest-host ethic that was sacrosanct in the Greek world. He cautions, however, that "with one possible exception . . . there is no evidence for this story earlier than or contemporary with Aeschylus." It is impossible, he maintains, to place it earlier than Euripides, in whose lost play *Chrysippos,* the rape is portrayed as the cause for the fall of the House of Labdakos. And he asks: "Can Aeschylus earlier have done the same?"

> Certainty is clearly impossible. Yet the lack of extant pre-Euripidean sources for the myth is not decisive, and there is one scrap of evidence which might give it greater antiquity. That is the scholion on line 1760 of Euripides' *Phoenissae,* which gives a version of the story and attributes it to one Peisander . . . a Rhodian epic poet of the sixth century. . . . If he is the one meant by the scholiast, then there is evidence of epic treatment of the myth before Aeschylus. Perhaps, as several scholars have argued, the scholion contains some later additions to the myth.

Even so, the gist of the story is given in the first sentence, and the rest of the note elaborates on it. That sentence refers the tale definitely to Peisander.

As it happens, most if not all contemporary critics and commentators take the text of the passage of the second ode quoted above at face value and, interesting as the question Thalmann raises may be, accept Apollo as the source of the curse on Laïos and his descendents. The present commentary will accept the possibility of the curse that issued from Pelops that concerns only the House of Labdakos for three generations to its extinction, and then it will accept the oracle of Apollo that Thebes would be safe if Laïos had no children, an arrangement that allows for the entanglement of house and city that is at the center of *Seven Against Thebes.*

In any event, Laïos, one may assume, unhappy with Apollo's advice (command?) journeys three times to Delphi and each time receives the same oracular pronouncement: that if he is to maintain Thebes in safety he must die without children. Laïos disobeys and in time Apollo puts Thebes in danger, perhaps from the Sphinx, but ultimately from the Argive invasion by Polyneikês. Whether the child was had by Laïos' own design, or his wife's, or by virtue of their mutual "frenzy," as the ode says, is unclear. The child is then exposed to die on the mountain, but, unknown to the parents, it is somehow saved. In Sophokles both Laïos and his wife, as well as the grown Oedipus, know from another oracle of Apollo that their son will kill his father and marry his mother, and that is the parents' reason for exposing him, and the adult Oedipus' reason for fleeing his supposed parents, the king and queen of Korinth. Whether that is the situation in Aeschylus is open to question. In any case, there is no allusion to it in *Seven Against Thebes,* and if it was mentioned in either of the preceding plays there is nothing to indicate it. Why, then, do the parents in Aeschylus try to kill their child? A guess is that Laïos had second thoughts regarding Apollo's advice/command and attempted to reverse his error by killing the child. Unfortunately it was too late, the deed was done and a son was born.

In *Laïos,* the first play of the trilogy, we know that Laïos goes off on a journey, that he meets and has an altercation on the way with his now grown but unknown son, and that he is killed by him, along with most of the royal retinue. A surviving member of the king's guard takes the news back to Thebes.

In Aeschylus, why Thebes is held hostage by the Sphinx is not known. It may be a part of Apollo's punishment, and yet there is another possibility. We know that a sixth-century source mentions Hera as the one responsible, as retribution for Thebes' failure to punish Laïos for his guilt in the rape and death of Chrysippos. "If," writes Thalmann, "Aeschylus incorporated this into his story (and it is possible, though of course not certain, that he did), it would be one way in which the city was implicated in the misfortunes of the individual family [the House of Labdakos]." It would also coincide with Thalmann's deduction that the crime "implies a violation of divinely sanctioned limits on human conduct." Considering that Hera is a patron goddess of marriage, and thus, by implication, of the family, Laïos' strike at the family of Pelops was answered by Hera's strike at his own family as well as at Thebes for its failure to punish Laïos' "crime." But does Hera's punishment also include the Argive invasion in the third generation of *Seven Against Thebes*? What we have here, then, are multiple reasons for the fates of family and city to be entangled, quite apart from the offense to Apollo. In any event, the Labdakos family has been deeply wounded, and this may account for Aeschylus' "major rearrangement of the family relationships."

In the epic version Oedipus unwittingly marries his mother, but has no children by her, as he does in Aeschylus. It is unknown whether this is an invention of Aeschylus or a non-epic variation on the myth, but "his choice or invention of it is remarkable." Thalmann continues:

> The curse, working through the generations, cut off Laïos and his descendants from the normal rhythm of life; Aeschylus therefore must have wanted to make the family's composition strikingly abnormal. By making Oedipus not only the father but also the brother of Eteocles and Polyneices, he made their birth unnatural; more important, he presented a picture of a family in which the generations were confused and the relations between them ambiguous.

There is another aspect of Aeschylus' use and elaboration of the Oedipus myth that deserves attention, and that is Oedipus' self-guilt and blinding as punishment for his crime. In *Oedipus Tyrannos* he blinds himself in remorse for his "crime," but in *Oedipus at Kolonos* he retracts his guilt and defends himself as the victim of the gods, as one who acted unwittingly. But in Aeschylus (perhaps for the first time, according to Thalmann) the personal guilt of Oedipus is indeed an issue, for it is "crucial to the notion of an inherited curse which affects both the individual and the community." And that Curse, that Fury or Erinys, inherited by Oedipus is in turn passed on to Eteoklês and Polyneikês in the form of their father's curse that will end in their death at each others' hands.

III

After Oedipus' self-blinding, it is logical to suppose that the rule of Thebes most likely fell to his sons, who in time somehow abused their father (there are extant several possibilities—from dispossession, to being served an inferior cut of meat at table, or with the wrong table service) and were made the victims of his own curse on them that is to play itself out in *Seven Against Thebes.*

It is in the second choral ode, after Eteoklês' final exit on his way to do battle with his brother Polyneikês, that Aeschylus begins a grand summing up of the entire trilogy: the fall of the House of Labdakos and the fate of Thebes, both of whose fates are so entangled by the Pelops/Hera/Apollo/Oedipus curses. He begins at the end, which is just about to eventuate as the Fury of Oedipus presses on to the mutual destruction of his two sons. Then, progressing generally rearward in time, over the course of three generations, he speaks of the means of their destruction, Iron, the "stranger from Skythia," the sword that Oedipus in the previous play predicted would arbitrate and mete out their equally divided inheritance and fate, their graves; of the crime of Laïos and the curse to last for three generations; of Laïos' triple denial of Apollo and of Oedipus' birth; of the death of Laïos at his son's hands; of the son's marriage to his mother and the birth of a terrible brood from that union. Then the ode begins to reverse direction as it speaks in the present of the city as a ship tossed perilously by the triple-crested waves of ancient curses, the ship whose only chance of survival is to empty its hold or it will founder— an image that suggests what was part of the myth for the three generations concerned: Apollo's word that Thebes would be spared if Laïos had no children. The Chorus then speaks again of Oedipus as the most honored of men by man and god, for he purged Thebes of the Sphinx; of Oedipus who discovered the evil of his acts, the killing of his father, the marrying of his mother, and the curse of mutual destruction put upon his sons. The Chorus finally ends up back where it began, with the Fury that is now come to see that curse fulfilled, namely the extinction of the last of the House of Labdakos: the third generation of the descendents of Laïos: Eteoklês and Polyneikês.

City and House are about to be disentangled in a terrible battle between brothers; and Aeschylus, it appears, this time around, allows Apollo to do what was denied him in the first generation, to save Thebes despite Laïos' disobedience and the (attempted) killing of the child. The second ode follows in its entirety.

I shudder,
shudder at the house-destroying god,

god unlike any other god,
infallible god that prophesies evil,
the Fury that Oedipus called upon,
Avenging Spirit,
to slay two brothers at each others' hands.
And now it happens,
now it comes true,
among us now,
Fury cried up by a father's curse,
wrathful Oedipus,
shouted in madness,
son-destroying Fury that spurs it to its end.

A stranger comes,
a stranger in a dream,
a stranger from Skythia,
savage-hearted Iron,
ruthless arbitrator of wealth,
keen-tempered Iron,
razor-sharp blade,
allottor of land,
but only so much as the dead require,
none of their vast plains and fields,
but only the space of a grave.

When they are dead,
when brother murders brother,
when their land's dust has
drunk down their blood,
black blood of slaughtered brothers,
who will come then,
who will give cleansing,
who will purify their hacked limbs,
wash them clean of evil pollution?
I weep for the miseries
old and new
that mingle in the history
of this house!

I tell of a crime of long ago,
one swift in retribution,
yet with us still,
to the third generation,
when Laïos defied Apollo
who three times told him at Delphi,
at Earth's navel,
if he chose to save his city,
he must live his life childless.
But Laïos listened to the folly of his own counsel
and sowed his own disaster,
Oedipus, son,
Oedipus, father-killer,
who sowed the sacred soil where he was sown,
and harvested a bloody crop;
Oedipus,
son of parents caught up in frenzy.

The sea rises,
waves of evil crash,
another rises,
rises high,
triple-crested,
crashes,
crashes hard on the city's hull,
a thin defense between us and doom,
the width of our walls.
I fear,
I tremble for our safety,
our city's and our princes'.

For ancient curses,
come home,
demand heavy payment,
and never depart.
Disaster knows poverty
and passes by.
But the rich grown fat
must pay their toll by

emptying out the
wealth of their hold.

Who was ever more honored
by man and god
than Oedipus
who purged our land
of the man-eating Sphinx?

But when at last
he knew the horror of his marriage,
overwhelmed with grief,
in misery,
he did two deeds,
two terrible deeds,
two deeds of evil.
First, with the hand that slew his father,
he ripped out his own eyes,
dearer to him than his sons.

And then when those sons disowned him,
he lashed them with wrathful curses,
saying the day would come
when with blades of iron
they would divide his property.
But now I tremble,
for now a Fury has come,
a swift-footed Fury,
to see it fulfilled!

IV

For all of the contempt and hostility that the last century and a half has exhib-
ited in regard to *Seven Against Thebes*—much of it wrongheaded and perverse,
expecting of it what its author never intended, disgruntled that it is not like
other Aeschylean plays—it is nonetheless a great play and the product of an
extraordinary mind.

It differs in one major respect from the extant play that precedes it in
time, *Persians,* and from the play that is to succeed it, *Suppliants,* and that is
in the introduction of an individual, Eteoklês, who will serve as the dramatic

focus of the action. In the other two plays it is the Chorus that serves as the focal point.

Eteoklês has been called by Kitto in his *Greek Tragedy* "the first man of the European stage," and the play he singles out as "our earliest tragedy of character." Eteoklês is quite simply one of the most arresting figures of the Greek theater. He may not be Oedipus in the plays by Sophokles, but, then, Aeschylus was his own man and his own thinker, just as Sophokles was his own; and just as Sophokles was not of a temper to have written the *Oresteia,* so Aeschylus could never have written anything that resembled a character of Euripides. In a word, Eteoklês is the paradigm of the Heroic Man, one who dazzles not only the people of mythical Thebes who inhabit *Seven Against Thebes,* but audiences as well. He is, in another word, one of the finest examples of the *areté* hero in extant Greek tragedy. The operative word here is "finest," for Aeschylus treats him almost as a symbol, much as Shakespeare treats Henry V as a symbol of the ideal warrior king. It is not too much, perhaps, to say that Eteoklês is the exemplar of what the Greek warrior of the fifth century strove to be. Central to that striving is the concept of areté, a word that is not a product of fifth-century Greece, but as old as the earliest beginnings of Greece of which we have any knowledge, and is a major factor in the Homeric epics *Iliad* and *Odyssey.* But before continuing, something must be said about areté, for no equivalent term for it exists in English.

V

Areté is the product of the ancient concept of nobility. According to Werner Jaeger in his *Paideia,* "its oldest meaning is a combination of proud and court-ly morality with warlike valour. But the idea of areté is the quintessence of early Greek aristocratic education," as described by Homer. At its root the word means exceptional, indeed unrivaled, ability and superiority. Jaeger continues:

> In Homer, the real mark of the nobleman is his sense of duty. He is judged, and is proud to be judged, by a severe standard. And the noble-man educates others by presenting to them an eternal ideal, to which they have a duty to conform. His sense of duty is *aidos.* Anyone is free to appeal to aidos; and if it is slighted the slight awakes in others the kindred emotion of *nemesis.* Both aidos and nemesis are essential parts of Homer's ideal of aristocracy. The nobleman's pride in high race and ancient achievement is partnered by his knowledge that his preemi-nence can be guaranteed only by the virtues which won it. The aristoi

are distinguished by that name from the mass of the common people: and though there are many aristoi, they are always striving with one another for the prize of areté. The Greek nobles believed that the real test of manly virtue was victory in battle—a victory that was not merely the physical conquest of an enemy, but the proof of hard-won areté. . . . The hero's whole life and effort are a race for the first prize, an unceasing strife for supremacy over his peers. . . . In peace-time too, the warriors match their aretai against one another in war-games: in the *Iliad* we see them in competition even in a brief pause in the war, at the funeral games of Patroclus. It was that chivalrous rivalry which struck out the motto of knighthood throughout the centuries:

αιεν αριστευειν και υπειροχον εμμεναι αλλων.
["To act always with valor, always to be the most noble."]

That line from the sixth book of *Iliad* clearly indicates that the Homeric poet had progressed beyond the older Greek ethic that defined areté as "warlike prowess" only; for now, in Homer's time, it combined noble action with the workings of a noble mind, which is another way of expressing the advice of Phoenix, the old teacher of Achilles when he advises him "to be both a speaker of words and a doer of deeds," for words and the ability to use words became a part of areté and was the sign of intellectual superiority. The rationale, then, behind the constant broadening of the meaning of areté was to keep pace with a society whose ideals of human perfection were expanding and growing ever more exalted in terms of morals and honor. "Men," says Aristotle in *Nicomachean Ethics,* "seem to pursue honor in order to assure themselves of their own worth—their areté. They strive to be honored for it, by men who know them and who are judicious. It is therefore clear that they recognize areté as superior."

"Here, then," writes Jaeger, "we can grasp the vital significance of early aristocratic morality for the shaping of the Greek character. It is immediately clear that the Greek conception of man and his areté developed along an unbroken line throughout Greek history. Although it was transformed and enriched in succeeding centuries, it retained the shape which it had taken in the moral code of the nobility. The aristocratic character of the Greek ideal of culture was always based on this conception of areté." And he continues:

Under the guidance of Aristotle, we may here investigate some of its further implications. He explains that human effort after complete areté is the product of an ennobled self-love, φιλαυτια. This doctrine is not a mere caprice of abstract speculation—if it were, it would be misleading to compare it with early conceptions of areté. Aristotle is defending the ideal of fully justified self-love as against the current beliefs of his own enlightened and "altruistic" age; and in doing so he has laid bare one of the foundations of Greek ethical thought. In fact, he admires self-love, just as he prizes high-mindedness and the desire for honour, because his philosophy is deeply rooted in the old aristocratic code of morality. We must understand that the Self is not the physical self, but the ideal which inspires us, the ideal which every nobleman strives to realize in his own life. If we grasp that, we shall see that it is the highest kind of self-love which makes man reach out towards the highest areté: through which he "takes possession of the beautiful." The last phrase is so entirely Greek that it is hard to translate. For the Greeks, beauty meant nobility also. To lay claim to the beautiful, to take possession of it, means to overlook no opportunity of winning the prize of the highest areté.

But what did Aristotle mean by the beautiful? Our thoughts turn at once to the sophisticated views of later ages—the cult of the individual, the humanism of the eighteenth century, with its aspirations towards aesthetic and spiritual self-development. But Aristotle's own words are quite clear. They show that he was thinking chiefly of acts of moral heroism. A man who loves himself will (he thought) always be ready to sacrifice himself for his friends or his country, to abandon possessions and honours in order to "take possession of the beautiful." The strange phrase is repeated: and we can now see why Aristotle should think that the utmost sacrifice to an ideal is a proof of a highly developed self-love. "For," says he, "such a man would prefer short intense pleasures to long quiet ones; would choose to live nobly for a year rather than to pass many years of ordinary life; would rather do one great and noble deed than many small ones."

These sentences reveal the very heart of the Greek view of life—the sense of heroism through which we feel them most closely akin to ourselves. By this clue we can understand the whole of Hellenic history—it is the psychological explanation of the short but glorious aristeia of the Greek spirit. The basic motive of Greek areté is contained in the words "to take possession of the beautiful." The courage of a Homeric nobleman is superior to the berserk contempt of death in this—that he subordinates his physical self to the demands of a higher aim, the beautiful. And so the man who gives up his life to win the beautiful, will find that his natural instinct for self-assertion finds its highest expression in self-sacrifice.

In discussing *Seven Against Thebes* it is important to remember that it is the culminating play of the Theban trilogy, and what went before can largely be only guessed at. Needless to say, how the play would look if it were played in its original sequence can also only be surmised. It behooves us, then, to see it as a single play, and to judge it on its own merits. As it stands in its truncated form, apart from its two earlier segments, it is only tangentially the pitiless working out of the original curse put upon Laïos and discussed above. That can be seen as the theme that unites the plays of the trilogy. In its current form the tragedy of *Seven Against Thebes* is not so much that of a man, Eteoklês, who is the victim of a curse put on his House three generations ago, but of a man who by virtue of everything Aeschylus tells us and shows us about him deserves better than he gets. He is everything the areté hero can possibly be. The concept of an unfair and cruel punishment is utterly different from the more benign, though terrible, punishment of Xerxês in *Persians*. There the dramatic pulse is a much simpler and less complex matter; it is the punishment of personal and national hybris. In *Seven Against Thebes* the dramatic pulse beats as feverishly as it does anywhere in extant Greek tragedy. In *Persians* the punishment was just, in *Seven Against Thebes* it is cruel and vicious and perhaps even unjust.

VI

The scene of *Seven Against Thebes* is the high hill of the Theban Akropolis, that walled seat of government and religion that is the center of all that is vital to the State. Not far outside the walls is the massed army of Argos, assembled by Polyneikês, the exiled brother of Eteoklês. It is a moment of enormous tension as the invaders get ready to move closer and surround the walls that they have long held at siege. The stage is most likely packed with tense male citizens milling about, uneasy at the sounds of military preparation without, the clash and clanking of metal weapons and armor, the positioning of heavy armaments, the rumble of wheels on stony ground, and not least the sense of thousands being marshaled to formation by shouted voices of command. It is a sound that pervades the scene of action from beginning to end.

Onto this scene comes Eteoklês, ruler of Thebes, and from the first he demonstrates the aptness of an image that is frequently associated with him in the play, that of captain or helmsman, "of your Ship of State," as he says, a rock-steady guardian who knows what leadership can be and is for him. His is an entry as forceful and energetic as any in Greek tragedy, and one the text of which is so reminiscent of the opening page of Sophokles' *Oedipus Tyrannos* as to suggest that the thirty-year-old Sophokles witnessing this play in 467 vividly recalled it three decades later when he wrote his own Oedipus play. Tone, value, progress of thought and quality of kingship, and paternal concern are the same. Like son, like father. The only difference is that Eteoklês is, given the siege of Thebes, a warrior as well, more immediately pressed than even the Oedipus of Sophokles with a plague at his doorstep, and so he is seen at the peak of his readiness, and, like his father by that other playwright some thirty years in the future, he is sleepless in his paternal concern for his people.

> Thebans!
> Children of Kadmos!
> I stand before you here, helmsman
>   of your Ship of State,
>   my hand on the tiller, sleepless
> and unblinking, as should any captain
>   when a fateful decision is required!
> And such a decision stares us
>   down at this moment.

But Eteoklês is also a realist, he is pragmatic. He realizes what is owed to the gods, and he gives them their due, asking for their aid. He knows that if Thebes is victorious the gods will be praised, and if Thebes is defeated and enslaved it will be he who is blamed. And he says it:

> If all goes well, it is the gods'
>   doing, and praise to them.
> But let disaster strike—which
>   heaven forbid!—and one name only
> will be on every man's tongue,
> one name will swell like an angry
>   wave,
> muttered cries, groans,
>   curses from every man's
>   throat,
> a wailing lament of discord:
>
> Eteoklês!

So he doesn't wait for the gods to respond or not to respond. He does what is required, he gives Zeus his due: "Zeus Protector, save us from this fate! Fulfil your name!" The next moment he is a realist once again, or perhaps he never stopped being one for we can suspect a bit of irony in that "Protector," not to mention the challenge to Zeus to "fulfill" his name. That done with remarkable efficiency, his focus is immediately back on track—the city's safety:

> But now to you, to your
> > task.
> I call on you all to come to your city's aid.
> Boys, not yet men, men now
> > past their prime, and those of you now
> > in your glorious peak of
> > > manhood.
> Your city needs you,
> > needs you all, to defend her and her
> > > temples and altars, her
> > gods, who must never lack your
> > > > devotion.
> Rescue her, and rescue your
> > children, and earth, your
> > mother, your fondest nurse, who
> shirked no toil of nurture,
> but bore you on her breast as
> > tender saplings, so that when the
> > > time comes—and it has
> > come!—you will take up the
> > > shield and fight in her
> defense as loyal repayment for her
> > > love.

And then, sounding every bit like Henry V at Agincourt, Eteoklês gives his own "Once more unto the breach" speech to his "citizen army" as we might call them (the real army being at the gates, ready to be attacked).

> Hear me, all of you!
> Thebes needs you, now!
> Man the battlements and city gates!
> > Take up arms!

Hurry! Run,
run to the bulwarks and the towers'
platforms! Be brave! Hold your
ground! Stand up to this foreign
invader face to face! The gods are
with us!

This opening speech of the play by a leader who knows with near-certainty that this is his last day, and that it will end with his own and his brother's death at each others' hands, paints verbally a vivid picture of a surpassingly brave and noble warrior whose sole concern is his people and not himself.

As the men of Thebes run off to their posts, a Scout enters with news that intensifies an already tense situation. He describes the invading Argive army outside the walls; the ritual slaughter of a bull by its leaders, dipping their fingers in the black gore of its blood, those men with "the hearts of lions . . . flashing from their eyes, and wills of iron," swearing oaths to a trinity of gods he identifies as "wargod Arês, Frenzy and Fear."

They would
either, they said, smash this city and
pound it into dust, or with their
dying blood make a paste of the
earth of Thebes.

Having vividly described the scene and the temper of the men thirsting for battle, the Scout concludes with advice that might seem overly forward of a regular soldier to be offering to his general, except that it is offered with such confidence and directness that it tells of a commander who is known by his army as by his citizenry as one willing to listen and to take advice. It is advice offered without fear, the polar opposite of that trembling messenger in Euripides' *Bakkhai* who asks a tyrannical Pentheus if he has permission to speak freely. "Hurry, sir," says the Scout,

there's no time for delay;
assign the best of our men,
the city's finest,
at our seven gates.
Every second counts.

The Argives are approaching in full
        force, raising clouds of
                dust, and the field is flecked with foam
        from their stallions' throats.

And then, master theater craftsman that he is, Aeschylus tells us in the close
of the Scout's speech, the degree to which Eteoklês is respected for his benevolent and successful rule. And he does it in one sentence: "Be the helmsman
you are, sir."

Be the helmsman you are, sir.
Batten down our
        city before the squalls of wargod
        Arês swoop down and
                        destroy us.
There's a flood of men rushing toward us
        like waves of the sea.
It's now or never, sir.
        We have to act.
        Trust me, sir.
I'll keep my eye peeled, and my
        news from outside will be clear as
                        day.
You'll know what's
        happening, sir. You'll be
                safe, sir.

There can be little doubt that all of Thebes (as well as everyone in the
audience of that Theater of Dionysos in Athens) knows of the curse that Pelops
placed on the House of Labdakos, and that the final blow of that curse is about
to strike. If the heat of the moment has made the Scout forget that the brothers are to kill each other before the day is out, or at any rate very soon, he is
surely reminded of it when he describes the enemy as drawing lots to see who
goes to which gate, and tells Eteoklês to "assign" or marshal "the best of our
men, the city's finest, at our seven gates." First of all, the fact that the verb is
in the Greek "middle" voice suggests that Eteoklês will arrange the assignments
but not himself participate as one of those assigned. Given the Scout's respect
for him, it is not unlikely that he knows that Eteoklês will indeed assign himself to one of the gates. The Scout's desire for this not to happen causes him

in the thought process of formulating his sentence indeed to suggest that. But it is the repetition, "best of our men," and "city's finest," that suggests the Scout intuits what will happen and, knowing the honor and moral integrity of Eteoklês, repeats the encomium that so aptly defines his master's heroic areté. The repetition is most likely punctuated by only a second's hesitation. But whatever it is, it is meant to convey to the audience his love for his ruler. His last sentence, as he leaves to return to the walls, is: "You'll be safe, sir." A wish that most likely he knows is futile.

In these two opening segments of the prologue Aeschylus has gone to considerable effort to inform the spectator of the nature of the hero of his tale. He shows him, first, as a man of action acting—on the spot and in public—responsibly and heroically at a desperate and uncertain moment in his city's history. He then shows him to us in something close to a private moment, only he and the Scout are on stage, as he listens to the Scout's battlefield report, in which we see the respect his men, and, by extension, the city have for him. The third stroke in the portrait of his hero comes with the exit of the Scout, leaving Eteoklês alone on stage, a moment totally to himself. From the mass scene of the opening, to the intimate scene of the meeting with the Scout, to the scene of total isolation, the focus on Eteoklês grows sharper and sharper, as if a lens were zooming in for a close up or a magnifying glass were being held up to him, and not only does his public image not erode with the greater focus, but his stature grows immeasurably. He prays, while the noise of war preparations is heard outside the walls:

> O Zeus and Earth our mother
>> and the city's gods, and you,
> Fury, Spirit Curse of my father Oedipus,
>> for you are powerful,
>>> spare,
>>>> spare my city at least,
>>>>> don't
> tear us up root and branch, homes, temples,
>> the victim of enemy hands!
> We're Greek, we're free,
>> as is our city, Thebes,
>> the children of Kadmos,
> slavery must never bind her in its chains!
>>>>> Be with her!
>> Defend her!

> I plead for us both! A prosperous state
> deals prosperously with the gods!

Are the opening lines of this prayer a cry of anguish, or, considering the obvious contraction, the pulling in, the focusing of attention on Eteoklês on an empty stage. Is he calm in contrast to his active, highly verbal mode in the opening crowd scene, and also in contrast to his total silence during the Scout's speech? I suspect calm, collected, if also passionate. Alone on stage with only one thought in mind, he may well not move at all. That is, after all, the direction in which Aeschylus' stagecraft appears to have headed.

Eteoklês first implores, as is only proper, Zeus and Mother Earth and the city's gods. Then, for the first time in the play, he addresses his father's gods, the Fury, the Spirit Curse called down on him and his brother, that he knows will destroy them both. But even before finishing that sentence, he has gone beyond that momentary thought of himself, and pleads for his city: "spare my city at least, " he says—and that "at least" says everything. In Greek it has to do with the positioning of a particle that stresses what precedes it. So what is stressed here is "city." There is not a "spare me" anywhere to be found. His "us" and "we" and "our" in the concluding lines are not self-centered, but city-centered; he is as much one with his people as Sophokles' Oedipus is to be thirty years later.

Even his closing lines, "I plead for us both! A prosperous state deals prosperously with the gods!" are in keeping with the tone of the prayer. Some critics have taken them as faintly irreverent, but I suspect they are not. On two separate occasions the chorus says virtually the same thing, a kind of bartering with the gods, which, according to Hutchinson, the play's major contemporary editor, is not unusual: "Men may remind the gods that only if they are delivered can they continue to offer sacrifice." He also points out that "prosperous" here is not necessarily the opposite of unprosperous, but rather "a reticent expression for 'not destroyed by the enemy.'" If that reticence did not surface in public, but only in this private moment, it merely adds to Eteoklês' stature for presenting to his people a face to inspire hope rather than its opposite. That reticence is also a subtle attempt on Aeschylus' part to show his hero as one who is human as well as the noblest of leaders. Shakespeare does the same with his Henry V, who, in the dark of night, before the battle of Agincourt, prays for the God of Battles to steel his soldiers' hearts.

VII

The quiet, somber moment of the prayer concluded, Aeschylus shocks us into recognition with one of the most active and effective Chorus entrances in Greek tragedy. The Chorus of Young Theban Women does not enter as most choruses, in an orderly dance or march (as we wrongly used to believe), but in what must have been an elaborate choreography designed by Aeschylus, an entrance of enormous disorder and agitation, lunging, spiraling every which way to make visual the agitation and wild frenzy present in the dochmaic meter of their chanted utterance that later erupts into song and a mixture of dochmaics and lyric iambs (in the Greek). The center of attention of these frenzied women is the multitude of altars and statues that dominate the scene and that they will later fall in front of and cling to in their terror. They describe the martial sounds of the Argive enemy outside the walls. Here is the opening:

> I hear the hoofs.
> Hard on the land.
> Echoing, echoing.
> Listen. Hear it?
> Listen.
> Clashing shields.
> Closer, closer.
> Coming.
> Tumbling, thundering.
> Pitiless crash.
> Mountain torrent.
> IOOO! IOOO!
> Gods. Goddesses.
> Turn them,
> the evil,
> rushing,
> the walls,
> war cry,
> turn, turn back disaster.
> Shields, coming,
> white shields,
> dazzling.
> Ready.
> Ready for battle.
> Full speed.

What god, what goddess?
Who will save us?
Gods, do you hear?
Down on your knees, women.
Fall to the earth.
Bow to the gods.
Grab, cling to the statues.

The entrance song of the chorus is a long one (just over one hundred lines in the Greek) in order to create an atmosphere of chaos that contrasts violently with the play's opening, and especially with the subdued passion of the prayer only now ended. It is important, too, in establishing an atmosphere utterly in opposition to what Eteoklês believes must prevail in order for Thebes to survive. He bursts onto the scene with a forcefulness, indeed violence, that has not been seen before, and it comes as a shock.

Vile, insupportable creatures!
Is this how you help the
        city, your city, a city that needs
                                help?
Is this how you fuel the
        hearts of your defenders with
        courage? The spirits of those
                defending you under siege?
By throwing yourselves at the
        feet of the city-gods' statues?
By groveling before them?
        Howling, shrieking?
        An outrage to decency!

He then launches into what has become a most problematic part of what is perceived as his character: virulent anti-feminism.

Save me from the female sex,
        bad times or good!
Give them the upper hand and
        they're insufferable; frightened, they're a
                danger to the home and even more
        to the city!

And it goes on. One must wait for Euripides' Jason and Hippolytos to find more virulent condemnation of the female. Jason and Hippolytos have obvious reasons for their attitudes, and so does Eteoklês, and the reason is as simple as saying that the chaos and anarchy the women are creating is pushing Thebes to the brink of extinction. Their shrieks, their yells, their frenzy are undermining, from within the walls, the city's morale and capacity to respond to the threat of invasion as surely as the enemy is destroying it from outside the walls. They are encouraging cowardice, he says, and he will deal with them, if they continue, as he would deal with any man who did the same, "with death by stoning in the public square!" Though he doesn't use the word treason regarding the women's actions, he might as well have, for they are striking at the heart of the city. He is, in fact, more lenient, if also more enraged, than Henry V on his way to war in France, who never blinks as he condemns to death the nobles Cambridge, Scrope, and Grey for an act of treason. Neither Henry's action nor Eteoklês' in any way lowers their value as areté heroes, but in fact shows them to be vigilant at every turn, an ancient attribute of kings.

Eteoklês then continues in a mode that would not have shocked the fifth-century Greek.

> Matters outside the home are affairs of state
>   and we want no women here!
> This is men's work, and
>   men's work it will remain!
>
>   Go inside, now,
> inside with you, and stay there,
>   inside your houses, and make no
>   trouble!

The position of women in fifth-century Greece was not the best. It was a male society, and women's function was to bear and raise (male) children till their fathers could take charge of them at age seven or eight and introduce them into the male world. For the rest, woman's place was in her section of the house, much as Eteoklês says.

When he has finally quieted them, he makes another point that helps to define his character for us. Even further, he tells the women that they must change their prayers. Rather than simply ask the gods to *avert* disaster, merely to shield them from the enemy, they must ask the gods to *join* the Thebans in defeating the enemy. He believes in the gods, but when it comes to action it is, ultimately, man who must act if he is to survive. Again he is the pragmatic warrior; again he is the areté hero, whose basic moving force is, as Aristotle says, "to take possession of the beautiful." And the beautiful here for Eteoklês is to win victory and safety for his city. "And so," continues Aristotle, "the man who gives up his life to win the beautiful, will find that his natural instinct for self-assertion finds its highest expression in self-sacrifice." That is what Eteoklês now does. With his prayer concluded, he turns, as always, to the duty at hand, to action.

> I'm going now
> to assign six men to six
> gates, reserving for myself
> the seventh.
> Seven champions at seven gates to
> fight the foe heroically.
> And I go before the arrival of a scout
> to tell us the urgency of the
> need.

According to Christopher Dawson, "in revealing and characteristic fashion, he turns to action: he offers himself as the seventh defender, to engage physically and prominently in the city's defense—in fact, because of the Chorus' irrationality, deserting his post as the ship's helmsman . . . So, in making what seems to be an appropriate immediate decision, he leads to his own downfall."

But that isn't necessarily so, not if what we are dealing with in Eteoklês is an areté hero, one determined "to take possession of the beautiful." And here we have to expand "beautiful" to refer not merely to an action and its result (the delivery of Thebes) but to a reputation, his, the reputation of Eteoklês. As an areté hero, Eteoklês has no choice but to take vengeance for an offense done to him. To fail to do so would bring disgrace and dishonor, and with that there comes loss of areté, loss of reputation and moral superiority. That offense against him (and Thebes) is invasion by a treasonous brother.

The great central scene of the play over—the brilliant, perceptive, and moral matching of six Theban warriors against their Argive opponents at the first six gates, and then the inevitable matching of Eteoklês against Polyneikês at the seventh—the great transformation in Eteoklês begins, or rather the full blossoming of the areté hero. But before embarking on this culminating sequence of *Seven Against Thebes,* the ritualistic fitting out of Eteoklês in his warrior's armor, the final realization of the warrior before our eyes, it is necessary to pause and consider first the implication of the portrait of Eteoklês' opponent, his brother, at the seventh gate—Polyneikês. What does Aeschylus offer as the opposite of the areté portrait he has painted of Eteoklês?

VIIII

In Sophokles' *Antigonê* we have no picture of Eteoklês except as defender, nor any of Polyneikês except as invader, though we know from *Oedipus at Kolonos* that both brothers are culpable in their treatment of the blind Oedipus, and so both are guilty of bringing on themselves their father's curse. For all that we come to learn of Eteoklês in *Seven Against Thebes,* we learn precious little of Polyneikês, but what we do learn is potent material, a lifetime packed into a comparatively few lines spoken by Eteoklês. Before that, however, Aeschylus, in the words of the Scout, presents a most unflattering picture of Polyneikês as the assailant at the seventh gate: a blustering, loudmouthed, irreverent invader intent on destroying not only his brother, as the curse has it, but all of Thebes and its people.

> Now for the seventh man at the seventh gate,
>> the final champion,
>>> your brother.
> I'll tell you of the curses and the
>> fate he calls down on the city.
> He declares that once he stands
>> mounted on our walls,
> once he is proclaimed victor and conqueror of Thebes,
> he will shout his wild cry of conquest,
> his war-whoop at the city's fall,
>> at its desolation and over its vanquished corpses.
> And then, hand to hand, he will
>> fight and kill you, and, in killing you,
>> lie beside you in death;
> or, if you live,
>> he will banish you to dishonorable exile
>> as you once banished him.
>>> Bellowing,
> he calls to witness the gods of your
>> race and the gods of your fatherland,

Polyneikês,
          violent warrior Polyneikês.

These descriptive lines are crucial in evaluating the nature and the legitimacy of Polyneikês. To begin with, he is a traitor, as Amphiaraös, the honorable Argive prophet-warrior at gate six makes clear, one intent on invading and destroying his father's land and his father's gods, and this cannot be taken lightly. No less significant is the suggestion that he doesn't take Oedipus' curse quite seriously. He first boasts of killing Eteoklês and then lying beside him in death. But then he says "or, if you live," and if he does live Polyneikês will banish him as he has been banished. In saying "or, if you live," he virtually denies the efficacy of the curse on the two brothers, an efficacy that one must assume is an element so basic to the myth that Aeschylus would not have been permitted to alter it. In the matter of such a curse, Winnington-Ingram writes, "for a man to lie beneath a father's curse was to the Greek a most terrible thing: it had the force of an Erinys . . ." Can Polyneikês' denial, or doubt, of the curse be anything but sacrilegious in the classical Greek world, let alone in the mythic world of this fable?

Polyneikês' emblazoned shield is then described in some detail and for good reason:

          His shield,
     newly-fashioned and a perfect round,
     has emblazoned on it in beaten gold
          a twofold device.
     A man in full armor led on modestly
          by a woman.
     Her motto says in gold letters:
          "I am Justice. And I will restore this man
          to his city and to the home of his fathers,
          rightfully his own."

Justice, daughter of Zeus, has now entered the picture and will be a major concern in Eteoklês' response as well as in the remainder of the play. But before that let us look at the conclusion to the Scout's speech.

     Now you know all the devices of the enemy.
          It's for you, helmsman,

to choose and send the warrior to answer him.
You will find no fault in my report.
                              Yes,
it's for you to determine the city's
                    course.

As with so much in this most subtle of plays, Aeschylus bridges gaps of
time to remind his audience of attitudes expressed earlier. He does so here,
when the Scout for the second time calls Eteoklês "helmsman," a term of
respect for his leadership, which he used at the end of the prologue. But there
is another repetition here as there was in the prologue. Just before his exit after
his speech describing Polyneikês at the seventh gate, the Scout says to Eteoklês: "It's for you, helmsman, to choose and send the warrior to answer him,"
and "Yes, it's for you to determine the city's course." Editors have frequently
assumed the repetition to be unnecessary and redundant. But the same kind
of repetition occurred in the Scout's speech in the prologue. There the repetition was two juxtaposed phrases: "[1] assign the best of our men, and [2]
the city's finest, at our seven gates." Here, as earlier, he has no doubt what
will happen, that Eteoklês will post himself at the seventh gate, all the others
having been assigned. That knowledge so moves him that here, as before, he
repeats himself in order to hide his embarrassment at his visible or invisible
emotional response. Even more telling, perhaps, is his departure before Eteoklês makes that assignment. Many editors choose to delete one or the other of
those lines, and that is certainly a solution, though perhaps not the best, and
a bit shortsighted when it comes to an assessment of Aeschylus' psychological understanding, not to mention his stagecraft.

   This repetition of an emotional moment by the same character accom-
plishes three things. It reasserts close to the play's end the city's love for its
ruler; it reasserts the honor of his areté status; and it gives credence to his evaluation of Polyneikês in the speech to come, the speech that begins with the
climactic moment of the tragedy. Always in charge, despite his full awareness
of the events to come, Eteoklês cries out in anguish for the first time in the
play. Some critics maintain that prior to this he has hidden from himself the
realization of what is to come, and that here, for the first time, he allows himself to acknowledge it. This, I think, contradicts the honesty and honor of the
areté hero that Eteoklês has been shown to be. Aeschylus has put on him too
great a value for him to fail to be anything less than totally honest with
himself.

God-hated house of Oedipus,
> house cursed by the gods,
> house maddened by gods,
> > house of tears,
now the curse of Oedipus is fulfilled!

But no time for tears or wailing now,
giving birth to even worse suffering!

As in his prayer at the end of the prologue, Eteoklês immediately rejects his personal concern and returns to the matter of Thebes and her people, turning his full attention to Polyneikês:

> > > As for him,
Polyneikês,
> > so well named,
> > > strife-bringer, we will
see if his sign is fulfilled; whether golden
letters on a shield will do what they say;
or are they the babble of a demented
> > > > mind?
If Justice, virgin daughter of
> > Zeus, had ever been with him in
> > > thought or deed, his boasting might have come
> > > > > > true.
But never, never once, never—not when he
> > fled the dark cavern of his mother's
> > > womb, not in childhood or adolescence, not when the
hair of manhood grew on his chin,
> > did Justice ever, even once,
> > > turn her eye on him or ever acknowledge him!
Nor does she now,
> > now as he rapes his city, his parent
> > > land, in this violent, criminal assault!
For if she did, if Justice looked
> > kindly on him, she would be justly misnamed
> > > for championing one who brings death on his city!

Harsh words. Words that inevitably raise the question: Do we have any reason to doubt this damning report? The answer is, not if we take seriously the honor of Eteoklês—but to leave it at that is to settle for too easy an answer.

In Eteoklês' speech quoted above, he speaks of Justice as never once in Polyneikês' life having cast an eye on him, never having acknowledged him, not as a child, not as an adolescent, not as a man. But there is one period that we have failed to account for that Eteoklês has not. Justice also failed to look on and acknowledge Polyneikês from the time "when he fled the dark cavern of his mother's womb," and this may be the most viable clue to the polar opposition that these two brothers represent. If Polyneikês was born "evil" from his mother's womb (a theory that violates science but not the world of myth) what is there against saying that in that same womb, simultaneously, Eteoklês, Polyneikês' twin (as many have believed), was created "good"? It suggests that this twinship of polarities is fated to destroy itself in violent conflict, which is, after all, what the curse is out to accomplish.

In any event, we must admit that we know nothing about the brothers' fraternal relationship in Aeschylus' trilogy, information we would almost certainly have derived from the *Oedipus*. This means that we know nothing about why Eteoklês is on the throne and Polyneikês is in exile; we know only that Eteoklês has banished him. But given the honor and nobility of Eteoklês, and the fact that Aeschylus will consistently ally him with Justice, may we not assume that the banishment of Polyneikês was warranted, and not necessarily for reasons that the Erinys has imposed, but for personal reasons unique to them as living beings whose only fate is to be enemies? Nor do we know anything about why the blind Oedipus curses them, nor what could the "good" Eteoklês have done to deserve it?

One answer might be: nothing. Aeschylus has drawn his areté hero so convincingly that for him to have been guilty of the insult to Oedipus is virtually unthinkable, whereas it is believable of the Polyneikês he has given us. Is it possible, then, that the insult to Oedipus that led to his curse on his sons was the doing of a less than honorable Polyneikês and not of Eteoklês, and that the aged and guilt-ridden Oedipus, irrational in his outrage, and/or ignorant of Eteoklês' innocence, cursed them both? If this is the situation, then the implication of the innocent Eteoklês in his father's curse is a tragedy twice over. First of all, because he didn't deserve it; and second, because it was inevitable in the course of the all-inclusive curse on the House of Labdakos, which he also didn't deserve.

IX

The great central scene of *Seven Against Thebes,* known as the shield scene, consists of seven pairs of speeches. The Scout enters to report on which Argive warrior is at which of the seven gates, describing the character of each, as well as the scene embossed on each man's shield. Eteoklês then assigns to each gate the Theban warrior best suited to meet his opponent, not only as a warrior but as one superior of character and moral fitness. It is a scene of powerful ritualistic proportions and profoundly theatrical. But Aeschylus makes it serve another function as well: He continues to define the character of Eteoklês, and he prefigures the character of Polyneikês at the seventh gate.

Up to the beginning of the shield scene, the play and our attention have been focused on the larger scene—the siege of Thebes, the frenzied women, the need to keep morale high despite the growing danger, the noise of war just outside the walls. But now the expanding direction of the drama begins slowly to reverse, from large to small, from the public war of two states to the private war of two brothers. The play's focus begins to tighten. What's more, we have reached the middle of the play, but haven't yet even heard mention of the name Polyneikês, let alone the word "brother." That first audience in 467, having seen the two preceding plays will, of course, have seen Polyneikês in the *Oedipus* (where, perhaps, he had a role commensurate with that of Eteoklês in this play) and will know from exposure to the myth in various forms that Polyneikês was banished by Eteoklês, that he fled to Argos, married into the royal family, assembled an army led by King Adrastos, and attacked Thebes. All of which are elements of the original myth that could not be altered, and all of which take place between the end of the second play of the trilogy and *Seven Against Thebes.* In any event, the absence of Polyneikês' name until two thirds of the way through the play is not unintentional. Even within that shield scene his name is delayed (in the Greek) for two-hundred-and-eight lines.

As far as is known, Aeschylus is the first to make use of Thebes' seven gates—his addition to the myth. The reason for this innovation may well be that it allows him more time for delay, not only to increase tension as we approach the subject of the seventh gate, but to give himself time in which slowly to change the play's focus. The original curse of Pelops was on the family line of Labdakos for three generations. It is now the third generation and it is that concluding event, the annihilation of the house and the end of the curse, that Aeschylus is methodically, and subtly, making his way toward. And he begins this refocusing in the descriptions of the Argive and Theban warriors at the seven gates.

The descriptions of the Argives at the first four gates are much the same. Though each has individual characteristics, they share a general profile. They are arrogant, boastful, immodest, raging, and frequently impious, while their Theban counterparts are noble, modest, brave, pious, men of action rather than braggarts. Most important in the Thebans is that they are allied with Justice. Considering what we already know of the character of Eteoklês, and our foreknowledge of Polyneikês at the seventh gate, we must conclude that the Theban warriors have characteristics that are predominant in Eteoklês, whereas the Argives, save for one, have the characteristics of Polyneikês.

At the first gate "raging" Tydeus the Argive is met by the "noble and modest" Theban Melanippos. Most important is the fact that Melanippos is armed by Justice. Aeschylus' design is subtle; he begins by using words and phrases that are loaded with reference to Eteoklês even though they are not precisely directed at him but at Melanippos. Justice is described as being "blood of his [Melanippos'] blood," and as sending "him out to fight for the motherland that bore him." As we will see at the seventh gate, Justice, never an ally of Polyneikês, is in strong alliance with Eteoklês. The "blood of his blood" is that (metaphorically) shared between Melanippos and Justice, but Aeschylus is also saying that Justice and Eteoklês are (metaphorically) of one blood, and, perhaps of equal importance, he is reminding us of the (literal) blood relationship between the two brothers, blood that will mutually be spilled today. Eteoklês, like Melanippos, is also born of Theban soil, the "motherland that bore him" (literally: "the mother that gave him birth"). So, if Melanippos represents Eteoklês armed by Justice, then it is not too much to say that Tydeus represents Polyneikês who is not armed by Justice. What we have, then, in Eteoklês' reply is a series of references that begin to turn the play's focus onto the curse of the House of Labdakos in its final stage, the battle of the brothers.

At the second gate is Kapaneus, arrogant and boasting, a man who "exceeds what is proper to humans," who scorns Zeus' lightning bolt and will defy his wrath in attacking Thebes. He, too, is a prefiguration of Polyneikês at the seventh gate. Step by step Aeschylus is putting the power of Zeus and Justice on the side of the Thebans.

Eteoklus at gate three is a rather colorless Argive unless we are to associate him with the behavior of his horses who snort and "rage and wheel in their eagerness to throw themselves at us at the gate . . ." But on his shield is a device showing a man mounting a ladder to reach the top of the city's walls," his war cry "that not even Arês could hurl him from the battlements," a device that prefigures Polyneikês' boast at gate seven as described by the Scout:

He declares that once he stands
> mounted on our walls,
once he is proclaimed victor and conqueror of Thebes,
he will shout his wild cry of conquest,
> his war-whoop at the city's fall,
>> at its desolation and over its vanquished corpses.

The Argive Eteoklus will be matched against Theban Megareus whose "hands will do his talking for him; they are his only boast," an attribute that is deeply rooted in Eteoklês' character as a man of action.

At the fourth gate is Argive Hippomedon, a roaring, war-possessed man "raging for battle like a frenzied Bakkhant . . ." His Theban opponent is Hyperbios:

> A man eager to
learn his fate in this time of crisis,
> he is irreproachable in form and spirit
> and the bearing of arms. Hermês did
well in matching this pair.

And so is Eteoklês "eager to learn his fate in this time of crisis." What's more, in the next sentence we see the archetype of the areté hero: Eteoklês as Hyperbios. At its root, remember, areté means exceptional, unrivaled ability and superiority. The Scout uses the term "irreproachable." It appears almost as if the entire war were being fought by clones of Eteoklês and Polyneikês, and in a certain sense that's what is happening as the play's focus alters. That the gods are on the side of Thebes is clearly stated in the quotation's final observation that "Hermês did well in matching" them, as if Hermês working through Eteoklês were making the assignments. It should also be noted that the allusions to Eteoklês and Polyneikês are becoming increasingly more pointed with each Theban and Argive warrior assigned.

Not only is "irreproachable" Hyperbios (whose name means something like super-life, or life over and above the normal) as areté hero a reference to Eteoklês, the devices on the shields of both warriors are predictive of the outcome of the encounter at the seven gates. On the Argive Hippomedon's shield we see

Typhon belching black smoke from his fiery mouth,
> flame-flecked smoke, the sister of fire.

The rim is a tangle of writhing, intertwining
   snakes that holds the framework fast.

On Hyperbios' shield is Zeus enthroned with a thunderbolt in hand. Typhon
was a hundred-headed monster who when he tried to dethrone Zeus was struck
down by the god's thunderbolt. Of the encounter of these two warriors Eteoklês says:

                    Just as
         both men will meet as enemies,
            so too will enemies meet on their shields.
   One with fire-breathing Typhon,
         the other, Hyperbios,
               with Zeus enthroned, a flaming
         thunderbolt in hand.
   Zeus invincible, champion of our
                          champion.

It is perhaps significant that this device on Hyperbios' shield is the only Theban device described, whereas every Argive shield is dealt with fully. Its significance may be suggested by the fact that it is situated directly in the middle,
at gate four, of the seven gates and appears to serve as a foretelling of the Theban victory.

The Argive warrior at gate five is Parthenopaios, a riddle of a man, a
youthful beauty, still a boy, yet a man of strength, but also a man of impiety
and great savagery, with gorgon eyes. He is clearly doomed by his impiety for:
"He swears by the spearshaft he reverences more than god and even his life
that he will raze the city of Kadmos in spite of Zeus." He is a man of con-
tradictions, but it is his shield's device that speaks loudest,

   for on it is the shame of Thebes, the Sphinx that
         ate men raw, burnished bronze and
               cunningly riveted in place.
   In her claws she shamelessly clasps a
         Theban destined to receive the shower of
         missiles hurled at him.

That device takes the conflict back to where it began in the first generation,
the House of Labdakos. The man-devouring Sphinx in Thebes was Hera's

punishment for Laïos' sin, the rape and death of Chrysippos, and that takes us back to the curse of Pelops. But it also calls to mind the second generation and Oedipus who freed Thebes of the Sphinx after unknowingly killing his father and subsequently marrying his mother. The image of a Theban in the claws of the Sphinx, the Theban that will be struck by many Theban missiles, is a clear and so far the most pointed reference to the battle of the brothers, both Thebans—Theban striking at Theban. Furthermore, the fact that Parthenopaios is not an Argive, but an Arkadian who is in Argos as a foreign guest, presents a parallel with Polyneikês who is also not an Argive, and also a guest.

In the midst of all the self-dooming impiety displayed by the Argives, Aeschylus has Eteoklês begin and end his reply to the Scout's speech describing Parthenopaios with implorations to the gods, putting him securely on the proper, the just side of the conflict. As each time before this, Eteoklês places at the fifth gate a warrior with characteristics reflective of his own character: a man of action.

At the sixth gate is the Argive prophet-priest-warrior Amphiaraös, a man of honor, bravery, and wisdom who is a vigorous dissenter in the Argive cause against Thebes and as avid a hater of Polyneikês as is Eteoklês. In every respect he is an image of Eteoklês as areté hero, thus putting him in a position of considerable moral authority in his judgments regarding Polyneikês.

Amphiaraös' first act in the Scout's speech is to berate the "raging" Tydeus at gate one for his complicity with Polyneikês in inciting the invasion. He calls him "murderer, man of great mischief . . . rouser of the Fury [of the House of Labdakos]." He might as well be speaking to Polyneikês, for both of them share the depravity of the treasonous invasion. And then it happens, with one word, "Polyneikês," and the real Polyneikês emerges for the first time in the play.

> He [Amphiaraös] then tosses up another name,
>   Polyneikês, your brother,
>   mighty Polyneikês,
>   sown from the same womb,
> stressing again and again the
>   strife buried in his name,
> finally addressing him with these words:
>
>   "What do you expect
>   from this maneuver of yours? The divine
>   favor of the gods? Praise for your noble

deed in times to come? You're sacking your
father's city and its native gods with an
    army you recruited in a foreign land!
The mother-source of you! How can you
    block that, how with any justice,
        how?
And your father's land—will it become your
    ally once again when you have
    destroyed it at spear point?

"Polyneikês," "brother," "same womb," "strife in his name," "mother-source,"
and then "justice." With the juxtaposition of Polyneikês' name with a *lack* of
Justice (reminding us of Eteoklês' alliance *with* Justice) the refocusing begun
at the first gate is complete. What began as a war between states has now nar-
rowed to the Erinys-driven war between two brothers. But that's not all that
Amphiaraös' condemnatory speech to Polyneikês reveals. Inasmuch as
Amphiaraös is a reflection of Eteoklês, it is, in effect, Eteoklês speaking, and
there can be no question that its mode is sheer hatred. Aeschylus is saving time,
as it were, paving the way for the third round of invective directed at Polyneikês,
this time by Eteoklês himself. (The first was directed by Amphiaraös at
Polyneikês as Tydeus at the first gate.) Now that the refocusing is complete,
it is incumbent on Aeschylus to raise to fever pitch the hatred between the
two brothers.

Immediately Eteoklês turns, as always, to the matter at hand, and the
matter at hand is Polyneikês: Polyneikês strife-bringer, Polyneikês enemy of
Justice, Polyneikês born "evil" from his mother's womb, Polyneikês who "rapes
his city, his parent land, in this violent, criminal assault!" That last accusation
is prominently placed at the end of the list because it is the matter that is of
the greatest personal importance to Eteoklês: the invasion of Thebes, the city
that it is his duty to keep safe, and the damage it has done to his reputation.
With Polyneikês now at the seventh gate, Eteoklês is passionately resolved to
right the grievous wrong done to him. His most passionate wish is about to
come true—to right a wrong done to his reputation, for reputation is everything, and without it he is nothing. In short, it is a matter worth dying for,
and that price Eteoklês is happy to pay. Equally important, however, is that
the decision to fight for his name is made freely. He knows that death will
happen in the course of the working out of the curse, but he is little concerned
over that. It is his personal agenda that guides him resolutely into conflict:
Everything hinges on the name that he leaves behind. That this is so is, if not

entirely certain, then at least suggested by a response he makes to the Leader of the Chorus as he is being ritually fitted-out in warrior's gear during the arming scene:

> My father's Curse appoints me to this ritual,
>> tearing at me with tearless eyes,
>>> whispering:
> "First comes profit, then death!"

Something very odd is happening. His father's curse, his Erinys, is at Eteoklês' ear, whispering to him something that has to do with "profit," Erinys whose sole concern should be for his and his brother's fated death. The word for profit (gain, advantage) is κερδος, the same word used only a few lines earlier in the same context, namely death:

> If a man must suffer evil,
>> it must be without dishonor.
>> That alone profits us in death.
> But evil and dishonor together bring no
>>> glory.

What is that profit, one asks? The only answer in keeping with the warrior ethic and the demonstrated character of Eteoklês is "honor," which is to say: areté. What Eteoklês is determined to accomplish before he dies is, as Aristotle says, to take "possession of the beautiful." Beauty in this case is the restitution of Eteoklês' honor. And how otherwise to carry out that restitution in the case of the Homeric warrior that Eteoklês is than the death of the enemy, even if it means his own death? Not to do so is cowardice, an alternative of which the areté hero is incapable.

There are two quarrels in progress, it appears, and they are on a parallel course. The one driven by the Erinys of Oedipus' curse, and the personal one driven by Eteoklês' concern for his reputation after death, in perpetuity. And both will find fulfillment in the brothers' hatred of one another. But why is that advice in the mouth of the Erinys whispering into Eteoklês' ear?

One possible answer is that the Erinys' advice means one thing to the Erinys, and quite another to Eteoklês who is so obsessed with his reading (and for good reason) that he fails to see that of the Erinys. To the Erinys "First comes profit, then death!" most likely means "First you will kill Polyneikês, then you will die!" It urges him into action. To Eteoklês it almost certainly means: "First clear your reputation by killing your enemy, then you can die, for you will die vindicated." If one needs a reason for this misreading by Eteoklês of the Erinys' prodding message, it is not difficult to find. Time is running out, Polyneikês is at the gate, and the fated mutual fratricide pursued by his father's curse is about to be fulfilled. But if that is all that happens, if his *fated* death is what ends his life, rather than his areté-driven revenge which will also lead to his death, then he will have died in a state of pollution unacceptable to the Homeric warrior ethic. Eteoklês knows that whatever happens he will die. But if he goes to his death as the victim of fate rather than as the vindicator of his honor, he is doomed to an ignoble death of shame and dishonor. Jaeger in *Paideia* expresses it better than anyone, and it deserves repetition here, for it is at the core of the Eteoklês that Aeschylus has given us.

> We must understand that the Self is not the physical self, but the ideal which inspires us, the ideal which every nobleman strives to realize in his own life. If we grasp that, we shall see that it is the highest kind of self-love which makes man reach out towards the highest areté: through which he "takes possession of the beautiful." The last phrase is so entirely Greek that it is hard to translate. For the Greeks, beauty meant nobility also. To lay claim to the beautiful, to take possession of it, means to overlook no opportunity of winning the prize of the highest areté.

How, then, does Eteoklês go to his death except with rage, rage no less than that of Achilleus at the opening of *Iliad,* that greatest of Homeric warriors whose honor is slighted and he will have none of it, a rage that sends hordes of fighting men to their deaths. How Aeschylus prepares for this rage in Eteoklês has already been discussed—the condemnatory speeches of Amphiaraös to Tydeus and Polyneikês, and Eteoklês' own tirade directed at his brother. And that is the tone that not only continues from that point onward, but that grows steadily. Even the Leader of the Chorus calls attention to it: "Dearest son of Oedipus . . . don't become like your brother who cursed us so violently," and "Dear son, why so eager? You must never resign yourself to the wild lust for battle."

The Leader does everything possible to calm his passion, pleading with him twice not to bring pollution on Thebes by spilling a brother's blood, for which there is no purification. She says to "avoid evil and honor the gods and the black-robed Fury will flee your house." And again: "In time the Spirit may cease to rage, and blow more kindly. But now she rages." For Eteoklês to take this advice would, of course, condemn him to a life of shame, deprived of areté, a living death, for even though the curse were averted (were that possible), there would be no confrontation with Polyneikês, and therefore no restitution of his honor. And so, each time, as step by step he is transformed into a warrior before our eyes, he responds with increasing force in his passion to do what must be done:

> Winds of the gods that drive this on,
>> let us set sail on the Sea of Death
>> to Kokytos' stream,
> the end of all for the race of Oedipus
>> so hated by Apollo!

He is addressing both issues here: the fated confrontation with Polyneikês that will lead to their mutual fratricide and the extinction of the House of Labdakos, but also, and singularly important to him, to the freely chosen confrontation that is essential for his self-redeeming vengeance to be realized, and in doing so, to assert the meaning of his name—man of true glory. When Eteoklês says:

> Gods?
> The gods have abandoned me by now.
> Only one gift would please them.
>> My death.
> Why cringe before death any longer?

he is again speaking on two levels. The first level is that of the curse, that his fate has been set and the gods are no longer concerned, perhaps because an Erinys is pursuing it. But what does he mean when he says that his death is the only gift that would please them? If he speaks ironically, he means that in their cruelty the gods will be pleased with his death. However, if he speaks not despairingly, but with enlightenment, he may mean that the gods would be pleased if he were to die not his fated death, but a heroic death, a death that would restore his areté status. A statement that is most often taken to demonstrate Eteoklês at his most fatalistic suddenly becomes a forceful determination to regain his honor and nobility, a gain, a "profit," as discussed earlier, that would please the gods. That this speech is the next after describing the Erinys whispering in his ear "First comes profit, then death!" makes this deduction fairly persuasive. And "Why cringe before death any longer?"

indicates how he once despised the fated death that was his inheritance, but which now he embraces because in addition to being fated (no escaping that), it is also, and to him solely, a death of beauty following the confrontation that will have restored his areté.

Rather than being undone when the Chorus Leader remarks that the Erinys of Oedipus' curse "rages" still but with time will leave off "and blow more kindly," he accepts it, not in anguish, as frequently assumed, but boldly:

> Rages?
> Yes, rages, blown on by the
> Curse of Oedipus!
> My dreams,
> the phantoms I see in nightly
> visions, are true—my father's
> heritage divided!

These are the facts, he implies, facts that may once have tormented him because they were undeserved, the result of a sin long ago that was not his and that would lead to a petty and miserable death for him. But that has all changed, his death now will be glorious in his victory over evil.

The arming of Eteoklês complete, he stands before us fitted-out to fight for his honor; and in fighting for his honor, also for his city, for he knows that with his and his brother's deaths and the end of the Labdakos line, Thebes will be saved. Again, inevitably, we come back to beauty and the beautiful: the nobility of the Homeric hero that rises above the mean and contemptible scorn of death. What he scorns is not death but his physical self, and what he rejoices in is the use of his physical self to achieve the highest aim: to take possession of beauty—and that achievement is worth the extinction of his physical self. He finds that his nature, the inherent quality of his being, asserts itself most nobly in the act of self-sacrifice.

Eteoklês' last statement in response to the Leader who still tries to persuade him defines Eteoklês as an areté hero of the first order.

> When god sends evil there's no escape.

Again he speaks on two levels. By "evil" he means, first, the curse sent by the gods that cannot be averted; and second, by "evil" he means the wound to an honorable man's reputation that no man of honor can fail to restore at any cost, even his own death. It could be said, however, that it was not the gods who wounded Eteoklês' honor but Polyneikês, and that would be true. At the same time, one never knows. Aeschylus not infrequently permits the gods to work their designs through human motivation. So, when Eteoklês meets Polyneikês at the seventh gate it is an act of the noblest self-sacrifice for the salvation of his city, and at the same time an act that reasserts his personal nobility for all time: his areté.

X

With the exit of Eteoklês, the great second ode is sung that sums up the entirety of the three-generation curse of the House of Labdakos. At its end there enters the Scout to tell of the battle of Eteoklês and Polyneikês at the seventh gate. That completed, he exits and the Chorus splits into two sections to lament the fate of the House of Labdakos. The corpses of the two brothers are then brought in and the Chorus laments at length the fate of both brothers at each others' hands.

There is, however, a major difficulty with the ending of the play that will probably never be settled, making of the ending a matter of choice or conviction. At line 861 in the Greek text there enter Antigonê and Ismenê, the sisters of Eteoklês and Polyneikês, and they remain onstage for the concluding two-hundred-and-seventeen lines. Until 1848 that concluding scene was largely accepted as an Aeschylean text. But in that same year the discovery of the *didaskalia* gave information to suggest otherwise. Prior to 1848 it was believed that *Seven Against Thebes* was the second play of Aeschylus' Theban trilogy, and that the late entry of Antigonê and Ismenê onto the scene was a means of linking the second play with the third. The *didaskalia,* however, from the best manuscript of Aeschylus, the Medicean, indicated that *Seven Against Thebes* was in fact the final play. At that point debate arose about the authenticity of the ending inasmuch as it made the trilogy end with a question mark, without a final resolution. In addition, language and the matter of style were seen not to suggest Aeschylus as author. It is an involved issue and needn't be overly exercised here except to say that the Antigonê-Ismenê ending was most likely added sometime after Aeschylus' death for a revival of the play and in an effort to bring in into conformity with Sophokles' very popular *Antigonê.*

The most salient reason for rejecting the present ending, other than that it is bad playwriting, is that nowhere in *Seven Against Thebes* are the two sisters of Eteoklês and Polyneikês referred to. If they were mentioned earlier in the trilogy we have no way of knowing. Furthermore, the curse of Pelops in the first generation was on the whole of the House of Labdakos, not merely on its male descendents, and if Antigonê and Ismenê lurk in the wings the curse has not yet worked itself out to its inevitable conclusion, and that is no way to end a trilogy united by that same curse.

The decision made for this translation was to jettison the ending as interpolated and allow the play to end with a highly impressive and theatrical scene of lamentation over the corpses, a scene, by the way, that is fully sung to the accompaniment of aulos and lyre—a scene, finally, that bears a great resemblance to the concluding scene of *Persians.*

* * *

SUPPLIANTS

I

Until a major discovery in 1952, *Suppliants* was considered the earliest surviving play of Aeschylus as well as the oldest surviving Greek tragedy, a play that was relegated to the 480s or even the 490s B.C.E. Then in 1952 a papyrus fragment was published that clearly indicated that Aeschylus had won first prize with a tetralogy that comprised *Suppliants, Egyptians,* and *Danaïds,* as well as the satyr play *Amymonê* (the Danaïd tetralogy) in the year 463, which is to say in the last decade of his long life. With the discovery of the *didaskalia* papyrus, Aeschylus' earliest extant tragedy and the earliest extant Greek tragedy became *Persians* produced in the year 472.

This discovery was not universally welcomed. Too many hard and fast academic theories had been formulated regarding, for example, the development of Aeschylus' style from *Suppliants* to *Oresteia,* or the origins of drama as we know it. "One had only to work backward from the *Suppliants,*" according to Podlecki's description of the situation, "reduce the actors' importance and emphasize the chorus', and bring the action to an almost complete standstill, in order to arrive quite automatically at a true picture of 'primitive' drama. Such a picture may still be true, but the *Suppliants* can no longer be used to prove it." And then there were the diehards who, while not doubting the evidence of the papyrus, theorized that, even though *Suppliants* was first produced in 463, it had "obviously" been written decades before, in Aeschylus' early formative years, and only in 463 pulled from a drawer into the radiant light of an Athenian spring day. Not a very likely prospect, according to Podlecki, inasmuch as tragedies were almost certainly to have been produced in the year of their composition.

The conventional critical attitude, even after the discovery of the *didaskalia,* has been to see *Suppliants* as a strange and archaic work, one "that has an overwhelmingly choral quality, that aura of 'archaic oratorio,'" as William Arrowsmith has put it. The reason for this being, of course, that the play doesn't follow the rules of playwriting that we expect of Greek tragedy in the classical age. Since we know virtually nothing about the origins of tragedy it is easy to make assumptions about what preceded it. Even Aristotle in the fourth century, in his *Poetics,* relied mainly on guesswork and deduction, and there was nothing to prove that he was right or wrong. So to say that Aeschylus—even if he wrote *Suppliants* for production in 463—looked back to the early form of tragedy, is to ignore one very important fact: that Aeschylus seldom followed the rules of contemporary playwriting, choosing, rather, to suit the form of his drama to its content.

If most Greek tragedy conforms to the rule that the focus of the dramatic work (then as now) is the individual, what does a playwright do when a subject arises that demands another approach? To reject it is one response, or another is to recast it so that it focuses on the individual as opposed to the group. Yet that solution is to destroy the very nature of the subject at its root. Can we imagine what Lope de Vega's *Fuenteovejuna* or Hauptmann's *The Weavers* would be without the crowd as focal point? Take away from *Suppliants* its mass focus and we deprive it of its strongest factor: Choral writing that is poetry of such brilliance that it has little competition in extant Greek tragedy. Those who see the play as looking backward to earlier times criticize, among other things, the denseness of the imagery as being more akin to poetry than to tragedy, as if poetry of the classical period (let alone from the time of its origins in prehistory) were not written to be recited as opposed to read. Michael Ewans has an answer:

> This drama has more choral lyrics than most other tragedies for two reasons: neither of them has much to do with its date of composition. The central character is a group of people, not an individual . . . and the Danaides are in a state of heightened emotion for most of its length, and therefore naturally express themselves through the medium of lyric. The pervasive modern assumption (usually among scholars unfamiliar with opera) that lyric expression can never be socially and politically subtle, and must therefore necessarily be early and archaic, will not stand sustained examination in the context of early fifth-century Greece. Aischylos performed his tragedies in the same culture in which complex, allusive odes composed to celebrate victories in Olympic and other games made Pindar a millionaire.

II

The myth that Aeschylus chose to reinterpret in his tetralogy is particularly barbarous and grisly, one that begins in the remote mythical past and is laid out in considerable detail in several of the odes sung by the chorus. In this super-plot, as it has been called, the Argive princess Io, who is the keeper of the keys at Hera's temple in Argos, takes the fancy of Zeus who amorously pursues her against her will. Hera, his wife, being fully cognizant of Zeus' frequent philandering, takes the matter in hand and in a rage of jealousy turns Io into a cow. Zeus, undaunted by the transformation, promptly assumes the form of a bull, causing Hera, in turn, to station as watch over Io the hundred-eyed giant Argos, who, as it happens, is killed by Hermês and turned into a peacock. Hera, not to be outdone, retaliates by dispatching a gadfly to torment and pursue Io in her madness across continents, from Greece to Asia, swimming seas, the width of the Bosporos (cow-ford), until finally she reaches the Nile Delta where, in a meadow sacred to Zeus, she collapses in exhaustion. Zeus restores her to human form and, with a divine breath and a gentle touch (no sexual violence this time around), impregnates her with a son named Epaphos (meaning "touch" or "caress") who will become progenitor of a line of gods and heroes. Five generations later, two brothers, descended from Epaphos, fall into disagreement when one of them, Aigyptos, tries to force his brother Danaös to allow a marriage between his fifty sons and Danaös' fifty daughters. At which Danaös, in fear and trembling, gathers his closely guarded brood and flees with them from Egypt to Argos, the land of their original mother Io.

It is at this point that *Suppliants* begins, in the same marshy Argive meadow from which Io was once cruelly chased by Hera's gadfly. The scene is desolate except for a sacred mound that serves as an altar sanctuary with symbols of Greek gods. It is to this sacred place that the women of the chorus will retire in their plea for sanctuary from the raging pursuit of their fifty Egyptian cousins.

King Pelasgos of Argos enters at the head of his army to investigate the daughters' landing, and they appeal as suppliants in the name of their common Argive ancestry. This places Pelasgos in an agonizing bind. If he disagrees and rejects them he will offend Zeus as guardian of suppliants, and yet if he agrees it means war with the pursuing Egyptians.

The daughters increase the pressure of their supplication even to the point of threatening to hang themselves from the symbols of the gods in the sacred precinct. Pelasgos, however, refuses to make a judgment, maintaining that only the citizens' assembly can do so, and he goes off with Danaös to try to gain the consent of the people of Argos. After a choral ode, Danaös returns with word that the Argive assembly has voted unanimously to take them in. Soon after, Danaös sights the Egyptian fleet in the harbor and hurries off to find help. There then enter an Egyptian Herald and a Chorus of Egyptian Soldiers who in a scene of frantic song, speech, and intricate dance attempt to capture the daughters and return them to Egypt. At that moment Pelasgos enters, the Herald and Egyptians are driven off threatening war, and after a choral finale the daughters go off with Pelasgos toward Argos.

III

It becomes apparent that the numerous choral odes that tell of Io and her wanderings are meant to point up a parallel with the plight of the daughters fleeing the unwanted sexual attention of their Egyptian cousins. And the conclusion of the play with the daughters going off to Argos in safety is meant to parallel the happy resolution of Io's flight in which with a gentle touch Zeus fills her with Epaphos.

What happens in the other two plays of the trilogy is virtually impossible to determine apart from a few deductions made on the basis of suggestions in *Suppliants.* It is fairly certain, for example, that in the next play, *Egyptians,* a sex-war between the daughters and their Egyptian cousins ensues, and that somehow by the end of the second play the male cousins manage to win, most likely by force, their claim to the marriage. Based on the few fragments that survive from the third play, *Danaïds,* it is possible to suggest that the grisly climax of play two is the mass murder in the bridal chamber of the Egyptian cousins by the daughters. All but one, that is: Hypermêstra does not kill her husband Lynkeus. Why is not known, though one alternate version of the myth suggests that it might have been that he was the least violent of his brothers and that Hypermêstra loved him.

Fragments of the final play also suggest that there was a trial, but of whom is unknown. One possibility is that Hypermêstra was tried for failure to live up to the daughters' oath to kill their husbands. Another possibility is that the forty-nine daughters who carried out their oath were the ones tried. In any case, the gods are drawn into the issue, a fact that is substantiated by the *didaskalia* in which was found part of a speech by Aphroditê, goddess of love, that appears to resolve the culminating trial and end the trilogy.

Holy Heaven yearns to pierce the Earth,
and Earth, too, is seized by desire for marriage,

and rain falling from Heaven like showers of love
impregnates Earth that gives birth to grass for herds
and grain, Dêmêter's gift, to all mankind.
The showers of this marriage make trees grow flowers
and fruits. And I of all this am the cause.

IV

Suppliants is most frequently criticized as being static, mainly because of its
abundant choral odes, and then there is complaint about the use Aeschylus
makes of the three speaking parts, Danaös, Pelasgos, and the Herald. One complaint is that of the three only two are ever on stage together, and that they
scarcely ever speak to each other. In the scene, for example, of Pelasgos' first
entry Danaös says nothing for 258 lines (in the Greek) and then only when
drawn in by the chorus. To say there is no action in that scene in which the
daughters plead for protection on the basis of their Argive roots, of their relationship to Io, of being on the side of Justice, and then threatening to pol-
lute the altar of the gods by committing suicide if they are not sheltered, is
nonsense. "Action," after all, can exist in the tense of a verb.

In the conventional dramaturgy of the fifth century Danaös would have
been the daughters' spokesman, but that would have taken the focus from the
daughters, even though much of the heated, impassioned one-on-one dialogue
with Pelasgos is (in this and other translations—how the Greeks handled it
we don't know) with the Chorus Leader. What's more, the Chorus Leader is
a female (though played by a male), variety in itself, and who better and more
passionately to plead the case than the victims, the fleeing women. How, for
example, would Danaös have threatened Pelasgos with the women's extreme-
ly potent threat of suicide at the sacred altar-mound? Far less effectively, if for
no other reason than that Danaös is old and not directly involved in the sexual threat to the women. But in addition Aeschylus appears to have made
Danaös something of a doddering character, over-solicitous regarding the
daughters' adherence to his much self-extolled advice. And can we overlook
the quite foolish assurance he attempts to give by telling them to stay in the
sanctuary when the Egyptians arrive (at any moment!), that they will be perfectly safe as suppliants, that their pursuers will never dare to violate the sanctuary, while he goes off to find protection for them? It's a moment that borders
on the ludicrous in its simplemindedness. The portrait that Aeschylus has painted of his Danaös is not a failure on his part, but a stroke of genius inasmuch
as it allows for a truly aggressive scene between the Chorus Leader and Pelasgos

by empowering her/them to plead for their own safety. Perhaps the most conclusive evidence for use of the daughters (in place of Danaös) is that roughly half way through the scene the Chorus Leader and finally the chorus as a whole burst into song, while Pelasgos speaks over the accompaniment of the aulos and lyre—a scene of enormous tension and brilliance, one which could never have happened with Danaös if for no other reason than that his excitement could not have reached the pitch required for lyric (which is to say musical) utterance. What, now, of Pelasgos in this same scene?

Pelasgos enters without visible indication concerning who he is. The Chorus Leader has to ask him:

> But how do I address you?
> Private citizen?
> Spokesman?
>   The city's leader?

He appears not to be a vain man but one seriously concerned with their plight. After a brilliant exchange between them regarding the history of Io and Argos and her divinely imposed suffering, it isn't long before Pelasgos begins to come apart. That he is a deeply feeling man there can be no doubt, but when they ask for protection as suppliants, he immediately notes that that action on the part of Argos would lead to war. They respond that Justice is on their side, to which he replies that the Egyptians may also make that same claim. "I tremble before this shaded altar," he says. The Chorus Leader then describes herself and the women of the chorus, singing:

> Listen to me,
> hear me,
> son of Ancient Earth.
> Listen with a kind
>   heart,
> lord of
>   Argos.
> See me,
> your suppliant,
> an exile,
> fugitive,
> a wolf-hunted
>   calf

on jagged rocks,
trusting,
trusting the herdsman's
                    strength.
Be that
          herdsman.
Hear our cry.

He all but collapses at the thought that the conflict with the Egyptians may bring disaster, "unwanted strife," war. With music under him, he speaks:

I see the gods nod in the
          shadow of your branches.
I see strangers who are citizens,
                    our kin.
I pray to the gods they bring no
          disaster. Let them not bring
                    strife.
          Unwanted.
Unwanted strife.
          Not war.

He states that if they were at his private hearth, he would have no fear in accepting them into his house, but they are at the city's hearth, not his, and

                    it is
          the city that would suffer, and
the city that must find the cure.
It is the people's risk.
          I must ask the people.
Only then can I act
                    justly.

To which she replies, singing:

No, Lord!
No, Majesty!
You are the
          people!

You are the
> state!
No king can be judged!
You rule the
> altar,
you rule the land's
> hearth!
Your will is one vote,
your will is
> rule!
When you sit enthroned,
you speak for all!
Beware heaven's curse!
Beware
> pollution!

And on it goes in an impassioned and dramatic confrontation. One can hear the shrill screech of the *aulos*. But what can one say except that Pelasgos is a weak character, contrary to the critics who see him as agonized but noble, and to prove that point quote his famous:

We must take counsel,
> deep counsel,
> to find salvation.
Like a diver into the deep of the
> sea,
we must be clearsighted and
> sober, to find a way
> unharmful to the city,
> but also to me.
War must not seize us,
> our lands,
> our goods.
If we give you to them,
> you,
> here,
> in this holy place,
we open our house to the

burden of Vengeance, all-destroying
god who even in Hades sets no man
                                    free.
We need deep counsel to
    find salvation.

A far cry from a decisive ruler in a situation that is desperate, that needs immediate resolution. One automatically thinks of the decisive and heroic and
unconflicted Thêseus of *Oedipus at Kolonos* who, when an urgent decision is
needed to be made in the kidnapping of Antigonê and Ismenê by Kreon, makes
it without recourse to the city, because he knows the city and the city knows
him, and that's why he is king of Athens. But what does Pelasgos say except:

I'm withered by this dispute.
I would rather be ignorant than
            expert in evil.
But I hope against all hope that
    all will be well.

And when finally Danaös is brought into the picture, Pelasgos, still refusing
to act (because the people not he must make the decision), tells Danaös to go
to the city's altars and distribute the wool-wound suppliants' branches so that
the people will know he and his daughters are begging for protection. In doing
so, he reneges on his obligation and, like a coward, passes it off onto Danaös.
He then himself defines unknowingly the terrified pettiness of his nature when
he says to Danaös:

It will be seen that you come as
    suppliants and the people will not
    take me to task.
They're quick to criticize their leaders,
        these people.

To which Danaös responds:

We thank you for championing our cause,
        and for the respect you show toward
                strangers.

And one wants almost to ask: "Is he joking?" Except we know, of course, that he isn't. What would have been the result if Pelasgos had been created a strong, decisive, assertive ruler like Thêseus? Quite a different scene, with quite a different degree of mounting tension. Pelasgos, like Thêseus, would have accepted the women as Argive kin and led the army he has brought with him to meet the soon-to-arrive Egyptian pursuers. The scene would have been a brief one, as opposed to the lengthy but impassioned one we have, where tension mounts incrementally as the chorus grows more insistent and Pelasgos grows increasingly more tormented and defeated by his fear to the point of becoming, as he says, "withered by this dispute." As it is, the scene with a strong and determined though fearful chorus and a weak and indecisive Pelasgos is an agon of the first order. Aeschylus unquestionably knew what he was after.

V

The opening of the play is a splendid ode sung by the chorus in which they narrate in sensuous and delicate poetic terms the story of their legendary mother, and then call on Epaphos to come to their deliverance.

> I sing now,
> I sing,
> and call on the Zeus-calf
> from across the sea,
> child of Zeus,
> by the breath of Zeus,
> breath and touch that
> ripened in her womb,
> that brought forth a son
> to our first mother,
> a son,
> Epaphos,
> to our flower-grazing mother,
> ancestress,
> Io,
> Epaphos,
> Caress-child.
> Epaphos,
> Epaphos,
> come,
> be our defender.

I call him to come,
I call from these pastures
where once she grazed,
great mother of us all,
and in remembering her long-ago agonies,
the pain she suffered,
Argos will know,
her people will learn
from the tale I will tell,
the truth that time alone can prove,
that we are Argives
who come to these shores.

Before this, however, they chant information more immediate, of their present plight, their flight from Egypt from the fifty lusting and insolent sons of Aigyptos who are in hasty pursuit.

Zeus,
god,
Lord of Suppliants,
Zeus Protector,
hear me,
hear my cause,
and be favorable to me,
to me and these women,
sisters,
who set sail where Nile slips
languidly to the sea
through dunes of salt-washed sand.
We left behind a land Zeus loved,
sun-blest pastures that stretch to Syria,
left it exiles,
but not for blood-guilt,
but willing fugitives fleeing our pursuers,
sons of Aigyptos who
want us in marriage,
unholy marriage,
loathsome, detestable,
kinsmen,

cousins,
an unwanted marriage.

Danaös,
father, leader,
advised this rebellion
as the best of the evils that promise
sorrow.
And so we fled,
unchecked our flight,
across the tremulous salt sea,
to Argos,
her harbor,
here to these meadows,
where our race first saw
the light of day.
For we are Argive.
In flesh, in blood, in heart, in mind,
Argive.
Sprung from Io,
fly-maddened cow,
whose womb quickened with
the touch and breath of Zeus.

Not only do we learn of their situation but of their near-frenzied fear and
loathing of their male cousins in pursuit, a terror at the prospect of marriage
that recurs so often that it takes on the aspect of phobia. We learn, too, that
it was not the young women themselves who instigated the flight from marriage, but their old father Danaös who "advised this rebellion as the best of
the evils that promise sorrow," and it was they who assented, calling themselves "willing fugitives." Throughout the play they will constantly refer to sex
in derogatory metaphoric terms. "Death before they foul this marshy land! . . .
Kill them before they make our beds unholy, before they mount our beds of
innocence . . ." They appeal to Justice and hate the "pride" (hybris) of their
pursuers, asking that "force" not make their marriage bed. They then invoke
Artemis as defender of chastity to come to their aid:

Virgin daughter of Zeus,
help us.

> Give us protection.
> As you guard the gates of your
> hallowed shrine,
> so guard ours with all your might.
> Unconquered maid,
> unbroken goddess of chastity,
> guard our gates,
> deliver us unconquered.

And if the sky gods fail to heed their pleas to be saved from marriage and sex with their cousins they declare that they will invoke the "Zeus of the world below, Hades," and hang themselves. Zeus, it must be noted, is mentioned unusually often in this play and for a good reason: In effect he is their Father; it was his breath and gentle caress that made him the father of Epaphos, Io's son, and the progenitor of their line; they are "children" of Zeus.

VI

Their opening lyric concluded, their father Danaös speaks, and we learn very quickly that he is an old man of much advice. We already know that he advised the flight of his fifty daughters, and early in his first speech we also discover that he wants them to "write his words" in their hearts or minds and to heed them. He ends his speech with advice on how to speak and behave when the Argives come to inquire regarding their presence on Argive shores.

> Now, when they ask you,
>   you must answer as is only
>   proper to suppliants.
> With reverence.
> With tearful voices.
> Make it plain that you're fugitives,
>   but not for any crime, not for any
>   shedding of blood.
> And show need.
>   As for boldness,
>   there will be none, and no
>   immodesty, your eyes will be
>   downcast at all times.
> Speak when spoken to,

and don't delay
unduly in your responses.
People here are easy to take
offense.
You're foreigners and fugitives.
Remember that.
Bend with the wind.
Arrogance has no
part in weakness.

Sounding a bit like a tedious Polonius, we derive the impression that Danaös advises perhaps a bit too frequently where his young daughters are concerned, and not infrequently on matters sexual. Here, when he speaks of "modesty," and tells them to keep their eyes "downcast at all times," he is telling them not to flirt or look with too much interest on the Argive men who will come to question them. Immediately they respond like worshiping dutiful daughters who are compliant in everything: "Your words are wise, father, and spoken to daughters who respect wisdom. We won't forget." Immediately following these words they invoke Zeus with: "And may Father Zeus, our first father, look down upon us!" There are times, as here, when the margins between Danaös and Zeus are so close as to be indistinguishable—a father-worship that at least suggests that the daughters' fear of sex and marriage may have as much to do with Danaös' protective caveat as with their impulsive cousins.

Danaös' "advice" and the daughters' constant need for it continues to the end of the play. They have won the Argive people's support and are invited into the city to live wherever they choose, yet they need their old father's advice and they ask Pelasgos "one more favor. Send our brave-hearted father to advise us. He's wise and we listen to his counsel. He'll know best where we should live." He arrives and in the course of his final lengthy speech manages to reveal some pertinent facts concerning his fatherly protectiveness. Early on he begins as we have heard him before:

Listen to me again now;
and to the other wisdom I have
given you, write these words in your
memory.

They are foreigners, he tells them, and they must manage themselves well or risk criticism from the people of Argos. But most important of all to him is, as several times before, the sexual demeanor of his young daughters. The imagery of his speech is wondrous in its expressiveness, and critics have rightly been thrilled by its delicate, nuanced beauty. And beautiful it may be, yet there is a deviousness to his words of advice that is at the very heart of this play and that has virtually been overlooked.

> So you must bring no disgrace on me with your
> youth that turns men's heads.
> Summer fruit is not easily guarded.
> Animals, beasts, birds come to
> plunder it, as well as men.
> What else?
> And in matters of love,
> Aphroditê spreads her feast in
> gardens of desire, and men when
> passing the charming beauty of
> girls, conquered by the sight,
> send out bolts of seductive glances to
> enchant them.

Nature imagery takes on a not unconventional reference to female sexuality, and Danaös comments on the inevitable: the plunder of those fruits by animals, birds, and beasts, "as well as men." What else can one expect of predators? he concludes. Men, conquered by the sight of beauty, enter Aphroditê's garden of delights to seduce. Again, he might ask, what else can one expect? Men will be men. So far so good. He has presented a ravishingly beautiful description of the inevitability of sex and love. But then comes the thorn in the finger. So far Danaös has spoken objectively, now he veers off into a most subjective and limiting path of "advice" to his virginal daughters.

> Never forget the seas we
> fled across to escape this lust of men,
> and the pain we suffered in doing so.
> Let us not fall to it again.
> Let us not shame ourselves, only to
> delight our enemies.
> A new life awaits, my dears,
> and the choice is yours.
> To live alone or in company with others,

as the king has offered.
And what's more,
at the city's expense.
That much is easy.
But remember to value
modesty even more than life itself.

And what else should we expect of the chorus represented by the Chorus Leader than:

I pray the great gods to rain down good
fortune upon us!
As for my summer fruit, father,
unless the gods have laid new
plans,
my path is set.

What else can "My path is set" mean but that sex will not be a part of their lives? Is it too much to say that old Danaös has effectively brainwashed his daughters into an anti-sexual mode? The advice he gives them so liberally in the play can't be new; they've heard it for years. One wonders, too, about their Egyptian cousins in such hot pursuit (they will arrive in the next play), but what do we really know about them? They have had many epithets leveled against them: arrogant, insolent, loathsome, detestable, but are they really? The mouths these terms of abuse emerge from are subjective to say the least. We have had no objective evaluation. Even if other versions of the myth denigrate them, that doesn't mean that Aeschylus necessarily does. He is, after all, invited to reinterpret.

There is, however, another fragment in the didaskalia papyrus (other than that from the Aphroditê speech) that is attributed to the third play of the Danaïd tetralogy and that may offer a clue regarding those lusty but elusive Egyptian suitors. It has no attribution, but Michael Ewans puts it tentatively in the mouth of Danaös. I quote it in Ewans' translation.

And then the clear light of the sunrise comes,
while I, singing the morning song with boys and girls,
awake the bridegrooms who are well disposed to us.

Some vast change must have occurred for Danaös (with all his advice) to look kindly on those Egyptian bridegrooms. Remember that at the end of the second play or during the break between the second and third plays, they were murdered by their brides in the bridal chamber on the wedding night. It isn't likely that Danaös should have been reconciled to them. The fragment more rightly perhaps belongs to Pelasgos who may not know of the murderous scheme, and so he comes to wake them. Let us also assume that the Egyptians are not the monsters they have been described as being, but, rather, decent as well as normally sexed adolescents. If this is the case, then their murder on their wedding night by the daughters whose anti-sex bias has been demonstrated is a doubly horrendous matter. It also says that the influence of Danaös on his daughters was disastrous.

VII

Immediately following the Chorus Leader's "summer fruit" acquiescence quoted above, the chorus breaks into a final ode that they share with an additional chorus of Argive women who entered with Pelasgos on his return to chase off the Egyptian Herald and his soldiers. It is a choral ode that represents two diametrically opposed views of sex: pro-sex by the Argive women and anti-sex by the daughters who once again implore Artemis to "spare us marriage that comes by force, for that way lies death." The Argive women, however, immediately warn them never to ignore Aphroditê.

> Never ignore Aphroditê.
> With Hera she stands next to Zeus.
> And that cunning goddess of love
> is greatly praised for her solemn rites.
> Dear to their mother are
> Passion and seductive Persuasion,
> to whom nothing is denied.
> And to Harmony is given love's
> whispers and cries
> and the gentle touching of flesh.
>
> But it is for you I fear,
> fugitives fleeing love's hot breath.
> Stormwinds rise,
> cruelty, suffering,

> bloody war threatens the future.
> Why was their pursuit so fast,
> your kin, your cousins,
> the fair crossing?
> What Fate has ordained
> Fate will see through.
> The mind of Zeus cannot be crossed.
> May this strife end in marriage.
> For many women
> marriage is destiny.

What basically they are saying is that Aphroditê is a force of Nature and not to be withstood—an attitude shared by the classical Greek; and that marriage is "fate," a law of Zeus—also a widely shared attitude of the classical Greek. That it should be so is not difficult to understand in regard to the Greek states of the time. Marriage produced numbers, and numbers are defense, and defense is survival, and so it was for the Greeks. In Athens, for example, it was an unwritten law that the male was to marry at least by age forty.

But the daughters protest: "Not with Aigyptos' sons! . . . You will never charm me, never!" "Then pray a more moderate prayer," advise the Argive women as the daughters are led off to Argos still calling for justice to be done.

VIII

That love and sex are at the core of *Suppliants* can scarcely be denied, although there is little doubt that it contains other vital themes as well. The problem is that it is the first play of a tetralogy, and an unusually lyrical one at that, and as such it suggests more than it tells; it is a very light and graceful touch; and only the remaining lost plays can tell us whether one speculation or another is right. In the meantime we can only guess. One thing, however, is certain: It is a play of poetically brilliant odes that are generally considered the most beautiful lyric poems in classical Greek. But is it a theatrical failure? That, of course, remains a subjective issue whether on page or stage. But that it represents the boldest theatrical experiment among all of the seven extant plays of Aeschylus, and of the extant Greek tragedy in general, is very close to being beyond question.

• • •

PROMÊTHEUS BOUND

I

Just as *Suppliants* confounds critics with its strangeness of form and style to the point that its date of composition is debated, *Promêtheus Bound* has in modern times been believed by some, by virtue of form and style, not to have been written by Aeschylus at all.

Production information regarding *Promêtheus Bound* is lacking, though certain characteristics of the play suggest a date following *Oresteia,* produced in 458 B.C.E., therefore sometime between then and Aeschylus' death in 456, a date that would make it his final tragedy. Knowing what we know, there is no solution to the conundrum of the play's authorship. If it is not by Aeschylus, then we have a surviving work by a fourth great tragedian of the fifth century. If it is by Aeschylus, then we have a seventh extant play by him. Although it would be gratifying to know which of these possibilities is the correct one, in the long run it makes little difference (as little difference as knowing whether Shakespeare wrote Shakespeare). What is important is that we have extant a play from the fifth century that has played a significant role in the theater of the Western world, a play whose subject has left a lasting effect. Furthermore, to discuss the question of authorship that the issue raises is a subject dealt with at length by many scholars and need not be exercised again here.

II

Fire, it is safe to say, is the *sine qua non* of civilization. It protects from the unpitying onslaughts of cold that assail us. It cooks and makes palatable the food we eat, and it makes possible the transformation of the natural world that surrounds us to serve our needs. We might almost say that Time begins with fire. There is no mythology that doesn't in some way memorialize its advent. In some cases this divine spark arrives as a theft from the gods through the medium of a bird, an animal, or even a man. From the Far East to the North American Far West, from the Arctic to the Antarctic, it is everywhere imbedded in the human collective unconscious. In the *Rig-Veda,* the oldest and most sacred of the Hindu Vedas, the god Matarisvan, by rubbing, gives birth to the fire-spirit Agni and then introduces him to earth. In Greece it is the pre-Olympian Titan Promêtheus who serves the earth's population in that function.

Hesiod, in his poem of the eighth century B.C.E, *Theogony,* gives a foreground position to Promêtheus. He tells at length how he dares to give Zeus a less than excellent piece of meat in order that he might give the better piece to man. In retaliation, Zeus refuses to give fire to humans, thus prompting Promêtheus to steal it on man's behalf. In a second retaliatory move, Zeus creates woman, Pandora, as punishment for humanity, and Promêtheus he has bound to a post for an eagle daily to tear out and consume his ever-renewing liver. In a way, that myth is a cautionary tale never to attempt to get the upper hand on Zeus. In spite of his name, which means "forethought," Promêtheus was scarcely more than a petty comedian, even in Hesiod—more clever than wise, myopic rather than visionary, one who played virtually no role in the religious life of archaic and classical Greece. Even Aeschylus at first conceived of Promêtheus as a semi-comic trickster figure, "an impudent wag who tempted providence," as C. J. Herington has it, "in unusually ingenious ways, and was promptly put down for it." And he adds:

> It is a remarkable fact that almost all the ancient Greek literary accounts of Prometheus that survive, whether complete or in fragments, are either overt comedies or at least written in a humorous manner. There was a lost comedy by Aeschylus' Sicilian contemporary, Epimarchus, entitled *Prometheus or Pyrrha,* and Aristophanes' extant *Birds* contains an uproarious Prometheus-episode toward its end. . . . Even the great myth of Protagoras about the creation of mankind (as reported in Plato's *Protagoras* 320C–322d), profoundly serious as its implications are, does not treat Prometheus with any great respect, and treats his brother Epimetheus with outright levity. Strangely enough, Aeschylus himself seems originally to have shared the general attitude toward Prometheus. His earliest extant play, the *Persians* of 472 B.C., formed part of a trilogy of tragedies, which was followed according to the custom at the Dionysiac competitions, by a light-hearted satyr-play. The title of the satyr-play in that production was *Prometheus,* almost certainly with the subtitle *Pyrkaeus* ("the Fire-Lighter"). Not so long ago, a song probably sung by the satyr-chorus in this play came to light in a papyrus. Fragmentary though it is, it allows glimpses of a wild dance, in which the Satyrs caper round "the unwearying glare" of the fire newly given by Prometheus, and praise him for his boon to mankind; they also hope that they'll be joined by a Nymph or two, to complete the pleasure of the occasion.

Out of this clever but minor mythic figure of Promêtheus Aeschylus created an icon that has captured the world's imagination and passion far beyond its original mythic status. A primitive creation-story has been put dead-center in human consciousness, not only of the ancient world, but of the modern. As Podlecki says: "The *Promêtheus Bound* can be considered from many points of view: as an anguished cry of the human spirit, a quarrying ground of archetypal images, a Marxian treatise illustrating the class struggle; even as 'pure' drama."

III

Promêtheus Bound is set somewhere near the beginning of time at the farthest reaches of earth, Skythia, on a desolate mountain crag of the Kaukasos. Power and Violence, functionaries of a tyrannical Zeus, enter dragging the rebel Titan god Promêtheus. With them is the fire-god Hêphaistos who at the brutal insistence of Power chains Promêtheus to the mountain crag. Isolated, he is visited by a Chorus of the Daughters of Oceanos, to whom he reveals his "crimes" against Zeus that have brought him to his present condition. This exposition is interrupted by a visit from a fellow Titan, Oceanos, father of the Chorus, who offers to serve as intermediary between Promêtheus and Zeus, an offer that Promêtheus rejects. Then Io enters, a human victim of Zeus' cruel lust, half-girl, half-cow, forced to wander the earth, driven on, frenzied, by a gad-fly—a vivid testimony of Zeus' cruelty to the despised race of mortals. With Io's departure Promêtheus reveals that he knows the secret that will allow Zeus to escape overthrow if only he possesses it, an occurrence that is possible only upon Promêtheus' release. Then Hermês, Zeus' messenger, appears and tells Promêtheus that unless he gives up the secret he will be plunged into the bowels of earth, only to be brought back to light so that Zeus' eagle can eat at his liver. Promêtheus refuses and at the play's conclusion the earth opens in a cataclysmic storm of earth and sky and he is engulfed.

IV

Of the two main characters of this play, one of them doesn't appear. But unlike the reclusive Godot, we have drawn for us a portrait of him so vivid that Zeus (who appears in no extant Greek tragedy, and possibly never in any) virtually stands before us in form as palpable as the onstage Promêtheus. He is a tyrant pure and simple, and Aeschylus wastes no opportunity in defining him as that at every turn. We may not see Zeus, but we see his henchmen, Power, Violence, Hêphaistos and Hermês at work. We see the effects of his tyranny, Promêtheus chained to the crag, Io suffering a cruel persecution, image of his hatred for humankind. What's more, even the gods of Olympos are subject to Zeus' tyranny. In his opening command to Hêphaistos, Power speaks of Promêtheus having to learn to accept Zeus' "sovereignty," an introductory euphemism for tyranny. Hêphaistos, who pities Promêtheus, and balks at his onerous task, continues, as a god, to define the gods' position, that not even they are free; and Power concurs. They all are slaves, they all know pain, all except Zeus, the god at the top. "Only Zeus is free," he concludes.

What has happened to the Zeus of Hesiod and the Greek tradition, the Zeus of the archaic and classical worlds: the Great Father, the Wise Ruler, the Enlightened One, the source of all justice and fair-dealing? And what of the "wag" Promêtheus of Hesiod's tale who disappeared for three hundred years only to reappear in the fifth century, again as his old self in comic or semi-comic depictions in Greek literature and drama, only to be transformed into a defender of human dignity and freedom from oppression? Clearly neither Zeus nor Promêtheus in their traditional guise fit into Aeschylus' plans for the final tragedy of his long career.

V

There have been several attempts to plumb the reasons for this radical change, and though a definitive answer is not to be expected, some are particularly worthy of consideration, in particular that by Herington, who accepts Aeschylus as the play's author and places its composition in the last two years of his life, which is to say after *Oresteia*. He writes the following:

> In the *Suppliants*-tetralogy, and even more in the *Oresteia,* we become
> aware of two related tendencies in Aeschylus' imagination: a growing
> preoccupation with the nature of Zeus, and an insistence on the idea
> of a split between the divine powers of the universe. Neither of these
> tendencies is visible in the two earliest plays, the *Persians* and the *Seven
> Against Thebes;* on the other hand they are brought to a crashing cli-
> max in the *Prometheus Bound,* where the human action has become
> almost insignificant, the split between the divine powers is apparent
> at the very opening of the play, and the nature of Zeus is questioned
> as fiercely as it ever was in any ancient pagan work. If this view of the
> matter is right, then Aeschylus discovered, very late in his life, that
> the lowly Prometheus who had been on his imagination for at least
> fourteen years might now be made to serve him in his last and most
> radical effort to convey his vision of the human and divine state.

To do that Aeschylus, in a considerably less optimistic mood than in *Oresteia,* required a newly established despotic ruler who dominates a self-serving, egocentric, and solipsistic universe; and to match him he needed a worthy adversary that the Promêtheus of Hesiod and the tradition did not provide. By the same token, the Promêtheus of mythology needed as radical a reconstruction as Zeus. The "impudent wag," as Herington calls him, "who tempted Providence in unusually ingenious ways, and was properly put down for it," lacked significance. As the adversary of the tyrannical new Lord of Olympos, Aeschylus needed a hero of archetypal proportions, a powerful Titan capable of defending a humane cause—the survival of a threatened humanity—even against insurmountable odds. Aeschylus therefore proceeded to transform the Promêthean pedigree as radically as he had the nature of the traditionally benevolent Zeus.

First of all, the sly trickster is given a birth more commensurate with the demands made of him by his re-creator. No longer is Promêtheus the grandson of Earth (Gaia), rather he becomes her son, one of the original Titans; and Gaia's significance is equally boosted by taking on the identity of her daughter Themis, goddess of prophecy, allowing Promêtheus to speak of "Our mother Themis . . . Themis who is also Earth, many names but one form." And as a result of his mother's new status, Promêtheus himself is gifted with prophecy, permitting him to prophesy the future wandering of Io and her eventual reconciliation with Zeus.

Although these are the principal reasons for the alteration of Promêtheus' pedigree, Aeschylus goes even further in redefining the traditional family ties. Of his brother Titans only Atlas remains, the heroic Titan unmercifully condemned for eternity to support on his shoulders the pillars of the universe. His brothers Epimêtheus and Menoitios are eliminated probably as being not up to standard with their brother's new dignity. "In this way," Herington sums it up, "Promêtheus becomes a member of the older divine generation, the Titans, and uncle to Zeus instead of an obscure cousin." And so, urged on by the Daughters of Oceanos, Promêtheus, chained to his rock, launches into the narrative of a past that was new not only to him but to every member of that first, undoubtedly fascinated, audience.

He speaks of a civil war on Olympos. The Zeus faction wants to depose Kronos; the Titan faction opposes Zeus. Promêtheus, originally on the Titan side, defects with Themis when his brother Titans insist on winning by brute force, despite their mother's warning that only cunning and not violence will prevail. "Thanks to me and my strategy," Promêtheus tells the Daughters of

Oceanos, "dismal Tartaros is now the dwelling place of ancient Kronos, the Titans, and all his allies." He continues:

Zeus now sits on his throne
    as king of the
        gods—because of me;
    and this is how he repays me:
    with pain and humiliation.
There is a disease shared by tyrants:
    they cannot trust their friends.

But you asked me why he tortures me,
    what is my guilt, and why he
    treats me with such
                    outrage.
I'll tell you.

The war no sooner over,
and he now seated on his father's
    throne, he began dispensing
        privileges to each of the gods,
    a different power to each.
But to man he gave
    nothing, nothing for mortal
    humans—except loathing—loathing and the
        resolve to stamp them out,
to start again,
    a whole new race.

And who stood in their
    defense, this race of humans?
No one.
    Only I.
    Only I dared.
And because I dared, the race of
    humans was saved from being thrust into
Hades,
    destroyed utterly.
And for that, you see me now,

wracked,
> tormented,
>> tortured,
pitiable to behold.
I who pitied humans am shown no
> pity.
You see here a sight that does
dishonor to Zeus.

He then defends his disobedience of giving fire to man: "I knew what I was doing. I knew I was doing wrong. I needed no one to tell me, and I don't deny it. I willed it. I did it. Of my own will I did it. By helping mortal man I condemned myself to misery."

New, as well, was the revelation of Promêtheus' gifts to helpless man, man before fire: intelligence, reason, thought, enlightenment, numbers, letters, animal husbandry, ships, medicine, sacrifice to the gods, metallurgy—a magnificent litany of wonders never before enunciated. "All human skill and science was the gift of Promêtheus," says he. Here, then, was the birth of a new mythological hero, or, better yet, the re-birth to a higher purpose.

VI

Tyrants were not unknown to archaic and classical Greece. What one must remember is that the concept of tyrant changed in the course of time. M. I. Finley in his *The Ancient Greeks* describes an aristocracy not always united:

> . . . factious and ambitious individuals often brought about struggles
> for power within their ranks, exacerbating the troubles [of the lack of
> civil reform]. Out of this civil strife, and aided by the new military
> developments, there arose the specifically Greek institution of the
> tyrant. Originally a neutral word, "tyrant" signified that a man seized
> and held power without legitimate constitutional authority (unlike a
> king); it implied no judgment about his quality as a person or ruler.
> Individual tyrants in fact varied very much: some, like Peisistratus in
> Athens, reigned benevolently and well, and advanced their cities in
> many ways. But uncontrolled military power was inherently an evil;
> if not in the first generation then in the second or third the tyrants
> usually became what the word now means.

What is interesting in this regard is that Aeschylus' description of Zeus as tyrant anticipates the first full-scale portrait of the tyrant in Greece by approximately a century. It was not until the middle of the fourth century that Aristotle in his *Politics* was to lay out in vivid terms the characteristics of the "bad" tyrant as Greece had come to know him. And he did so in the typically Aristotelian manner: by observation of current tyrannies, and by a study of tyrannies of the past. Yet there is also the attractive possibility, and by no means a distant one, that he also tallied his list against that of Aeschylus in *Promêtheus Bound.*

Before looking into the *Politics,* we might first consider a short passage from Aristotle's *Rhetoric* that is as succinct a description of Zeus in Aeschylus' play as any. "This tyranny," writes Aristotle,

> is just that arbitrary power of an individual which is responsible to no one, and governs all alike, whether equals or better, with a view to its own advantage, not to that of its subjects, and therefore against their will. No freeman willingly endures such a government.

Not only do we find Aeschylus' Zeus in that statement but Promêtheus as well, the freeman who cannot willingly endure such a government.

VII

To Aristotle everything has a purpose; to exist without a purpose is not a possibility. Or, to put it another way, all things have a goal, and that goal is perfection: what Aristotle calls the "final cause." Nothing is what it is until it has reached perfection; and perfection for Aristotle is the achievement of an end result, and that end result, that "final cause," is the Good. Nature, therefore, does nothing in vain and every development is progress. This is the basis of his *Physics.*

> By gradual advance in this direction we come to see clearly that in plants, too, that is produced which is conducive to the end—leaves, for example, grow to provide shade for the fruit. If, then, it is both by nature and for an end that the swallow makes its nest and the spider its web, and plants grow leaves for the sake of the fruit and send their roots down (not up) for the sake of nourishment, it is plain, therefore, that this kind of cause is operative in things which come to be and are by nature.

On the human level, Aristotle believed that the perfection of the human organism is possible only in community, only in the polis, the city-state, where, in friendly combative manner, men associate and in concert urge each other on to achieve the moral end not only of the individual but of the collective: Virtue. Or, to use another term, *excellence,* an attribute striven for by the Greek from archaic times in the form of the *agon,* contest, conflict, the urge to achieve the pinnacle whether in athletics or rhetoric or tragedy or war or—and here is the most important of all these terms for Aristotle—the *polis,* that congregation of male citizens whose aim is collectively to achieve the highest moral development it is in its nature to achieve. It is no accident that the term *politics* is derived from "polis." In the contemporary world "politics" has about it a suggestion of the underhanded or manipulative, the not quite aboveboard. To Aristotle, on the other hand, it meant something quite different. It concerned public or social ethics; it was that branch of moral philosophy that dealt with the state or social organism as a whole. The operative words here, of course, are "ethics" and "moral," a dimension of politics now effectively obsolete, as the entry in the Oxford English Dictionary sadly observes. Here we have the opening paragraph of Aristotle's *Politics* to serve as a guide against which to measure the reign of Aeschylus' Zeus.

> Observation shows us, first, that every polis (or state) is a species of association, and, secondly, that all associations are instituted for the purpose of attaining some good—for all men do all their acts with a view to attaining something which is, in their view, a good. We may therefore hold that all associations aim at some good; and we may also hold that the particular association which is the most sovereign of all, and includes all the rest, will pursue this aim most, and will thus be directed to the most sovereign of all goods. This most sovereign and inclusive association is the polis, as it is called, or the political association.

Sir Ernest Barker puts it quite well in his study of Plato and Aristotle when he describes Aristotle's polis as "an association of friends mutually provoking one another to virtue."

Aristotle's description of the proper polis and its proper functioning is the very opposite of what Aeschylus describes as the rule of Zeus in *Promêtheus Bound,* never mind that it is divine Olympos, indeed the universe, that is in question. Roger Boesche in his brilliant *Theories of Tyranny,* in summing up

Aristotle's view of tyranny, defines precisely the nature of the state that Aeschylus' Zeus presides over.

> In effect, tyrants turn the political world upside down. Even though freemen should share in the government of the polis, tyrants treat freemen as slaves and rule despotically; even though citizens should govern as equals, tyrants rule hierarchically; even though government should be in the common good, tyrants rule selfishly; and even though the political rule of the polis should be the proper soil in which human excellence can flourish, tyrants transform the polis itself into a household, which can sustain mere life but not the good life. Aristotle noted that monarchy greatly resembled household management. "For as household management is the kingly rule of a house, so kingly rule is the household management of a city." By extension, he certainly regarded tyranny, the perverted form of monarchy, as the cruel misrule of a household. Just as the master of a household uses his servant as a tool, or an "instrument," by using the labor of the servant to provide himself with leisure, so servants use their subjects as tools in their selfish pursuits.

Three times in his writings Aristotle refers to a tale of the tyrant Periander of Korinth regarding how best to preserve a tyranny. Asked for such advice by an envoy of the tyrant Thrasybulus, Periander "said nothing, but only lopped off the tallest ears of corn till he had brought the field to a level." In another place he comments on the same story with "the tyrant should lop off those who are too high, he must put to death men of spirit." Elsewhere Aristotle notes that the tyrant often undoes himself by displaying no regard for the public interest that does not also serve his own personal advantage. His aim is his own pleasure, whereas the aim of a king is the Good. The result being that the tyrant covets riches, whereas the king seeks what is honorable, what leads to renown. Instead of fostering and aiding the polis in its search for the Good, the tyrant oppresses the common man, disperses the people, forcing them into the countryside, expelling them from the city, and therefore diverting the people from its innate mission to achieve the highest value of the polis: Virtue. In Zeus' case, he determines to annihilate the human race.

The tyrant is also the enemy of notable men because they are his greatest hindrance. It is the man of honor and conscience and the determination not to be sidetracked by the self-seeking of the tyrant, who raises conspiracies against him. "Some," says Aristotle, "because they want to be rulers themselves

[we must assume better ones]; others because they do not want to be slaves."
The wise tyrant, therefore, the one who wants to maintain his tyranny, is the
one who takes seriously the advise of Periander: Lop off the heads, from time
to time, of outstanding citizens.

One might say that Periander's advice would have been followed by Zeus
in regard to Promêtheus if it weren't for the untidy fact that, being a god,
Promêtheus wasn't susceptible to death, a point made by Promêtheus himself
to the Daughters of Oceanos when indicating the length of his suffering. As
for public interest that does not also serve his own personal advantage, we see
none in Zeus' administration. His aim is his own pleasure as opposed to the
pleasure of his peers, the other gods. Even Power and Violence who bring
Promêtheus to the mountain crag to be chained say explicitly that they, who
themselves are gods, are slaves to the regime. The profound distrust of the tyrant
even of his peers leads him, as Aristotle notes,

> to get regular information about every man's sayings and doings. This
> entails a secret police [sent] to all social gatherings and public meet-
> ings. Men are not so likely to speak their minds if they go in fear of
> a secret police; and if they do speak out they are less likely to go unde-
> tected.

What else can we call Hermês near the play's conclusion but an eavesdrop-
per, a member of Zeus' secret police, a spy? His arrival is swift, suspiciously
swift, after the news from Promêtheus that Zeus' time is limited because of
an action still to come, which only Promêtheus knows.

VIII
Then there is Oceanos, friend, Titan relative, once involved with Promêtheus
in his reforms. When he enters the scene on his winged monster, he arrives
as a figure in a Medieval morality play, not precisely like a villain or devil tempting the virtuous Christian to betray his faith, but perhaps something not totally unlike, because Oceanos is no freedom fighter, not any more at least, but
rather one who sees submission as the most politic way of saving his own (and
his Titan friend's) skin.

> I see you, Promêtheus.
>   Indeed I see you.
> And I want you, for all your

cunning and cleverness, your
            intelligence—I want you to
hear some good advice I have for you—
            no, in fact, the best advice,
            the best I have to give.

Know yourself.
            That's it.
It's that simple.
Know yourself, adapt yourself.
These are new times, and new
            times have new ways. And
                        this new time has a new tyrant, a new
            ruler of the gods.
You must change, my friend,
            change to suit the
                        times, to fit in.
If you continue in the way you're going,
            hard, harsh words with every breath,
Zeus can't help but hear you,
            far off as he is, up there in the sky.
And when he does,
            when he hears you, your
                        present suffering will seem like
            child's play.
Give it up, my friend,
                        give up this attitude, this
            anger of yours.
                                    You're in pain,
so learn control and find a way
            free of your misery.

Tempter? Oceanos certainly doesn't see himself in that way. He's well motivated, honorable, you might say, at least in his own eyes, and his intentions
are better than Satan's; do as Oceanos says and you will survive, that's true,
just as Oceanos is currently surviving. The question, of course, is: How would
Promêtheus as hero survive, especially in his own eyes? How would the hero
(passionate in his need to defend honor, freedom, and personal as well as soci-
etal integrity) survive by simply "surviving"? Back again, then, to Oceanos as

prototypic Devil. A wolf dressed in sheep's clothing? No. For Oceanos believes what he says to Promêtheus, it's his nature, he's being true to himself: He's no hero and wouldn't know how to be one even if he wanted, at least not on his own. His intention is not evil; he has no desire to snare Promêtheus' soul, which is to say his heroism; he wants simply, in his simple way, to help his friend and fellow Titan see reason and save himself.

The problem with Oceanos is that he is lazy-minded as well as lazy-spirited. He's a courtier, a sycophant, whose advice to Promêtheus leads to nothing so much as complicity with the enemy, an alternative unacceptable to Promêtheus. Oceanos will be safe as long as he follows his non-intrusive, apolitical, unquestioning path, for that's what he is for Promêtheus, a courtier. "This is the reason," says Aristotle,

> why courtiers attain a position of honor under both these forms of government. Democracies are fond of demagogues, who may be called "the courtiers of democracy," and tyrants like obsequious associates—which it is the business of courtiers to be. Tyranny is thus a system which chooses bad men for its friends. Tyrants love to be flattered, and nobody with the soul of a freeman can ever stoop to that; a good man may be a friend, but at any rate he will not be a flatterer: they are also good tools for bad objects; "nail knocks out nail," as the proverb says. It is a habit of tyrants never to like a man with a spirit of dignity and independence. The tyrant claims a monopoly of such qualities for himself; he feels that anybody who asserts a rival dignity, or acts with independence, is trenching on *his* prerogative and the majesty of his sovereign power; and he hates him accordingly as a subverter of his own authority.

How else does one understand Promêtheus' response to Oceanos' "survival" tactics other than as ironic, particularly when it is couched in deceptively non-inflammatory language? To Oceanos' "The only thing, I think, you've never learned is that foolish words never escape punishment," Promêtheus responds with deceptive friendliness:

> How lucky you are!
>> You dared with me,
>> you shared with me.
>>> Everything.
> And yet you're free of blame and
>> punishment.

I envy you.
   Stay out of it.
   You're only heading for trouble.
He won't change.
   His mind is set.
Persuasion will get you nowhere.

Oceanos, of course, isn't quick-witted enough to perceive irony when it stares him in the face and he replies with: "You're better at advising others than yourself." Promêtheus then thanks Oceanos for his offer to mediate for him with Zeus, but behind that friendly façade of the following text is another text entirely:

Thank you, my friend,
thank you for your loyalty, your
   eagerness.
    I'm grateful.
But you mustn't trouble yourself on my
   account. I mean, well,
   if that's what you intend.
       You'll fail.
All that effort, and you'll
      fail.
My advice is to do nothing.
Stay clear of it all, for your
   own sake. Steer clear of
    harm. Keep your silence.
Over my head in misfortune myself,
   why should I want to drag my
   friends in after me?

"Know yourself," said Oceanos to Promêtheus early on. A splendid adage of the Greek world, widely admired, inscribed on Apollo's temple at Delphi. The irony here, of course, is that Promêtheus *does* know himself, knows why he was born, and knows without equivocation why he has done what he has done and will continue to do: oppose tyranny. It is nothing less than that knowledge that makes Promêtheus what he is. And that knowledge cannot but make Oceanos evil in not only the eyes of Promêtheus, but in those of Aeschylus and of those fifth-century Athenian males seated in the Theater of Dionysos on that Spring day.

IX

The entrance of Io, unexpected, out of nowhere, considered by many a scene utterly or largely unrelated to the play, is perhaps the most brilliant of Aeschylus' innovations, and in no way antithetical to his manner of working. He is again, as in *Seven Against Thebes* and *Suppliants,* not only telling, but showing his audience the subject of his tragedy, which is not so much Promêtheus, as what we see Promêtheus suffering: tyrannical injustice.

Here is Io, the helpless and unwilling victim of Zeus' brutal sexual predatory interest, a young woman whose very body is gruesomely deformed because of his lust, driven mad by the pain of the gadfly's sting, and condemned to a terror-stricken flight that swept her across continents. It is a long scene, the play's longest, its central panel, so to speak, and therefore, like the "shield" scene in *Seven Against Thebes,* the one that bears most solidly on the play's central concern. There is no reason to elaborate on it except to say that the subject of tyranny is *shown,* and if it takes a lot of words to convey the meaning of the scene's horror and injustice, the visual pain not only of Io, but the sight of the "crucified" Promêtheus, in tandem, far exceed the power, even of many words, to hammer home the effect sought by the playwright. It is a scene so powerful that it is difficult not to surmise that it prompted Aristotle a century later to write of the tyrant:

> He should also avoid all sexual offences: he should be personally free from any suspicion of violating the chastity of any of his subjects, boy or girl, and all his associates should be equally free from suspicion.

And a bit further on:

> . . . and when he indulges himself with the young [he should make it known that] he is doing so not in the license of power but because he is genuinely in love. In all such cases, too, he should atone for the dishonors which he appears to inflict by the gift of still greater honors.

That last sentence and the mention of "still greater honors," makes one think twice about the ostensibly benevolent end of the Io affair: the arrival in Egypt, the paternal, non-sexual touch of Zeus's hand and the gentle exhalation of the divine breath that implants the calf-child Epaphos in her womb.

X

Promêtheus needs no introduction to the structure of Zeus' regime. He knows it at first hand, and how it operates, just as he knows the nature of Hermês' mission. "Kowtowing ass-wipe of the latest tyrant," he calls him; and later: "Make no mistake: nothing could make me trade my misery for your servility." The very tone of Hermês' words, the bullying, the braggart mentality of the brute, defines his function in Zeus' scheme of things.

> You!
> You there!
> Yes, you who think you're so smart!
> Cleverer than clever,
> bitterer than
> bitter! You who have
> angered the gods by honoring those
> creatures of a day with the gods'
> privileges!
> You,
> you who stole fire from the
> gods, I'm talking to you!
>
> You boast of a marriage that will
> topple him from power.
> The Father demands to know what you
> know.
> These are his orders. And he'll
> have no riddling speeches from you.
> The truth and nothing but,
> all of it, you hear?
> And I warn you,
> I won't be called back
> a second time, Promêtheus.
> Zeus knows what he
> wants, and he gets it.

Hermês tries every means of breaking Promêtheus' spirit, but fails, only to become even more enraged, reminding him of the pain he must endure unless he relents. Finally Hermês capitulates, and in the process provides us with a description of the hero that is meant to show him as foolish, but doubles back on its speaker and serves as a brilliant tribute to Promêtheus' heroic endurance:

> You're like a young colt, new-harnessed,
> straining at the bit,
> struggling, bucking,
> fighting the reins.

And Hermês departs.

XI

And then again, once more (and finally), there is Aristotle ironically warning the ambitious tyrant what not to do if he wants to survive:

> . . . abstain from every sort of outrage, and from two forms above all others—the infliction of physical indignities, and violation of the chastity of the young. He should show a particular caution of behavior when he is dealing with men of sensitive honor. Arrogance in matters of money is resented by men who care about money; but it is arrogance in matters affecting honor which is resented by men of honor and virtue.

Zeus' outrage to fellow-god Promêtheus, the very one who secured for him his throne, who sided with him against his own brother Titans, has generated precisely what Aristotle warned of as the source of retaliation: hate and contempt.

> Hate and contempt are the two most frequent causes of attack. Hate is a passion all tyrants are bound to arouse; but contempt is often the cause by which tyrannies are actually overthrown. . . . Hate must be reckoned as including anger, which produces much the same sort of effects. Anger, indeed, is often a more effective stimulus; an angry man will attack with more fury, because his passion prevents him from stopping to calculate. . . . Hate can stop to calculate: you can hate your enemy without feeling pain. Anger is inseparable from pain; and pain makes calculation difficult.

An insightful observation and one he might well have learned from Aeschylus' Promêtheus, whose pain is not only from his abused integrity and sense of honor, but from the physical pain that wracks him. He is the victim of hybris on the part of Zeus, a shameless deed of violence against one not deserving. That is what Zeus' tyranny has perpetrated on Promêtheus, and this is the source of Promêtheus' anger as thunder, wind and storm tear earth and sky and he calls, chanting, for

no more words
deeds

IT IS!

earth staggers and writhes in agony
thunder bellows from the hollow deeps resounding
lightning's fiery tendrils flash and coil
winds whirl and dust in columns
dance a deadly dance on the wide world
sky and sea are one
all this is Zeus
Zeus this terror
Zeus this storm
down down on me this storm of Zeus

(Exeunt screaming in terror the DAUGHTERS OF OCEANOS.)

O MOTHER EARTH
my
MOTHER
and SKY
great SKY
whose glorious eye
sees all and
lights our way
behold me now
see how unjust
my

suffering

(Pandemonium. The mountain collapses.)

• • •

Carl R. Mueller
Department of Theater
School of Theater, Film and Television
University of California, Los Angeles

A Note on the Translation

Every translator feels obligated to explain his or her aim in making a translation, and that is a salutary endeavor, for at least it tells the innocent reader what to expect as well as what not to expect. As a translator for many years, I have always (perhaps even before deciding whether or not to buy a particular volume of translations), insinuated my fingers between the covers to peek briefly at the obligatory *Note on the Translation* that I know cannot help but be there. What am I looking for? Usually only one word—the word that must be the *bête noire* of the true translator: ACCURACY. What's accuracy to him or he to accuracy that he should lust for it? A flippant query perhaps, but perhaps not. For it is a question that boggles the mind of all but the pedant. And it is in the name of ACCURACY that many a translator's hour (lifetime?) has been wasted, not to mention the hours wasted on their product by the unsuspecting reader who sets out to enjoy a Dante or a Homer or a Goethe, only to plow his way through by means of will and in the end wonder what all the fuss has been about.

There is no question that there is a place for literal translation, for translation that is bound to the word. The most convenient example that comes to mind is the long-lasting and successful Loeb Classical Library that publishes the original text and the translation on facing pages. The aim of its volumes is to aid the reader with a little Greek (or Latin), or a lot of Greek (or Latin) but not quite enough, to read the original by casting a glance at the translation when knowledge fails or falters. David Kovacs is completing a new six-volume Euripides in that series that admirably fulfils its function as support in reading the original. He says about his translation: "I have translated into prose, as literally as respect for English idiom allowed." And he's correct. He's also "accurate." But that's what the series' mission is to be, and for good reason. Yet what his translations are not (and I suspect he would agree) are performable versions for the stage, and for one reason: "Accuracy" has destroyed the poetry.

But enough of this.

What is good translation? And the answer to that question is different with each "good" translator who has ever wrestled with the problem. Listen to St, Jerome, the great fourth-century translator of the Bible into the Latin Vulgate, in speaking of Plautus and Terence and of their translations of Greek plays into Latin: "Do they stick at the literal words? Don't they try rather to preserve the beauty and style of the original? What men like you call accuracy in translation, learned men call pedantry . . . I have always aimed at translating sense, not words." Fourteen hundred years later the body of translators of the King James Bible of 1611 expressed their thoughts on literal translation: "Is the kingdom of God become words and syllables? Why should we be in bondage to them?" And in the later seventeenth century, John Dryden, the translator of many a classical text, from Plutarch to Virgil and Ovid, expressed his theory of translation at length, but most succinctly when he said: "The translator that would write with any force or spirit of an original must never dwell on the words of the author."

To bring it now to our own day and to the prolific translator of many classical and modern texts, William Arrowsmith: "There are times—far more frequent than most scholars suppose—when the worst possible treachery is the simple-minded faith in 'accuracy' and literal loyalty to the original." To read an Arrowsmith translation, say, of a classical Greek play, side by side with the original, is to see a fertile and poetic mind undaunted by the mere word of the original. He realized that he was translating a fifth-century B.C.E. Greek play for a middle- to late-twentieth-century English-speaking audience and had one obligation: to make that ancient play work on the contemporary stage for an audience that had few if any ties to the play's original context or audience. His duty was to make it work, and to make it work with style and the best poetic means at his disposal.

And finally the contemporary Roger Shattuck: "The translator must leave behind dictionary meanings and formal syntax . . . Free translation is often not an indulgence but a duty." And to that one must add that dramatic texts require perhaps even greater freedom than non-verbal texts (and poetry in whatever form is a verbal text). On the stage, rhythm is every bit as important as what is being said—at times even more important. A stinging line has to sting not merely with what it says, but with how it says it, with its rhythm. One phrase, indeed one word, too many in a sentence, destroys a moment that in the end can destroy an entire scene. Effect on the stage is everything, whether one is Aeschylus or Tennessee Williams. What to do with that rebellious word or phrase? Cut it if it adds nothing of importance. And if it is important, and can't be cut, then write a new sentence that gets it all in, just be certain that it has grace and style and wit, or horror if that's what's needed, and serves the moment in the best and most theatrical way possible.

PERSIANS

(ΠΕΡΣΑΙ)

CAST OF CHARACTERS

CHORUS OF ELDERLY MEN *regents of Persia*

GHOST OF DAREIOS

ATOSSA *queen mother*

XERXÊS *king of Persia, son of Dareios*

PERSIAN HERALD

MALE AND FEMALE SLAVE ATTENDANTS

PERSIAN SOLDIERS *survivors from the Battle of Salamis*

PERSIANS

Susa, capitol city of Persia.
The palace of Xerxês in the background.
In the foreground the tomb of Dareios.
Autumn 480 B.C.E., shortly after the Battle of Salamis.
Enter the CHORUS OF OLD MEN dressed in rich Persian garments.
Music. Dance. Song.

OLD MEN: *(Chant.)*

We,
we men,
we,
we old men,
we men called The Faithful,
chosen by our master,
Lord King Xerxês,
son of Dareios,
Great King Xerxês,
Persia's king,
to guard his land,
his gold-rich land and gold-heavy halls,
we,
we who are trusted,
trusted in our years,
constant in our age,
guardians in his absence,
old men, old men,
faithful to our king,
while he, our master,
and our youth sail in conquest,
sails billowing,
bound to the land of the Hellenes.

But when will he come,
when,
our king,
with his golden army?

My heart quakes with portents of doom,
for all the youth of Asia are abroad,
Asia's youthful might is away,
clamoring after its young master.
But no courier comes,
no runner, no rider
to Susa's great city with news.

From Susa they went,
from Agbatana,
from Kissia's ancient, towering ramparts,
by horse, by ship, by foot,
in close-ranked columns of war.
Men like Amistrês and Artaphrenês,
Megabatês and Astaspês,
each of them kings,
Persian commanders,
but each of them also the Great King's servants,
marshals of Persia's massive forces,
surging, surging,
seething for battle,
archers, horsemen,
a sight to see,
fearful in the fight,
stern in the harsh resolve of their spirit.

Artembarês, high in his chariot,
and Masistrês,
and noble Imaios,
strong of arm with his archer's bow,
unyielding Imaios,
and Pharandakês,
and Sosthanês, driver of stallions.
And others, still others
great Nile sent forth,
teeming Nile's fertile flow:
Sousiskanês,
and Egypt-born, sun-dark Pêgastagon,
and towering Arsamês,

lord of temple-rich Memphis, and
Ariomardos, governor of age-old Thebes,
and marsh-dwelling oarsmen terrible in number.

And Lydians followed in throngs,
great bands of soft-living lovers of luxury
who hold in check the mainland race;
Lydians set going by Mitragathês
and noble Arkteus,
kingly commanders,
and gold-rich Sardis;
countless chariots,
column on column,
four and six steeds abreast,
a fearful sight to see.

And the men of sacred Tmolos,
of Tmolos' windswept heights,
are set on, too:
Mardon and Tharybis,
anvil-hard wielders of spears,
and javelin-tossing Mysians,
masters of the throw,
all of them,
all,
determined to cast on Greece
the yoke of slavery.
And Babylon,
golden Babylon,
sends motley hordes,
streams that snake across the far horizon,
sailors for the rowers' bench and galleys,
and bowmen certain in proving their warrior prowess.
And from the broad reaches of Asia,
from Asia's vast steppes and plains,
scimitar-bearing masses,
tribe upon tribe
throng in multitudes,
a terrifying escort for the Great King.

The youthful bloom of Persia's men has gone,
gone from the land,
and all Asia mourns,
the mother that nursed them
grieves aloud with longing.
And parents,
and young wives in empty beds,
count out the lengthening days,
days stretching thin,
and wait, and wait,
trembling.

(Sing.)

And it is
DONE!
DONE!
The yoke cast on the sea's broad neck!
The Great King's host,
our Great King's city-smashing force,
on alien shores!
The Hellespont crossed!
Rafts bound fast!
A bolted roadway sewn with flax!
It is
DONE!
DONE!

Now Great Xerxês,
now teeming Asia's lord,
godlike man of golden radiance,
man born of a golden race,
shepherds his godsped flock against the world,
by land,
by sea,
trusting their rugged, rock-bound strength,
his stubborn commanders' rugged rage.

His eye darkens,

a viper's glance,
flashing a murderous,
treacherous sting,
and men,
countless men,
and ships,
countless ships,
follow his hurtling Syrian chariot,
battling men famed for the spear
with an Arês mighty with the bow.

So great a flood,
so vast a cataract of men,
cannot be stayed with the sturdiest of defenses,
a force grand as the invincible waves of the sea.
Persia!
Persia's army!
Persia's people!
An irresistible force that cannot be conquered!
Men who are mighty and brave of heart!

Our ancient destiny is sent from god,
god-ordained:
to wage war,
to tear down walls,
to strike with thunderous cavalry charge
and lay great cities low in the dust.

But new knowledge now turns our eyes
to the white-flecked sea when the stormwinds pound,
and we tame its rage,
and we straddle its back,
and build a road bound tight with flax,
and surge across to alien shores.

But where is the man,
where is he so keen
as to cheat the snares of the gods with a leap?
Calamity lures him,

smiles,
seduces him,
into her net,
and no escape.

And so my black-robed heart is torn with terror.
I cry in pain for the army of Persia!
And for Susa's great citadel,
widowed,
stripped of her men!
Let her not hear my cry.
Nor Kissia hear,
and its hordes of women
sing in response an echoing cry,
and tear fine linen robes in grief.

Our men are gone,
on horseback and foot,
a stinging swarm of bees behind their master;
crossed over the sea's yoke,
making two continent's one.

And marriage-beds,
empty of lusty men,
are wet with the tears of gentle Persian girls,
each grieving softly for her mate,
the warrior mate she joyfully sped on his way,
grieving with aching love and desire for her man.

FIRST OLD MAN: *(Chants.)*
Persians!
Come!
Let us assemble here
and discuss deeply and
carefully what most
concerns us,
for the time is come,
and the matter
urgent.

How does King
Xerxês fare,
Xerxês
son of Dareios?
Have our Persian
bowmen
won the battle,
or have the pointed
spears of the Greeks
prevailed?

*(Enter ATOSSA, dressed in splendor, on a chariot drawn by
ATTENDANTS and accompanied by a large retinue.)*

But look!
Our King's royal mother!
Radiant as light from the eyes
of the gods she comes!
My Queen!
Prostrate yourselves before her,
all of you,
and address her with words
of welcome!

(They prostrate themselves as she approaches.)

Great Queen!
Loveliest of Persia's women!
We greet you,
your servants,
most venerable mother of Xerxês,
wife of Dareios,
spouse of Persia's god and a
god's mother!
Unless we are forsaken
by the ancient daimon
that led us always to victory!

(Music out.)

ATOSSA:

> Why else would I have left my golden palace
> > and the chamber where Dareios and
> > I once shared a bed?
> Care tears at my heart, anxiety
> > that I will share with you, my friends,
> secret fears that grip me, from which I see no
> > > > escape.
> Has our great wealth now tripped up prosperity
> > and in a cloud of dust
> > > slammed it to the floor of the palaestra—
> the prosperity won by Dareios with a god's help?
> This is the two-pronged fear I can scarcely utter:
> Wealth without the backing of men is useless;
> and the strength of men without wealth is a
> > > futile diversion.
> > > > No.
> Our wealth is secure.
> > Look around you.
> My fear is for the light, the guiding light of our
> > house, its master's presence.
> Without him we are blind,
> > > groping in darkness.
>
> And so, gentlemen,
> > matters being as they are,
> > counsel me from your age and wisdom.
> For you are my trusted and faithful Persians.

FIRST OLD MAN:

> No need to ask us twice, my Queen.
> Whatever word or deed you ask of us,
> > we offer it gladly,
> your faithful counselors.

(ATOSSA descends from the chariot. The OLD MEN rise.)

ATOSSA:

> > I have had dreams.

Dreams that haunt me in the
            dead of night. Dreams that have
                        come since my son marshaled his army
            and set out for Greece,
            to ravage it.
But never has a dream come so
            clear, so vividly, as what I
            saw last night.
                                    I'll tell it to you.

Two women appeared before me,
            both of them dressed in fine
                        garments, one in luxurious
            splendor as a Persian, the other in the
simple tunic worn by the
                                    Greeks,
            both of them taller than women are today.

And they were lovely,
            lovely without a fault, and sisters,
                        or so they seemed,
                        from the same parents.
They had both drawn lots,
            and one had allotted to her the country of
                        Greece, where she lived; the other,
            in Asia.
But a conflict seemed to arise between them,
            some bitter quarrel.
When my son learned of it,
            he tried to curb their anger and
                        calm them.
To do so, he hitched them under his
            chariot and yoked them beneath their
                                                    necks.

One of them stands tall and proud in the harness,
            her mouth submissive to the bit;
                        the other bucks and,
                        struggling, tears the harness

with her hands, dragging the chariot
    violently along without bit or
    bridle, and breaks the yoke in two.

My son stumbles and falls from the chariot.
Dareios comes then, his father,
            and weeps for him.
And when Xerxês sees him,
    in shame he tears at the
            clothes covering his body.

These are the things I saw in the night.

                        When I woke,
I rose and dipped my hands in the
    water of a fair-flowing stream
    to purify them of bad dreams.
Then standing at the altar with
    libations for those gods
    who avert disaster,
and to whom such rituals are due,
I saw an eagle headed for Apollo's hearth
    in search of safety.
Standing there speechless,
    I looked on in terror as a hawk came
            circling, and then rushing madly
straight at the eagle
    tore into his head with its claws.
And the eagle did nothing,
    nothing but cower and offer up its
            body to the assault.

It was a terrible thing I saw,
    and a terrible thing I've told you.
                        But I say this:
If my son succeeds,
    he will be the marvel of all men;
            but if he fails—
    he is not accountable to anyone.

If he lives, and returns home,
>	he will rule the country as before.
The country is his.

FIRST OLD MAN:
>		My Queen,
>	my country's Mother,
what I say is neither meant to
>		cheer you overmuch or
>	frighten you.
But if you saw some evil thing,
>		then go to the gods in supplication;
>		pray for them to avert the disaster
>			and to bless you, your children,
your friends and your city.
>			And second,
you must pour libations to Earth and to the Dead;
>		and ask with a kindly heart that your
>		husband Dareios, whom you saw last night,
>			send up to Light from the Dark below
>		blessings for you and your son,
and to snatch below the
>		evils here among us till they
>			molder in darkness and fade.
This is the advice I give you
>		from a kindly and prophetic heart.
I judge this dream to be for your own good.

ATOSSA:
>		My lord,
your words interpreting my dreams
>		favorably, show to me your
>			loyalty and support for my son and the
>		royal house.
>		I pray it may be so.
I will do as you advise.
>		Entering the palace,
>			I will perform the rites you suggest
>		for the gods above and for the beloved

dead beneath the earth.

> But first, my friends,
> tell me where in all this world can
> Athens be found?

FIRST OLD MAN:
Far in the west where our lord the Sun sets.

ATOSSA:
And can my son really want to destroy this city?

FIRST OLD MAN:
Yes, for then all Greece would be subject to him.

ATOSSA:
Can Athens have so large an army as that?

FIRST OLD MAN:
Large enough to have done the Medes great harm.

ATOSSA:
Besides men, what do they have? Are they wealthy?

FIRST OLD MAN:
They have silver springing from the earth.

ATOSSA:
And in battle, do they fight with bows and arrows?

FIRST OLD MAN:
No, in close combat they fight with spears and shields.

ATOSSA:
Who is it shepherds these people? Who is their warlord?

FIRST OLD MAN:
They're neither slaves nor subject to any man.

ATOSSA:

Then how do they withstand foreign invaders?

FIRST OLD MAN:

Well enough to have crushed the great army of Dareios.

ATOSSA:

Your words are cold comfort for our anxious mothers.

(Enter a PERSIAN HERALD, agitated, at a run.)

FIRST OLD MAN:

You'll soon know all there is.
For here comes a Persian herald,
    to judge by his run.
He brings news.
    Good or bad, we'll soon hear.

HERALD:

Cities of Asia!
    Listen!
Listen, Persian land!
Persia, great harbor of wealth!
        Listen!
In one stroke of fortune
    your great prosperity is destroyed!
The flower of Persia's youth is withered!
    Gone! All gone!
          OIMOI!
Cruel, too cruel, to be the first
    to tell cruel news!
But I must! I must!
      No other way!
I must unroll for you now
    the tale of the great disaster!
Persians!
       Hear me!
All the barbarian force of Persia is
          destroyed!

(Music. Song. Dance.)

OLD MEN: *(Sing.)*

> Cruel!
> Too cruel!
> Dreadful pain!
> Pain that stabs!
> Stabs!

HERALD: *(Speaks.)*

> Lost!
> Lost the barbarian force!
> I never hoped to see
> home again!

OLD MEN: *(Sing.)*

> Too long!
> Too long!
> I've lived too long,
> when these ancient ears
> must hear such pain!

HERALD: *(Speaks.)*

> Persians,
> I was there!
> I saw!
> I can tell you the suffering,
> the disaster!

OLD MEN: *(Sing.)*

> OTOTOTOI!
> In vain,
> for nothing,
> the arrows,
> the weapons!
> From Asia to Greece!
> For nothing!
> In vain!

HERALD: *(Speaks.)*
    The shores of Salamis,
          and all around,
              are glutted with corpses of
    men who died
              horribly!

OLD MEN: *(Sing.)*
                    OTOTOTOI!
                     Bodies!
                    Dear ones!
                     Floating!
                     Bloated!
        Their winding sheets their
            sea-drenched robes!

HERALD: *(Speaks.)*
    Our arrows were useless!
    Ship rammed ship,
          and the army went down!

OLD MEN: *(Sing.)*
              Raise up a cry,
            a cry of misery!
         Shout loud for the dead!
              Wail! Keen!
          The gods destroy us!
              AIIIIII!
              AIIIIII!
        Persians, lament
        for an army destroyed!

HERALD: *(Speaks.)*
    Salamis, Salamis,
        most evil of names!
    And Athens,
        I remember,
        and I groan with pain!

OLD MEN: *(Sing.)*

Athens!

Hateful Athens!

Hateful to her enemies!

Athens that makes our women
husbandless!

Athens that makes our mothers
weep!

(All look in silence at ATOSSA.)
(Music out.)

ATOSSA:

I listened to you silently
all this while, struck
dumb by the numbing
pain, no way to
ask or question suffering so
immense.
Yet what can we do but endure?
The gods send what the gods send.

Tell it to me now.
Tell me calmly, even with
groans and tears if you
must.
Unroll before me the whole
disaster. I must know.
Which of us has survived?
Which men, which leaders, which
commanders have died to
leave their posts vacant?
Tell me.

HERALD:

Xerxês himself is alive and sees the sun—

ATOSSA:

Your words have brought a great

radiance to my house, a bright,
dawning day after night's gloom!

HERALD:

      —but Artembarês, who ruled a
cavalry of ten thousand, is
      buffeted along Silêniai's rough
                    coast.
And Dadakês the chiliarch
      leapt from the ship in a nimble
      bound, never so
         effortlessly, struck midway between
         ship and shore.
And Tenagon the highborn
      Baktrian now haunts,
         bobbing in the sea, the shore of
Aias' island. And Lilaios and
      Arsamês, and, third, Argêstês,
         all now tumbled by waves,
      rammed headfirst onto rugged
rocks, round and round the
      island that brought them down,
         the breeding ground of doves.
Pharnouchos died, too, and his
      cohorts from the springs of Egyptian
         Nile, all from a single ship:
Arkteus,
      Adeuês and Pheresseuês.
And Matallos, leader of
      ten thousand men, from
         Chrysa, dying, dyed his tawny beard
      red in the bloody bath of the sea.
Dead, too, Magian Arabos,
      and dead Baktrian Artabês,
leader of thirty thousand dark
      horsemen, ruler now in a cruel
         land of one dark grave.
Amistris and Amphistreus,
      whose spear dealt death,

and noble Ariomardos, whose
  death will give great grief to Sardos, and
   Mysian Seisamês, and Tharybis,
commander of five times fifty
ships, a Lyrnaian and a man of
 great beauty,
   dead,
victim of an unhappy end.
And Syennesis, bravest of all,
  king of the Cilicians, greatest
thorn in the enemy's side,
  found and died a glorious
      death.

So much for the leaders who
  come to mind.
Of all we suffered,
I've told of only a few.

ATOSSA:

      AIIIII!
   AIIIII!
Can evil be so great!
And pain so unmerciful!
  Disgrace!
Disgrace to Persians!
  Shriek, shriek for
    shame!
Tell me,
  tell me again,
   again!
Had they so many ships, these Greeks?
Had they such daring to ram our
  ships with their prows?

HERALD:

If numbers could win,
  we Persians would have sailed
   home in triumph.

Of Greek ships there were
        ten times thirty, with a
        chosen group of ten in reserve.
                        Xerxês' fleet numbered
        one thousand strong, with
two hundred seven galleons more
        of surpassing speed.
I know this. I'm certain.
I know the facts.
This was the total.
In numbers was our strength.
But so much for numbers.
It was not by numbers they
        won, the Greeks,
        but some god, some
spirit, some daimon tipped the
        scales with a measure of
fate to keep safe goddess Athêna's
                        city.

ATOSSA:
    Then the city of Athens is not yet sacked?

HERALD:
    A city with men is a city defended.

ATOSSA:
    How did it begin?
    Tell me? The battle,
        the ships' first encounter?
    Was it the Greeks, or my son
        pluming himself for security in
                        numbers?

HERALD:
    The disaster began with the
        arrival of something evil, some
        daimon or deity from somewhere.
    A Greek appeared from the enemy camp,

whispering to your son that under
         cover of night every Greek to a man
would leap to his oar and row madly in every
         direction to save his skin.
Your son, at once,
         deceived by Greek treachery and the gods'
         jealousy, let it be known to all his
         captains that when the
sun descended below the horizon, and
         darkness covered the dome of the sky,
they were to divide the fleet into three divisions
         and block the Greeks' escape to the open sea,
         while other ships surrounded and circled the island.
He let it be known that if any Greeks
         foiled his plot and found some secret
                  escape from a horrid death,
his officers would pay with their heads.

These were his words,
         words from a light heart.
But little did he know the fate the gods had stored up.

The men obeyed in orderly fashion,
         getting their suppers, each crewman
         securing his oar-handle to the peg.
And when the sun sank down, and
         night crept in, each sailor boarded his
         ship, master of his own oar,
                  as did others,
         masters of their own weapons.

And then they sailed,
         calling to each other down the line of ships,
sailing according to instructions.
And so they sailed all night long,
         back and forth as ordered.
                           All night.
And not one sight of a Greek in attempted flight.
Day dawned with a sky-course of white horses.

And then a cry,
    a joyful song from the Greeks,
        loud, and a high-pitched
echo from the island rocks in antiphony.

Fear stood by us, man by man,
    left guessing in our tracks.
The shout was not a shout of
    flight, but a song of triumph as they
        surged into battle formation with daring
                confidence.
A trumpet, then, a shrill that cut the air with its
    blast and propelled them forward as
    one, at one command, oars slicing the
        sea with a single stroke.
And then they appeared,
        as one,
    in speeding flight, the entire fleet
bursting upon our sight.
              On they sped,
faster, faster,
    the right wing first,
        then the whole fleet chasing us down the
            seaways.
And then another great shout.

"Onward, sons of Greece!
Liberate your land,
    your children, your wives,
    the shrines of your gods and the
        graves of your fathers!
The fight is for them all,
    or all is lost!"

From our side then, cries, shouts in answer.
There was no delaying now.
    Ship struck ship,
    ramming with bows of brass,
    breaking away whole prows.

The Greeks began it.
    Men on opposing decks let fly their
        spears.
We resisted at first, holding our own;
    but soon our ships, so massed together,
    struck each other head-on in the narrow strait,
      bronze beak ramming bronze beak,
    destroying oars and benches.
The Greeks then circled round in perfect
    order and struck, and hulls were tumbled
      wrong-side up, and the sea was no longer
seen for all the wreckage and floating bodies.
And all the shores and reefs bobbing with corpses.

Every Persian ship now tried for escape,
    quick escape, no order, all confusion,
    and they kept pounding us,
      the Greeks,
with everything at hand,
    broken oars,
      wreckage from the sea,
as if we were a catch of fish,
    deboning us, a school of tunny,
    and moans rode on the air,
groaning, wailing,
    over that stretch of sea, till
      night's black eyes opened
and then there was silence.

Ten days are not enough to tell it all,
    the disaster I saw,
      disaster on disaster.
One thing is certain.
Never have so many died on a single day.

ATOSSA:
        AIIIIII!
A sea of troubles, wave on
    wave, breaks over us and
      drowns all the tribes of Asia!

HERALD:

    You haven't heard the half of it.
    Such suffering ensued, such ruin,
        that it unbalanced the scales twice over.

ATOSSA:

    What more is there?
    What greater pain? Tell me,
        what new disaster could have tipped the scales
                even lower?

HERALD:

    Those princes, the best of the lot,
        strongest of body,
        noblest of birth and heart and
            closest to my lord the king,
    died a shameful, inglorious death.

ATOSSA:

                AIIIII!
    Tell me! Tell me, for I
        tremble to hear! Tell me by what
        evil chance they died!

HERALD:

    There is an island off of Salamis,
        a small one, facing the
        sailor as he approaches,
    with no fit harbor for anchorage,
        where great god Pan dances along the
                shore.
    It was there Xerxês sent these men.
          Their mission,
    to make an easy killing of shipwrecked
        Greeks taking refuge there,
    and to save their own friends
        shipwrecked in the sea.
    So little did they understand what was to come.

When some god gave the
     victory at sea to the Greeks,
         that same day,
they armored their bodies in gleaming bronze and
     leapt from their ships circling the island
     and took our Persians off guard with
         nowhere to turn.
Stones thrown from Greek hands
     pounded them repeatedly, and arrows
     from bowstrings rained down upon them and
         destroyed them utterly.
In a final move, the Greeks plunged forward
     with a single roar from deep in their chests
     and lay into them with their
         swords,
slaughtering, butchering, hacking away at those
     poor wretches' limbs until every living
     one of them was dead.

         When he saw,
when Xerxês saw from the height of a cliff's
     vantage point, the degree of the
         devastation, he shrieked and
         tore his clothes and ordered his troops on land
     to turn and run for their lives in whatever
             disorder.

         Now, Majesty,
you have two catastrophes to
               mourn,
     disaster on disaster.

ATOSSA:
         O hateful divinity,
hateful daimon, how
     evilly you have deceived our
         Persian senses!
It was a bitter vengeance my
     son planned for fabled Athens, a

            vengeance that doubled-back and
      struck him bitterly!
Were the Persians destroyed at
      Marathon not enough?
Instead of retribution for the loss,
          he brought on himself and us a
      flood of afflictions.

                   But tell me,
tell me what ships escaped
      unscathed.
Where are they?
Where did you leave them? Tell me,
      tell me clearly,
          leave out nothing.

HERALD:
    The few ships that survived
          raised sail in a rush of disorder and
            fled wherever the wind blew them.
    What was left of the army
        began to die in Boiotia, gasping,
        thirst-parched, no water,
        or too exhausted to reach the spring
    so close at hand.

    Some of us made our way to
        Phokis, Doris, the gulf of Mêlia,
    where generous Spercheios waters rich farmland plains.
    Achaia, then, and the towns of Thessaly
        received us, starving, on our last legs.
    It was there most of us died,
        too weak to manage food or drink.
    But those still alive dragged on to Magnesia and
        Macedon, the ford of Axios and
          Bolbê's reedy marsh, as
    far as Mount Pangaion in Edonian territory.

    That same night god brought on winter

unseasonably and froze the sacred stream of
flowing Strymon.
Those who had never given the gods much
notice, fell prostrate on the ground and offered
prayers to Earth and Sky.

Our pleas concluded,
we raced to cross the ice before the sun.
We lost.
Only those swift enough made it. The rest
sank into icy water, tumbling,
falling upon each other,
struggling to keep afloat,
and luck was with those who gave their breath up soonest.

We few who survived after
dragging our way through Thrace with great
suffering are only now reaching our
country's borders and finally here to
home.

Persia has reason to mourn the loss of her youth,
flowering multitudes of beautiful young men.

All this is true.
But not all is told of the misery
hurled by god at the Persians.

(Exit the HERALD.)

FIRST OLD MAN:
Malevolent deity,
how viciously you have
leapt on the Persians!
How cruelly you have
stamped down our Persian race!

ATOSSA:
AIIIII!

I weep, I weep for the army,
      the many men lost!

O prophetic dream!
Dream in the night, so clear, so
      terrible, how surely you showed me
      the misery now come true!

But you, you, dear friends, you
      judged the evil vision too lightly.
Still, I will do as you say,
      you advise me well.
I will pray, first to the gods,
      the whole pantheon, and then to
      Earth and the Dead I'll make offerings,
and bring from my house libations.
      Not for the past,
            for that is done, over,
      but for the future, in hope of some
                              better time.

I look to you now for wisdom in what has
                        happened,
      for you are worthy and have our trust.
And if my son arrives before I return,
      comfort him and escort him to the palace,
before he adds more misery to his suffering.

(Exit ATOSSA in her chariot along with her retinue.)
(Music. Song. Dance.)

FIRST OLD MAN: *(Chants.)*
      Zeus,
      Great King,
      Majesty, you have
      destroyed us,
      destroyed our army,
      our Persian army of
      men

proud and powerful,
great hosts of men,
destroyed.
And Susa,
and Agbatana, too, you have
shrouded in the gloom of
grief.
How many women,
weeping, pitiable,
how many mothers,
beating their breasts,
breasts drenched with tears,
with tender hands
tear their veils,
sharing our pain?
New wives,
now widows, young
women of Persia,
longing for their
men,
their lusty men, their
marriage beds newly made,
soft sheets awaiting the
joys of youth, of youth's
voluptuous adventures,
weep bitter tears now
in grief and desolation.
And I, too, grieve unashamed
for the fate of the lost.

OLD MEN: *(Sing.)*

Asia weeps,
all, all Asia weeps,
her land stripped clear of men,
stripped naked her steppes and plains!
Xerxês led them!
Led them,
AIIII!
Xerxês destroyed them!

Destroyed them,
AIIII!
Xerxês in his madness misguided his ships!
AIIII! AIIII!
Dareios never harmed his men,
Dareios,
grand archer,
master of the bow,
beloved leader of Susa!
This king was no Dareios!

Soldiers, sailors,
dark-eyed, sail-winged ships led them off!
Led them off,
AIIII!
Ships destroyed them!
Destroyed them,
ships of death,
AIIII!
Ramming ships destroyed them,
AIIII!
Destroyed them,
destroyed,
AIIII! AIIII!
Greek ships destroyed them
with deadly ramming!
But our king escaped,
our king,
so we hear,
through Thrace,
through blustery Thrace.

They were the first,
AIIII!
the first to die,
the first to meet their fate,
AIIII!
caught up by Necessity,
AIIII!

by Necessity,
AIIII!
on the beaches of Salamis!
Smashed!
Destroyed!
AIIII!
Cry to heaven!
Shout your pain!
AIIII! AIIII!
Stretch high your wailing clamor
in a terrible howl!
AIIII!

Torn,
torn by the rock-sharp sea,
AIIII!
mangled by silent children
of the undefiled sea,
AIIII!
houses grieve,
grieve for lost men,
parents, childless,
bemoan empty houses,
AIIII!
lament the affliction god sent in their age!

No longer will Persia rule all Asia,
no longer will Persian law be the rule,
no tribute now to Persia's throne,
no more prostration to Persia's Great King,
for Persia's royal power is dead!

Now tongues are uncurbed,
now men speak freely,
a yoke is lifted and freedom rushes in.
The soil of Salamis,
Aias' isle,
holds all that is left of Persia's
greatness.

(Enter ATOSSA on foot and in unadorned mourning, accompanied by several FEMALE SLAVES ATTENDANTS carrying the makings of a ritual.)
(Music out.)

ATOSSA:
                    Friends.
The man who has lived through
        adversity knows that when a sea of
                troubles rises against him he is the
        victim of abject terror.
But when a beneficent daimon blows
                gentle good fortune, he is
        certain it will last forever.
                                As for me,
I have long suffered every kind of
                    fear.
Hostile visions visit me from the gods,
        and a roaring in my ears—
                no victory song.
                            These,
these are the evils that come with
        disaster and are driving me into
                    madness.
And so I have come again,
        come from my house,
        not as before, not in my
                chariot, not with the pomp and
pride of possession, but with
                gifts for my son's father,
        libations to soothe and
        appease the dead:
Milk, white, sweet to the
        taste, from an unblemished cow;
honey sucked by
        flower-working bees; lustral
        water from a virgin
                spring; and from an ancient
vine in the field, this unmixed draft of
                    radiant wine.

Olive oil, too, is here,
        golden-yellow, and
garlands of flowers sprung from
            teeming Earth.

Sing your songs, friends,
        songs for the dead, for
        Dareios below the earth, to
            summon him to us.
Meanwhile,
        I'll send these gifts for Earth to drink
in honor of the gods below.

(Music. Song. Dance.)

FIRST OLD MAN:
    Great lady, Persia's Queen,
        send your gifts to the gods
            below, and we will sing our
    hymns to ask the escorts of the dead
    to be kindly beneath the earth.

(Chants.)

    Gods of the world below,
    gods of the underworld,
    holy gods, Earth and
    Hermês, and
    Lord of the Dead,
    send him up from Earth's
    dark into the light.
    What remedy there is,
    perhaps he knows,
    cure for our pain,
    for ruin's
    suffering.
    If he knows, he alone
    can tell us, he
    alone of men can say.

OLD MEN: *(Sing.)*

> Does he hear me,
> my King,
> my blessèd King,
> my King equal to god?
> Does he hear my barbarous cries,
> my woeful cries of lamentation,
> deep, deep in the earth?
> Does he hear me in darkness?

> Earth,
> Great Mother,
> and all other leaders of the dead,
> let him come,
> the Proud Spirit,
> Persia's god born at Susa,
> send him, raise him,
> give him to us.
> Persian soil never covered such a man.

> Man dearly loved,
> dearly loved tomb,
> dear, too, the qualities buried here.
> Aïdoneus,
> release him!
> Aïdoneus,
> escort him!
> Our divine lord King Dareios!
> O-IIII!!

> He never killed a man of his armies
> in a war of deadly infatuation.
> We called him god's counselor
> who gave godly counsel,
> a leader who steered his army well.
> O-IIII!

> Shah,
> great Shah,

Lord King of past times,
come,
draw near,
appear!
Appear on the peak of your burial mound!
Raise your saffron-tinted slipper!
Show the plume of your kingly tiara!
Ever-benevolent Dareios, appear!
O-IIII!

Hear our pain,
our suffering,
our new sorrows!
Master of masters, come!
A Stygian death-mist
hovers about us,
for all of Persia's young men are dead.
Ever-benevolent Dareios, appear!
O-IIII!

AIIII!
AIIII!
We wept,
your friends,
we wept at your death,
we wept!
O lord, my lord,
why, why this terror,
this double,
this doubly-lamented disaster?
For all Persia's ships,
her triple-banked ships,
her ships are no more!

(The GHOST OF DAREIOS appears above his tomb.)

GHOST OF DAREIOS: *(Speaks.)*
Most faithful of the faithful,
companions of my youth,

elders of Persia,
what is this sorrow that grips the city?
The earth groans,
    hammered at,
        scratched open.
I see my wife near my tomb and am
    filled with fear.
        Her libations I received
    graciously and came.
But you here near my tomb sing a dirge,
    wailing, calling on me to rise,
        to appear, appear,
a shrill lament to raise the dead,
    calling me piteously.
The road from Hades is no easy one,
and the gods of the dead are better at taking than
                releasing.
But I exercised my authority there and came.
Let there be no delay.
I won't be accused of dallying.
What new and weighty evil crushes
              the Persians?

FIRST OLD MAN: *(Chants.)*
    Majesty,
    the sight of you
    awes me!
    I shrink with awe
    from speaking with you!
    The old fear of the
    past is revived!

GHOST OF DAREIOS: *(Speaks.)*
    I stand here now in response to your shrill laments.
    Be brief, say what you have to say;
        spare the awe you had for me in days passed.

FIRST OLD MAN: *(Sings.)*
    Fear freezes me!

How can I
            obey?
How can I say
words I would
fear to say to a
                friend?

(Music out.)

GHOST OF DAREIOS:
    Since ancient fear inhibits your minds,
    I ask my lady, Her Majesty,
        high-born companion of my bed,
            to dry her tears and put an end to her
    wailing, and tell me clearly the matter.
    To be human is to suffer,
                    nothing more.
            Sufferings come.
    Neither land nor sea is free of evil's sorrow.
    And the longer men stretch out life
                    the more evils come.

ATOSSA:
                    Of all men
    you were the most fortunate in prosperity,
        the envy of all while you
            looked on the light of the sun.
    Your life was happy here among
        the Persians, living like a
                    god.
        And I envy you now,
    for death came for you before the
            disaster fell.
                    You never saw it.
    But I will tell you, Dareios,
        I will now tell you the entire story in a word:
            All Persia,
    city-sacking Persia, is now
            destroyed!

GHOST OF DAREIOS:
>But how? Why? A plague? A revolt?

ATOSSA:
>No. The entire army was destroyed at Athens.

GHOST OF DAREIOS:
>Which of my sons led them? Tell me.

ATOSSA:
>Xerxês, impetuous Xerxês; all our youth gone.

GHOST OF DAREIOS:
>The stubborn fool! How? By land or sea?

ATOSSA:
>Both. Two forces on two fronts.

GHOST OF DAREIOS:
>But how did so vast an army cross to Greece?

ATOSSA:
>He yoked the Hellespont and made a road.

GHOST OF DAREIOS:
>Closed the gap of mighty Bosporos?

ATOSSA:
>Yes. But one of the gods must have helped.

GHOST OF DAREIOS:
>Some powerful Spirit to relieve him of his wits!

ATOSSA:
>And we see here the disastrous result.

GHOST OF DAREIOS:
>What happened? What evil fate that makes you groan?

ATOSSA:

    First the ships were destroyed, then the army.

GHOST OF DAREIOS:

    The whole Persian army destroyed by the spear?

ATOSSA:

    Yes; and all Susa mourns the death of its men.

GHOST OF DAREIOS:

    Our defense, our protection, lost, a great army!

ATOSSA:

    And every Baktrian man is dead, dead.

GHOST OF DAREIOS:

    O wretched fool, to kill our allies' young men!

ATOSSA:

    Xerxês, they say, alone, and with very few men—

GHOST OF DAREIOS:

    How did it happen? Where? Or did he survive?

ATOSSA:

    —reached the bridge that yoked the two continents.

GHOST OF DAREIOS:

    And returned to Asia alive? Is this true?

ATOSSA:

    True, yes, the accounts are clear as day.

GHOST OF DAREIOS:

    How swiftly god's oracles work!
    How swiftly Zeus hurls it
        down upon my son! I had
    hoped for more time,
            the distant future,

but when a man is a fool and loses control,
    the gods speed him on his way.
                A well of disaster
overflows for all I love.
And this was my son's doing,
    this his achievement, who in his
impetuous youth sought,
    like a slave, blindly, to
chain the sacred flowing Hellespont,
    god's holy spring, the Bosporos.
He made land of the sea,
    against all nature,
laying a great road for his great army.
How foolish to think he could master the
            gods, including Poseidon.
What was it but some disease that gripped his
                mind?
Now all I fought to win,
    the gold, the power,
are left to be plundered by anyone who wills.

ATOSSA:
    He kept bad company, our son,
        wild, raging Xerxês, and learned his
        lessons well from evil men.
    He wasn't a man, they said, a courtyard
        warrior, while you had fought and won vast
        wealth and fame and left it to your sons.
    But he, they said,
        said it again and again,
    did nothing to increase the prosperity you left him;
    said it till he determined to prove his manhood and
        launch this expedition against Greece.

GHOST OF DAREIOS:
    So now a deed is done that can't be
        undone, and done to us, so
        terrible, so vast, so unforgettable:
    the unmanning of Susa,

the fall of Susa's manhood.
Never since Zeus conferred on us the honor
     to rule all sheep-breeding Asia with a single scepter
          have we known such devastation.
                         First Mêdos
     led our men, and then his
     son, and third came Kyros,
a man blest, for he brought peace to his friends.
He brought to us, too,
     the men of Lydia and Phrygia, and
     all of Ionia that he won by force.
Being a wise and kindly man,
     god held no grudge against him.
                    The son of
Kyros was the fourth to lead our
     hosts; and fifth came Mardos,
a disgrace to the land; a usurper
          who stole and debased the throne.
A coup of loyal hands
     led by noble Artaphrenês did their duty
               and killed him in the palace.
Lots were cast for king and
     then it was my turn.
And I led my vast army on many
     expeditions, but I never brought such
          disaster upon the city.

Now it's young Xerxês rules.
          Barely a man.
     Inexperienced.
     Impetuous boy. He thinks
          as a young man
     thinks, and forgets my
                    advice.

          My lords,
you and I share an age, and we
     know one thing surely.
Not all the kings together who have ruled this country

have ever brought so much
suffering to these people.

FIRST OLD MAN:

What are we to do, lord Dareios?
Where do your words point us?
            To what good? Having suffered the worst,
how may we, Persia's people,
            win out to the best?

GHOST OF DAREIOS:

You must never again campaign in
            Greek territory; not even with a
            larger Persian army.
Greek soil is the Greek's staunchest
                                    ally.

FIRST OLD MAN:

Ally? But how?

GHOST OF DAREIOS:

It starves to death the invader with too many men.

FIRST OLD MAN:

But we'll muster a fine force, carefully picked.

GHOST OF DAREIOS:

                    No,
not even our ragged forces now in
Greece will return home in safety.

FIRST OLD MAN:

                    What are you saying?
Those Persians left behind
            will never cross the straits from
            Europe to Asia?

GHOST OF DAREIOS:

                    A few.

Some few out of many thousands,
        if one is to trust the gods'
                oracles.
Only look at how much they
        foretold has been fulfilled.
                Everything.
When Xerxês leaves his hand-picked
        troops behind, he's been
        persuaded by false hopes.
There they sit by the Asopos
        whose welcome waters make
                rich the Boiotian plain,
                        waiting,
        waiting for the crown of misery to be
put in place, just payment for
        terrible pride and godless
                arrogance.
They came to Greece and with no
        awe for the gods,
no shame, plundered images,
        torched temples, uprooted altars and
        pried up shrines, scattering them
                about in blind
                        confusion.
And so their suffering is no less
        evil than the evil suffering they
                caused.
And there will be more suffering.
Only the foundation of their
        evil is laid, the house is not yet
                built. So great will be the
bloody slaughter on Plataian
        land by the Dorian spear.
Piles of Persian corpses to
        generations hence will
                testify in silence to men's eyes
that mortal men should think only
                mortal thoughts.
Violence sown has reaped a harvest of

ruin and bitter
tears.
Behold these things,
behold these punishments,
and as you do, remember
Athens, and remember
Greece, and never
scorn the blessings heaven gives today
while lusting for others
tomorrow, and so pour out a
store of great
prosperity.
Zeus watches, and
Zeus is a stern chastiser of
arrogant minds,
nothing escapes him.

When he comes,
when Xerxês comes,
counsel him in your
wisdom; tell him in his
foolishness to listen to you and
stop offending god with
overboastful rashness.

And you, beloved and venerable
mother of Xerxês,
go home, choose a robe
becoming to him, your
son, and go meet him,
welcome him.
He'll need it, for in his
agony he has torn the
embroidered robes on his
body to shreds.
Be kind to him,
soothe his spirit, make him
calm, for you are the only one he will
listen to.

I must go now.
Back down to the land of
shadows.
Farewell, old friends, and
never let disaster conquer you.
Be glad for what you have:
your life: enjoy it
daily.
Wealth is of no use to the dead.

(THE GHOST OF DAREIOS disappears.)

FIRST OLD MAN:
I heard with pain the news of Persia's
pain and pains still to come.

ATOSSA:
O daimon,
evil Spirit, how cruel are the
pains I suffer, but this misfortune
stings my heart most of all:
to hear of my son's dishonor in tattered robes.
But I will go now to bring clothes from the house
and meet him on his way. I will
never betray my dear one in a time of crisis.

*(Exeunt ATOSSA and her FEMALE SLAVE ATTENDANTS in the
direction of the palace.)*
(Music. Song. Dance.)

OLD MEN: *(Sing.)*
How great,
how good was the life we lived,
the life of peace,
when our king of old,
our agèd ruler,
all-sufficing,
invincible and godlike,
who did us no harm,

Great King of Kings,
Dareios,
Lord Dareios,
ruled our land!
A country with armies famed in the world,
with laws strong as towered battlements,
a state well ordered,
and men returning,
unscarred, unscathed,
to happy homes.

And what cities he captured,
many, many,
and never left home,
never crossed the Halys!
Rivergod cities near Strymon's gulf,
hill-defended towns in Thrace,
knew him,
all knew him!
And cities with towers,
tower-walled cities,
cities outside the lake on the shore,
cities,
cities on the west coast of Hellespont,
and the Sea of Marmara
and the Thracian Bosporos!
And islands,
sea-washed,
islands near the headland:
Lesbos,
Samos where olives grow,
Chios and Paros,
Naxos,
Mykonos,
and Andros, nearest neighbor to Tênos!
Knew him,
all knew him,
knew Dareios as King!

And islands far out in the sea he ruled,
Lêmnos, Ikaria, Rhodos, Knidos,
and the cities of Kypros,
Paphos and Soloi and Salamis,
AIIII!
whose mother-city
now brings on our grief!
He ruled them,
ruled them all,
and all,
all knew him!

And Ionia he ruled,
Greek Ionia,
ruled in his wisdom,
cities teeming with men and many riches,
strength in men-at-arms,
undefeatable military might and many allies.
But now the gods turn all around,
we suffer defeat,
dreadful defeat,
defeat at sea,
the gods our enemies,
and we must endure.

(Enter XERXÊS in rags and on a near-destroyed ragged-curtained carriage pulled by several exhausted, almost naked SOLDIERS, remnants of the Persian army, a few others straggling along behind. XERXÊS carries an empty quiver.)

XERXÊS: *(Chants.)*
IOOOOO!
IOOOOO!
Hateful doom!
Hateful god!
Cruel god!
To descend so cruelly
on the Persian race!
No warning!

So savagely!
How do I bear this misery,
this unspeakable fate?
I see these agèd citizens
and all strength
is ripped from me!
Zeus!
Great Zeus!
I should have died with them!
Died with my men
now slaughtered!

FIRST OLD MAN: *(Chants.)*
OTOTOIIIIIII!
King!
My King!
I lament for your army,
your noble army,
for the greatness of Persia,
and her glorious men,
cut down now,
cut down, whom
god has destroyed!

The land,
the land cries,
cries aloud,
cries,
for her youth whom
Xerxês has
slain,
whom Xerxês has
crammed into dismal
Hades,
Persia's
youth from Agbatana,
great Persia's flower,
many, many,
thousands,

ten thousands,
archers,
masters of the bow,
a forest of men,
gone,
destroyed,
no more!

AIIII!
AIIII!
Weep for them,
weep,
our noble defense!
All Asia brought to her
knees in
shame!

(XERXÊS descends from the carriage.)

XERXÊS: *(Sings.)*
Behold me and weep,
I am your
misery!
The blight of my land,
the ruin of my
family!

OLD MEN: *(Sing.)*
I greet your return,
your unhappy homecoming,
with a cry of woe,
a lament of great sadness,
the ill-omened cry of a Mariandynian.

XERXÊS: *(Sings.)*
Sound your lament,
your ragged-voiced
grief,
for god now brings down

his blast on my
                    head!

OLD MEN: *(Sing.)*

                        I will cry aloud
                    my harsh-voiced noise
                    in honor of the pain,
                        the people's pain,
                pain for the sorrows suffered at sea.

XERXÊS: *(Sings.)*
    Killed by
                Greeks,
    Greeks killed them,
    war-god
                Arês
    gave them their strength,
    cutting a path through the
    night-dark
                    sea,
    and the fatal
    haunted
                shore!

OLD MEN: *(Sing.)*

                        OIOIIIII!
                        OIOIIIII!
                    Cry out, cry out,
                    ask all the questions!
                    Where are they now?
                Where are our dear ones,
            the hosts of friends who stood beside you?
            Men, comrades, like Pharandakes?
        Like Sousas and Pelagon and Agabatas?
        Psammis and Dotamas and Sousiskanês?
                All, all who left Agbatana!

XERXÊS: *(Sings.)*
    I left them there,

left them to
           death,
to death on
           Salamis,
they fell from our ships,
dead,
       dead,
washed ashore on the
rock-cruel
           coast!

OLD MEN: *(Sing.)*

                    OIOIIIIII!
                    OIOIIIIII!
         Where are Pharnouchos and noble Ariomardos?
                    And lord Seualkês,
                    and Lilaios, that noble man?
         And Memphis and Tharybis and Masistras,
                    and Artembarês and Hystaichmas?
                    I ask you,
                    ask you again:
                    where are they?

XERXÊS: *(Sings.)*
    IO IO MOI MOIIIIII!
    Hated,
    hated
           Athens,
    when they saw!
    Hated Athens!
    Ancient Athens!
    One stroke,
                one
    stroke, all at
    one
         stroke!
    ÉË!
         ÉË!
    Gasping,

          pitifully,
on the shore,
          gasping!

OLD MEN: *(Sing.)*

          But what of him,
          the flower of Persia,
          your faithful Eye,
          all-seeing,
          faithful?
          The thousands, he counted,
          ten thousand,
          ten thousands!
          Alpistos son of Batanochos,
          son of Sêsames,
          son of Megabates?
          And Parthos and mighty Oibarês?
          Did you leave them, too?
          Leave them behind?
          Poor men,
          poor wretches!
          You tell me of evils,
          evils beyond evils!

XERXÊS: *(Sings.)*
How I loved them,
loved my
          comrades,
my heart cries out from
deep in my breast!
Hateful
          memory!
Hateful
          remembering!
You tell me,
          tell me of
evils beyond evils!
My heart cries
out for my
          noble Persians!

OLD MEN: *(Sing.)*
And others? Others?
The others we long for?
Xanthes,
commander of ten thousand Mardoi,
and Anchares the Arian,
and Diaixis and Arsakês,
masters of the horse,
and Kegdadatos and Lythimnas,
and Tolmos whose spear thirsted in battle?
I'm stunned not to see then,
stunned,
stunned,
not here in your train,
these pitiful few,
these poor ragged remnants
that follow your curtained carriage!

XERXÊS: *(Sings.)*
Gone,
gone,
those warlords
of battle!

OLD MEN: *(Sing.)*
Nameless,
unnamed,
no more!

XERXÊS: *(Sings.)*
IË!
IË!
IO!
IO!

OLD MEN: *(Sing.)*
IO! IO!
O DAIMON! DAIMON!
You brought Disaster!

You brought Calamity!
Piercing is Ruin's glance!

XERXÊS: *(Sings.)*
    Struck down
    IO! IO!
    is Persia's
            power!

OLD MEN: *(Sing.)*

                            Down!
                        Struck down!
                            IO!

XERXÊS: *(Sings.)*
    New pain!
    New pain!

OLD MEN: *(Sing.)*

                        The Greeks!
                        Our fate!
                        On sea!
                    I weep for Persia!

XERXÊS: *(Sings.)*
    Great Persia's
                    army,
        gone!

OLD MEN: *(Sing.)*

                    Great Persia's power,
                            gone!

XERXÊS: *(Sings.)*
    Behold me now,
    a man of
            tatters!

OLD MEN: *(Sing.)*

                                     Rags! Rags!

XERXÊS: *(Sings.)*
    My quiver, empty—

OLD MEN: *(Sing.)*

                                     What was saved?

XERXÊS: *(Sings.)*
    that once held arrows!

OLD MEN: *(Sing.)*

                             So much now so little!

XERXÊS: *(Sings.)*
    Stripped!
             Naked!
    Nothing! No
               help!

OLD MEN: *(Sing.)*

                       Greeks stand fast in battle!

XERXÊS: *(Sings.)*
    I saw disaster!
    Calamity from
                 nowhere!

OLD MEN: *(Sing.)*

                       Greek ships struck
                   and thousands died!

XERXÊS: *(Sings.)*
    I tore my robes
    to see that
             disaster!

OLD MEN: *(Sing.)*
                          PAPAI! PAPAI!

XERXÊS: *(Sings.)*
    PAPAI!
             PAPAI!
    Worse than
             PAPAI!

OLD MEN: *(Sing.)*
                          Double and triple ills come at us!

XERXÊS: *(Sings.)*
    We mourn,
        our enemies exult!

OLD MEN: *(Sing.)*
                          Our strength destroyed!

XERXÊS: *(Sings.)*
    Stripped bare,
        naked of escorts!

OLD MEN: *(Sing.)*
                          Disaster at sea
                          destroyed our dear ones!

XERXÊS: *(Sings.)*
    Weep the
             disaster,
    then go to your homes!

OLD MEN: *(Sing.)*
                          AIIII! AIIII!
                          Agony! Agony!

XERXÊS: *(Sings.)*
    Cry out,
             cry,

echo my
>>> sorrows!

OLD MEN: *(Sing.)*
>>> A sorry echo to sorrowful cries!

XERXÊS: *(Sings.)*
Sing, sing
>>> sorrow!
Cry out with me!

OLD MEN & XERXÊS: *(Sing.)*
>>> OTOTOTOTOI!

XERXÊS: *(Sings.)*
O heavy grief!

OLD MEN: *(Sing.)*
>>> AIIII!
>>> The pain!
>>> I feel it too!

XERXÊS: *(Sings.)*
Beat your breast!
Mourn for me!
>>> Mourn!

OLD MEN: *(Sing.)*
>>> I weep my distress!

XERXÊS: *(Sings.)*
Cry out,
>>> cry,
answer my cries!

OLD MEN: *(Sing.)*
>>> We cry,
>>> we shriek,
>>> we weep!
>>> AIIII!

XERXÊS: *(Sings.)*
> Shout!
> > Shriek!
> Raise up your
> > > cries!

OLD MEN & XERXÊS: *(Sing.)*
> > > OTOTOTOTOI!

XERXÊS: *(Sings.)*
> And black blows fall,

OLD MEN: *(Sing.)*
> > > mingled with pain!

XERXÊS: *(Sings.)*
> Beat your breast,
> > beat,
> and cry a Mysian lament!

OLD MEN: *(Sing.)*
> > > Agony! Agony!

XERXÊS: *(Sings.)*
> Tear your white beards!

OLD MEN: *(Sing.)*
> > > We tear, we tear!
> > > With clenched fists we tear!

XERXÊS: *(Sings.)*
> Raise a shrill cry!

OLD MEN: *(Sing.)*
> > > We raise a shrill cry!
> > > AIIIIIII!
> > > AIIIIIII!

XERXÊS: *(Sings.)*
> Tear, tear your

              robes
with the points of your
fingers!

OLD MEN: *(Sing.)*

                        AIIII!
                        Tear!
                      We tear!
                   AIIII! AIIII!

XERXÊS: *(Sings.)*
    Tear hair from your head!
    Pity the
              dead!

OLD MEN: *(Sing.)*

                        AIIII!
                        Tear!
                      We tear!
                   AIIII! AIIII!

XERXÊS: *(Sings.)*
    Shed tears from your
                  eyes!
    Shed tears!
            Shed tears!

OLD MEN: *(Sing.)*

                        AIIII!
                        Tears!
                   I shed tears!
                        AIIII!

XERXÊS: *(Sings.)*
    Cry out,
           cry,
    answer my cries!

OLD MEN: *(Sing.)*

O-IIIIII!
O-IIIIII!

XERXÊS: *(Sings.)*
    Go home in tears,
    go home
          wailing!

OLD MEN: *(Sing.)*

IOOOO! IOOOO!

XERXÊS: *(Sings.)*
    IOOOO! cry IOOOO!
    IOOOO!
          through the city!

OLD MEN: *(Sing.)*

IOOOO!
IOOOO!
cry
IOOOO!
through the city!

XERXÊS: *(Sings.)*
Wail!
Tread
    softly!

OLD MEN: *(Sing.)*

This Persian earth is
painful to tread!

XERXÊS: *(Sings.)*
    ÉË!
        ÉË!
They perished in the ships—

OLD MEN: *(Sing.)*

ÉË! ÉË!
the three-banked ships—

XERXÊS: *(Sings.)*
Home, take me
home—

OLD MEN: *(Sing.)*

home, home,
with cries and tears—

(Exeunt OLD MEN and XERXÊS in the direction of the palace.)

Seven Against Thebes

(ΕΠΤΑ ΕΠΙ ΘΗΒΑΣ)

Cast of Characters

ETEOKLÊS *King of Thebes, son of Oedipus*

SCOUT *a Theban soldier*

CHORUS OF YOUNG THEBAN WOMEN

FIRST THEBAN WOMAN *leader of the chorus*

MEN OF THEBES *of all ages*

SLAVE ATTENDANTS

SIX THEBAN CAPTAINS

THEBAN SOLDIERS

SEVEN AGAINST THEBES

The Akropolis of Thebes.
Altars with ancient statues of Arês, Athêna,
*   Poseidon, Zeus, Artemis, Apollo, and Aphroditê*
A crowd of Theban citizens of all ages.
Enter ETEOKLÊS.

ETEOKLÊS:
    Thebans!
    Children of Kadmos!
    I stand before you here, helmsman
        of your Ship of State,
                my hand on the tiller, sleepless
    and unblinking, as should any captain
        when a fateful decision is required!
    And such a decision stares us
            down at this moment.
    If all goes well, it is the gods'
        doing, and praise to them.
    But let disaster strike—which
        heaven forbid!—and one name only
    will be on every man's tongue,
    one name will swell like an angry
                            wave,
    muttered cries, groans,
        curses from every man's
                throat,
    a wailing lament of discord:

    Eteoklês!

    Zeus Protector, save us from this fate!
    Fulfil your name!

    But now to you, to your
                task.
    I call on you all to come to your city's aid.

Boys, not yet men, men now
         past their prime, and those of you now
         in your glorious peak of
                  manhood.
Your city needs you,
         needs you all, to defend her and her
                  temples and altars, her
         gods, who must never lack your
                           devotion.
Rescue her, and rescue your
         children, and earth, your
         mother, your fondest nurse, who
shirked no toil of nurture,
but bore you on her breast as
         tender saplings, so that when the
                  time comes—and it has
         come!—you will take up the
                  shield and fight in her
defense as loyal repayment for her
                  love.

                  Until today,
the gods have inclined to us and to our
         cause, despite that the enemy has
long held siege to our walls,
         and for that we thank the
                           gods.
But now our prophet, our
         seer Teiresias, our expert
         augur, shepherd of birds, without
                  benefit of light or fire, with mind and
ear alone has read the sense of
omen-bringing birds with his infallible
                           science.
         Having heard,
he warns that in the night just passed,
         the Achaians have planned the strongest
assault yet on our city's walls.

Hear me, all of you!
Thebes needs you, now!
Man the battlements and city gates!
        Take up arms!
                Hurry! Run,
run to the bulwarks and the towers'
      platforms! Be brave! Hold your
          ground! Stand up to this foreign
      invader face to face! The gods are
                            with us!

I've sent scouts to reconnoiter the enemy's
      position. Their report will
tell me what I need to know.

(Exeunt THEBAN CITIZENS hurriedly in all directions.
Enter a SCOUT at a fast pace.)

SCOUT:
    Eteoklês, master of Thebes,
        I bring news of the enemy.
        Clear news, for I
           saw it myself. Seven enemy
captains, sir, warlords,
        slit the throat of a bull into a
           black-rimmed shield.
Dipping their fingers into the gore,
        they swore an oath to a trinity of
                gods,
        wargod Arês,
Frenzy and Fear. They would
        either, they said, smash this city and
        pound it into dust, or with their
           dying blood make a paste of the
        earth of Thebes.
Weeping they hung remembrances of themselves
          on Adrastos' chariot for their
        parents at home, but not one
cry of self-pity escaped their
                lips.

They have the hearts of lions, sir,
    flashing from their eyes, and
        wills of iron.
  I lost no time bringing this
news, for the attack will come
        anytime.
I left them casting lots who would attack
    which of our gates.

          Hurry, sir,
    there's no time for delay;
assign the best of our men,
    the city's finest,
        at our seven gates.
Every second counts.
The Argives are approaching in full
    force, raising clouds of
        dust, and the field is flecked with foam
    from their stallions' throats.
Be the helmsman you are, sir.
Batten down our
    city before the squalls of wargod
    Arês swoop down and
        destroy us.
There's a flood of men rushing toward us
    like waves of the sea.
It's now or never, sir.
    We have to act.
    Trust me, sir.
I'll keep my eye peeled, and my
    news from outside will be clear as
        day.
You'll know what's
    happening, sir. You'll be
    safe, sir.

(Exit the SCOUT.)

ETEOKLÊS:

> O Zeus and Earth our mother
>> and the city's gods, and you,
> Fury, Spirit Curse of my father Oedipus,
>> for you are powerful,
>> spare,
>>>> spare my city at least,
>>>>> don't
> tear us up root and branch, homes, temples,
>> the victim of enemy hands!
> We're Greek, we're free,
>> as is our city, Thebes,
>> the children of Kadmos,
> slavery must never bind her in its chains!
>>>>> Be with her!
>> Defend her!
>>>> I plead for us both! A prosperous state
> deals prosperously with the gods!

(Exit ETEOKLÊS. Enter the CHORUS OF YOUNG THEBAN
WOMEN in disorder and great agitation.)
(Music. Song. Dance.)

YOUNG WOMEN OF THEBES: *(Chant.)*

>> Shriek.
>> Terror.
>> Terror coming.
>> Terror.
>> Army loose.
>> On the march.
>> Floods.
>> Horsemen.
>> There, outside.
>> Outside the walls.
>> I know, I know.
>> I saw.
>> Dust.
>> To the sky.
>> Speechless messenger.

But true.
Clear. True.
I hear the hoofs.
Hard on the land.
Echoing, echoing.
Listen. Hear it?
Listen.
Clashing shields.
Closer, closer.
Coming.
Tumbling, thundering.
Pitiless crash.
Mountain torrent.
IOOO! IOOO!
Gods. Goddesses.
Turn them,
the evil,
rushing,
the walls,
war cry,
turn, turn back disaster.
Shields, coming,
white shields,
dazzling.
Ready.
Ready for battle.
Full speed.
What god, what goddess?
Who will save us?
Gods, do you hear?
Down on your knees, women.
Fall to the earth.
Bow to the gods.
Grab, cling to the statues.
Quick.
They're coming.
Listen, listen.
Shields pounding.
Why are we waiting?

Crown them with flowers,
the gods,
robe them,
now,
we can't wait.
Arês, Arês,
god of the golden helmet,
hear us.
This is your land,
you lived here once.
Will you deny us?
Abandon us?
You loved us once.

(Sing.)

Come, gods,
gods of Thebes,
come to us now,
come,
save us,
save us now from slavery.
A flood of white-plumed helmets
surges round our city,
a seething mass blown against us
by the blasts of War.
Zeus, Father, All-powerful,
protect us from the enemy.
Thebes is surrounded by the Argive armies,
and we tremble in terror of their weapons.
Bits in the mouths of their horses clatter destruction.
And seven men,
seven mighty warriors,
captains in command,
in armor,
their army's best,
stand ready for battle
at the seven gates
chosen by lots.

Athêna,
daughter of Zeus,
lover of battle,
save us,
save our city!
And Poseidon,
sea-lord,
trident-bearing god of horses,
save us from Terror!
And Arês,
IOOO! IOOO!
guard this city of Kadmos,
protect us,
prove your kinship!
And you, Aphroditê,
primal mother of Thebes,
defend us,
for your blood is our blood,
you gave us birth.
And Apollo,
you,
Wolfgod,
defend us,
true to your name,
devour our enemy.
And Artemis,
virgin-daughter of Leto,
ready your bow!

(Chant.)

É! É! É! É!
I hear it.
Listen.
The rattle.
Chariots.
Round the walls.
O Lady Hera!
Tormented axle-boxes shrieking.

Beloved Artemis!
The sky.
Mad.
Spears.
Bristling.
What will happen?
What? Our city?
What end will heaven bring?

É! É! É! É!
Stones.
Rain of stones.
On the battlements.
Beloved Apollo!
The gates, the gates.
Clanging, clanging.
Shields.
Bronze bound.
The gates, pounding.
Apollo who guides the battle's end,
Athêna, guardian of Thebes,
save us of the seven gates.

(Sing.)

IOOO!
Gods powerful in your defense,
you who fulfill all things,
you who guard our towers and walls,
do not betray us,
do not betray spear-tormented Thebes
to a foreign enemy.
Listen, hear us,
young girls of Thebes,
hear our prayers, as is right,
we who raise our hands to you.

IOOO!
Gods we love and cherish,

surround our city,
stand roundabout Thebes,
and show us your love.
Remember our offerings,
rich offerings,
splendid feasts of sacrifice.
Remember,
and remembering
bring us rescue.

(Enter ETEOKLÊS.)
(Music out.)

ETEOKLÊS:
Vile, insupportable creatures!
Is this how you help the
city, your city, a city that needs
help?
Is this how you fuel the
hearts of your defenders with
courage? The spirits of those
defending you under siege?
By throwing yourselves at the
feet of the city-gods' statues?
By groveling before them?
Howling, shrieking?
An outrage to decency!

Save me from the female sex,
bad times or good!
Give them the upper hand and
they're insufferable; frightened, they're a
danger to the home and even more
to the city!

What have you done here with your
mad storming about but
drained the people's hearts of
courage and given cowardice

a foothold?
While the enemy successfully attacks us
        outside the walls, you destroy us from
                            within!
It's the price we pay for living with women!

            I *will* be obeyed!
I demand *strict* obedience!
        And anyone, anyone, man or
            woman, who refuses my
authority will have a judgment of
        death passed against him and be
stoned to death in the public
                    square!
Death without reprieve!

Matters outside the home are affairs of state
        and we want no women here!
This is men's work, and
        men's work it will remain!

                Go inside, now,
inside with you, and stay there,
        inside your houses, and make no
                        trouble!
Do you hear?
Or have you gone deaf?
            Inside, I said!

(Music. Song. Dance.)

FIRST THEBAN WOMAN: *(Chants.)*
    O son of Oedipus,
    his dear, his
    beloved son,
    I was frightened,
    terrified by the
    terrible sounds,
    the rattle of chariots and the

screech of
whirling
wheels and screaming
axles, ῃd the
ringing bits in the horses'
mouths as they charged!

ETEOKLÊS: *(Speaks.)*
    No!
What good is the sailor who
  deserts his post for
   safety when the ship is in
danger of foundering?

FIRST THEBAN WOMAN: *(Chants.)*
  No, but it's here I ran,
  to the gods,
  to these ancient statues!
  I trusted them,
  trusted heaven,
  when the storm of stones
  thundered down the
  gates!
  In terror I had to
  beg the gods,
  the Blessèd Ones,
  to help our city!

ETEOKLÊS: *(Speaks.)*
  You pray that our walls should
   keep out enemy spears.
  Why should the gods not grant it?
  And yet, they say, when a city is
    conquered—as it will be if you
   continue as you are—the gods
  desert it.

FIRST THEBAN WOMAN: *(Chants.)*
  Never while I live,

never,
never may I see these
gods desert us.
Never, never may I
see our
city
ravaged by the
enemy,
our streets
devoured in
flame.

ETEOKLÊS: *(Speaks.)*
    Just don't call on the gods when
        reason deserts you.
    Obedience, they say, is
        mother to Success that will
    save us all.

FIRST THEBAN WOMAN: *(Chants.)*
    True.
    But still the
    gods rule over all
    things.
    When trouble comes,
    and hope seems
    helpless,
    they often lift us
    from our
    misery.

ETEOKLÊS: *(Speaks.)*
    It's men's work to
        sacrifice to the gods when the
    enemy pounds at the gate.
    It's women's work to
        stay inside and be
                silent.

FIRST THEBAN WOMAN: *(Chants.)*
It's thanks to the
gods
our city is still
unconquered and our
walls withstand the
enemy.
Why should this rouse
anger and
resentment in you?

ETEOKLÊS: *(Speaks.)*
Honor the gods all you like.
But do it quietly,
don't panic. Don't strike
terror in the hearts of our citizens.

FIRST THEBAN WOMAN: *(Chants.)*
It was when I heard
the terrible rattle
of sounds and
confusion
that I fled up here in
fear
to the sacred
citadel.

ETEOKLÊS: *(Speaks.)*
If you hear of men dying or
wounded, don't shriek out your
pain for all to hear.
It's common in war. Arês
feeds on slaughtered men.

FIRST THEBAN WOMAN: *(Chants.)*
Listen! Horses neighing! I hear them!

ETEOKLÊS: *(Speaks.)*
If you must listen, listen calmly.

FIRST THEBAN WOMAN: *(Chants.)*
> We're surrounded! The earth groans, the walls!

ETEOKLÊS: *(Speaks.)*
> Isn't it enough for you that I can handle this?

FIRST THEBAN WOMAN: *(Chants.)*
> Listen! Stones at the gate! Louder! I'm terrified!

ETEOKLÊS: *(Speaks.)*
> Silence! You're to say nothing of this in the city.

FIRST THEBAN WOMAN: *(Chants.)*
> Gods of Thebes, don't abandon our walls!

ETEOKLÊS: *(Speaks.)*
> Damn you! Keep quiet! Control yourself!

FIRST THEBAN WOMAN: *(Chants.)*
> Gods, gods of our city, save us from slavery!

ETEOKLÊS: *(Speaks.)*
> It's you making us slaves, you, me, all of us.

FIRST THEBAN WOMAN: *(Chants.)*
> Almighty Zeus, slay the enemy with your thunderbolt!

ETEOKLÊS: *(Speaks.)*
> Zeus, what a plague you created in woman!

FIRST THEBAN WOMAN: *(Chants.)*
> Women suffer the same as men when a city falls.

ETEOKLÊS: *(Speaks.)*
> How dare you talk of defeat with your hands on their images?

FIRST THEBAN WOMAN: *(Chants.)*
> Terror has taken hold of my tongue! I'm afraid!

ETEOKLÊS: *(Speaks.)*
    I beg you. Do me one favor. Do it now.

FIRST THEBAN WOMAN: *(Chants.)*
    Tell me, tell me quickly.

ETEOKLÊS: *(Speaks.)*
    Not one word more. Silence. Don't frighten your friends.

FIRST THEBAN WOMAN: *(Chants.)*
    I'm quiet now. I'll suffer my fate with the others.

ETEOKLÊS: *(Speaks.)*
                    Yes,
    I prefer these words to your
            earlier ones.
    Now, move away from the
                images, and pray a better
            prayer, that the gods will
            join in our
                        fight.
    Listen first to my prayer,
            then raise your own voice in a
                    shout of jubilation, Apollo's
            holy cry, as we do at
    sacrifice, giving courage to our
            friends, and defeating our
                        fear of the foe.

And now my prayer.

    I swear to the guardian
            gods of our country, gods who
            guard our fields and our
                    marketplace, to the
    springs of Dirkê and Ismênos'
            stream—if all goes well, and
    Thebes is saved and its
                        citizens,

we will stain with the blood of
sheep the hearths of their
 temples, raise trophies of
      victory,
and I will dedicate on the walls of their shrines
 the spoils of war
 won with spears from our
    enemy.

Make such prayers to the gods,
 but without frenzy or lamentation,
  for they will do nothing to
save you from your fate.

     I'm going now
to assign six men to six
 gates, reserving for myself
    the seventh.
Seven champions at seven gates to
 fight the foe heroically.
And I go before the arrival of a scout
 to tell us the urgency of the
    need.

(Exit ETEOKLÊS.)

YOUNG WOMEN OF THEBES: *(Sing.)*
    I hear him and I obey,
  but fear will not leave my heart,
   not let it rest.
 Dread floods my soul, and terror,
 terror of the army circling the walls,
  the terror of a timid dove
eyeing the circling serpent that threatens her nestlings.
  They crowd our walls,
   a host,
  a numberless horde,
attacking our battlements in full force.
 O god, what will become of me!

And others,
they surround us,
hurl rocks,
hurl jagged rocks at our men.
Great gods,
great children of Zeus,
save us,
save Thebes,
save the children of Kadmos,
for Thebes is in need of your help.
Bring us salvation.

What land,
what country
will give you what we can give you,
can give you better than we give you now,
if you abandon us to our enemies?
Dirkê's waters,
the sweetest of Poseidon's springs,
earth-embracing Poseidon,
and the children of Têthys.
Protect us, gods of Thebes,
protectors of Thebes, protect us.
Cast on the enemy outside our walls
Panic,
send Madness,
insane Destruction,
make them throw down their weapons and shields.
Do it, gods, and honor is yours.
Honor is yours from the people of Thebes,
for you will be my city's saviors,
throned in power and
answering my shrill appeals.

How piteous if this city,
this ancient city,
should be hurled down to the dark
of Hades' kingdom!
A war-spoil,

enslaved,
devoured by flames,
ashes merely,
destroyed at heaven's will
and the ravaging will of Achaians.
And piteous its women hauled off,
like horses, by the hair,
young women, old women,
clothes torn about them,
naked to the sight of rabid victors.
A cry will rise from the desolate city,
a wail as captive war-spoils are plundered
and led off to doom.
I foresee,
I foresee and I shudder.

Terrible is the sight of unwed girls,
not yet ripe,
forced from home on a bitter journey,
no rites, no hymns to make the road lighter.
The dead,
the dead are happier,
the dead are happier.
I pity the fate of a city captured,
disaster on disaster.
É! É!
Murder, rape, fire,
all the city fouled with polluting smoke.
Wargod comes,
Arês comes,
bringer of madness,
desecration, and death.

The town is alive with a
terrible noise;
the circling net of the
enemy pulls tight;
spearsmen defend against spears
and are gutted;

and babies wail at mothers' bloody breast.
Plunder, brother to rampage, begins.
Bargains are struck;
full-hands share with full-hands;
empty-hands hail down empty-hands:
partners in plunder;
everyone wanting
not less, not the same,
but more,
more,
more than their neighbor.
Easy to tell what happens next.

Stores of a kitchen
scattered about,
food become litter,
earth's crops fallen,
trampled at will.
A wife weeps to see such waste,
earth's gifts swept away in a torrent.
Young girls,
new slaves,
suffer a new misery:
serving the enemy
bed of the conqueror.
Will the night's consummation
ease their anguish?

(The SCOUT enters in haste, breathless.)
(Music out.)

FIRST THEBAN WOMAN:
Look! A soldier!
Running with news of the army.

(Enter ETEOKLÊS with a group of SIX CAPTAINS, fully armed, each with a small band of SOLDIERS.)

SECOND THEBAN WOMAN:
    And Lord Eteoklês, rushing to hear!

SCOUT:
    I've just come—just heard—
        the enemy's plans.
    I know which gate each captain drew by lots.
            I'll tell you all I know.

    Tydeus is already beating the ground
            near the Proïtid Gate, raging and
            straining at the bit to cross the
                            Ismênos.
    But he can't,
            not yet, the priest forbids it—unfavorable
            omens in the sacrifice.
    But Tydeus is possessed by his lust for battle
            and spits out insults at the cowardly seer like a
    serpent hissing in the burning noonday sun.
    "Gutless bastard!
            Afraid of battle!
            Coward!" he shouts,
    shaking his three-plumed helmet's towering
            mane, while from beneath the rim of his
            shield bronze bells clang loudly to strike
                    terror into the enemy.
    And his shield is all ablaze with an
            arrogant device:
    A sky of cunningly fashioned flaming stars;
            in the center, the eye of night,
                a glorious moon at the full,
            our oldest star.
    Inflamed by his rabid passion,
            boastful Tydeus rages at the stream,
    brandishing his braggart's shield,
    like a racehorse stomping the ground at the
            starting line, snorting, rattling the bit in
                    fury to begin, awaiting the trumpet's
            sound.

Who will you station at the Proïtid Gate, sir,
so when the bolts are pulled Thebes will be
championed by a hero?

ETEOKLÊS:
No man's equipment will ever frighten me.
And arrogant shield-devices
carry no spears, nor do crests and
rattling bells.
As for this night sky alive with
stars you say he sports on his
shield—some might find this
wild hope of his prophetic.
For if the "night" of death falls on his eyes,
the wielder of this arrogant, haughty device will
see its symbolic meaning turn back on him,
thus justifying itself.

To defend the gate against this Tydeus,
I name that noble and modest man,
the son of Astakos, a man who
detests boastful words, who avoids only
dishonorable deeds and is an enemy to
cowardice;
a man whose descent is from those
warriors Arês spared,
the Sown Men,
Melanippos,
a true son of Theban soil.
Armed with his dice, Arês will
determine the outcome; but Justice,
blood of his blood, arms
Melanippos today and
sends him out to fight
for the motherland that bore him.

*(After a formal salute, exit MELANIPPOS and his band of
SOLDIERS.)*
(Music. Song. Dance.)

YOUNG WOMEN OF THEBES: *(Sing.)*
Gods, grant him victory,
my champion;
with Justice beside him
he fights for his country.
But I shudder to see the bloody deaths
of men who fight for their people.

(Music out.)

SCOUT:
Yes, may the gods grant him victory.
As for the next,
the Êlektran Gate,
it was won by Kapaneus, a giant of a man,
bigger even than the former,
and so filled with arrogance and
boasting that he exceeds what is proper to
humans, launching wild
threats against our battlements—
which god prevent! Saying,
god willing or no,
that he'll sack Thebes and make havoc of the city.
Not even Zeus' wrath can stay him;
he likens the god's thunder and lightning
to the sun's heat at noon.
His emblem is a naked man
bearing a flaming torch as
weapon, and his motto written in gold is:
"I'll burn this town!"

You must send against such a man—
but who could face him in battle?
Who could challenge such terrifying
boasting?

ETEOKLÊS:
Having profited from Tydeus' boast,
here is another to our gain.

Foolish ambitions often betray themselves with
          foolish words.
Kapaneus threatens with deeds, he's
      prepared to act, to dishonor the gods.
Playing foolish games with his
tongue, a mere mortal, he directs his
          hot-air boasts against Zeus himself.
Firebringer, indeed!
He'll have his fire, all right!
A lightning blast from Zeus, and no mere
          warming ray of noontime sun!
I choose to set against this loud-mouthed
          braggart a man of fiery spirit,
Polyphontes, a warrior of great
          bravery, the champion of Artemis Protector and
                              other gods.

Name me the next man and the gate he picked.

*(After a formal salute, exit POLYPHONTES and his band of
SOLDIERS.)*
(Music. Song. Dance.)

YOUNG THEBAN WOMEN: *(Sing.)*
                    Destroy,
          destroy him who threatens Thebes!
              Zeus, destroy,
          destroy him with your bolt!
      Before he mounts my sacred place,
      before he rips with his thrusting spear
              my holy retreat!

(Music out.)

SCOUT:
    Now for the third, Eteoklus, whose lot
    leapt from the upturned bronze helmet
          to thrust his men against us at the Neïstan Gate.
    His snorting horses rage and wheel in their

eagerness to throw themselves at us at the gate;
their muzzle-gear moist with the harsh
        breath of their proud nostrils piping
an inhuman whine.
His shield is grandly decorated.
An armed man mounts a ladder at a city's walls,
        intent on destruction. His war cry
emblazoned in letters is that not even Arês
        could hurl him from the battlements.
Send against him a man who can save Thebes
        from the yoke of slavery.

ETEOKLÊS:

And here is the man I will send:
Megareus, son of Kreon,
        descendent of the Sown Men.
His hands will do his talking for him;
        they are his only boast. No wild horses
        stomping and neighing at the gate will
                frighten him off.
He'll never quit the gate.
Either he will die
        and pay back the land of his fathers for his
                nurture, or he will take two men,
the live man and the one on the shield,
        along with the city, a trophy to
        hang on his father's house.
                                So.
Let's hear another man's boast—
        and don't spare your words!

(After a formal salute, exit MEGAREUS and his band of SOLDIERS.)
(Music. Song. Dance.)

YOUNG THEBAN WOMEN: *(Sing.)*
                I wish you all success,
                        you,
                defender of my house,
        and I wish defeat on the enemy!

> As they howl their boastful
> threats against our city
> from a maddened mind,
> let Zeus Avenger look down on them
> in anger.

(Music out.)

SCOUT:
> Another is assigned the fourth gate,
>> the Gate of Athêna, and he
>> stands there, roaring,
> Hippomedon, a mighty bulk of a man.
> When he swung that threshing-floor he calls a shield,
>> the hair stood up on my head in
>>> fear, no denying it!
> He was no second-rate craftsman who
>> designed that shield. The emblem?
> Typhon belching black smoke from his fiery mouth,
>> flame-flecked smoke, the sister of fire.
> The rim is a tangle of writhing, intertwining
>> snakes that holds the framework fast.
> He shouted his war cry,
>> war-possessed,
>>> raging for battle like a frenzied
>>>> Bakkhant, terror glaring from his
>>>>> eyes.
> No easy task guarding against such a man.
> Panic incarnate stands boasting at the gate.

ETEOKLÊS:
>>> First of all,
> Athêna, who lives by the gate,
>> will see to it. She hates all
> violence and will drive the chill
>> snake from her nestlings.
> Then Hyperbios, Oinops' valiant son, will
>> meet and match him man to man in the
>> encounter. A man eager to

learn his fate in this time of crisis,
  he is irreproachable in form and spirit
  and the bearing of arms. Hermês did
well in matching this pair.
         Just as
  both men will meet as enemies,
  so too will enemies meet on their shields.
One with fire-breathing Typhon,
  the other, Hyperbios,
    with Zeus enthroned, a flaming
  thunderbolt in hand.
Zeus invincible, champion of our
           champion.

(After a formal salute, exit HYPERBIOS and his band of SOLDIERS.)
(Music. Song. Dance.)

YOUNG THEBAN WOMEN: *(Sing.)*
       I know,
    in my heart I know,
  that he who places on his shield
    the enemy of Zeus,
    earth-born power,
      serpent,
      repulsive,
  hated by men as by the long-lived gods,
  will break his head beside our gate.

(Music out.)

SCOUT:
  I pray it may be so!
  I speak now of the fifth man,
    at the fifth gate, the Borrhaian,
  beside it the tomb of Amphion, the son of Zeus.
  He swears by the spearshaft he reverences
    more than god and even his life
  that he will raze the city of Kadmos
    in spite of Zeus.

So boasts this offspring of a mountain mother,
this beautiful creature,
     a boy, yet a man, his cheeks
furred with the soft down of youth,
       soon a beard,
     spring-bloom of a boy.
He threatens at the gate with the savage-proud
     heart of a man and with his gorgon-eyes,
     belying his maiden name.
His bronze shield, too, is an affront,
     his body's full-length protector,
for on it is the shame of Thebes, the Sphinx that
     ate men raw, burnished bronze and
       cunningly riveted in place.
In her claws she shamelessly clasps a
     Theban destined to receive the shower of
     missiles hurled at him.
Having come so far, this warrior is not about to
engage in petty encounters,
     wasting his long trip,
     Parthenopaios the Arkadian.
He's here to repay his nurture in Argos,
     for he's a foreign guest, and so he hurls
       threats at our walls.
May heaven reject them!

ETEOKLÊS:
     God turn their boasting insults
       against themselves, and let them
     suffer the pain they'd inflict, and so die.
     But we have a man for him, too, this
       Arkadian, no braggart, a man whose hand
     knows instinctively what to do.
         Aktor.
     Brother of the man I just now spoke of.
     A man of few words, but deeds; and
       words without deeds he will
       never allow through his gate.
     Nor will he allow into Thebes that

monstrous and abhorred Sphinx.
She'll blame her bearer for the pounding she receives
    beneath our city's walls.
With heaven's help she will!

(After a formal salute, exit AKTOR and his band of SOLDIERS.)
(Music. Song. Dance.)

YOUNG THEBAN WOMEN: *(Sing.)*
> His words stab at my heart,
> my hair stands on end,
> to hear the loud threats
> of these boastful, evil men.
> I pray the gods destroy them
> in my land.

SCOUT:
The sixth man I will name is a man of
    honor. A brave warrior,
    he is also a prophet and wise man,
mighty Amphiaraös.
    At his station, the Homoloian Gate,
he berates the Lord Tydeus in the bitterest terms,
calling him "murderer, man of great mischief,
    confounder of the city, evil spirit of Argos,
    rouser of the Fury, bloodshed's servant,
and advisor to Adrastos in this evil venture!"

He then tosses up another name,
    Polyneikês, your brother,
        mighty Polyneikês,
    sown from the same womb,
stressing again and again the
    strife buried in his name,
finally addressing him with these words:

> "What do you expect
> from this maneuver of yours? The divine
>   favor of the gods? Praise for your noble

deed in times to come? You're sacking your
father's city and its native gods with an
        army you recruited in a foreign land!
The mother-source of you! How can you
        block that, how with any justice,
            how?
And your father's land—will it become your
        ally once again when you have
        destroyed it at spear point?
                            As for me,
I will enrich this soil with my prophet's wisdom,
        buried in enemy earth.
                            Come!
        To battle!
I expect no death without honor!"

These were his words, the prophet,
        shield in hand, a shield with no device, no
        emblem for all its bronze.
Never a man of show,
        his courage is in his arm.
He mines his mind for the gold of
            wisdom and common sense.

Best send against him a man who is
        wise as well as powerful.
Men of piety are dangerous
                        adversaries.

ETEOKLÊS:
    I lament the luck that
        links the just man with the unjust.
    There is no greater evil than evil relationships:
    no good harvest can come of them.
                    However pious,
    if you board a ship with pirates you're
        doomed along with them,
        good and bad alike;
            the gods spit you all out as one.

Or however honest you may be, if you
            live in a land that violates hospitality and
                  ignores the gods,
you're snared along with them, however unjustly,
and fall with them in the gods' all-inclusive
                                    scourge.

And so with this man, this prophet,
            the son of Oikleos. Here is a man
who is just,
            a man who is honest, pious, brave,
                  a mighty prophet, who has joined himself,
even against his better judgment,
            to unholy, bold-tongued, bragging men who have
            come too far on their road to turn back now.
And so, by the will of Zeus,
            he will be dragged down with them.
I doubt he'll even attack his assigned gate.
Not out of cowardice or baseness of spirit;
            no, for he knows his death, knows he must
                  die in battle, if Apollo's words
            are to bear fruit,
and when does Apollo not speak truth?
                                    Still,
I will send against this Amphiaraös
            the mighty Lasthenes, a surly gatekeeper
who is harsh to strangers, old in wisdom,
young in fighting-power,
            and keen-eyed to find the patch of flesh
            unguarded by the shield,
                  and strike home.
But only god can give good fortune to men.

(After a formal salute, exit LASTHENES and his band of SOLDIERS.)
(Music. Song. Dance.)

YOUNG THEBAN WOMEN: *(Sing.)*
            Gods, hear our prayers,
                  our just prayers,

and bring them to fulfillment
    for our city's good fortune!
   Turn back the horrors of war on the invader!
  Let Zeus slay them outside our walls with his bolt!

(Music out.)

SCOUT:
  Now for the seventh man at the seventh gate,
    the final champion,
             your brother.
  I'll tell you of the curses and the
    fate he calls down on the city.
  He declares that once he stands
    mounted on our walls,
  once he is proclaimed victor and conqueror of Thebes,
  he will shout his wild cry of conquest,
  his war-whoop at the city's fall,
    at its desolation and over its vanquished corpses.
  And then, hand to hand, he will
    fight and kill you, and, in killing you,
    lie beside you in death;
  or, if you live,
    he will banish you to dishonorable exile
    as you once banished him.
                      Bellowing,
  he calls to witness the gods of your
    race and the gods of your fatherland,
  Polyneikês,
    violent warrior Polyneikês.

            His shield,
  newly-fashioned and a perfect round,
  has emblazoned on it in beaten gold
    a twofold device.
    A man in full armor led on modestly
      by a woman.
  Her motto says in gold letters:
    "I am Justice. And I will restore this man

to his city and to the home of his fathers,
rightfully his own."

So.

Now you know all the devices of the enemy.
It's for you, helmsman,
to choose and send the warrior to answer him.
You will find no fault in my report.
Yes,
it's for you to determine the city's

course.

(Exit the SCOUT.)

ETEOKLÊS:
O god-hated house of Oedipus,
house cursed by the gods,
house maddened by gods,
house of tears,
now the curse of Oedipus is fulfilled!

But no time for tears or wailing now,
giving birth to even worse suffering!

As for him,
Polyneikês,
so well named,
strife-bringer, we will
see if his sign is fulfilled; whether golden
letters on a shield will do what they say;
or are they the babble of a demented
mind?
If Justice, virgin daughter of
Zeus, had ever been with him in
thought or deed, his boasting might have come
true.
But never, never once, never—not when he
fled the dark cavern of his mother's
womb, not in childhood or adolescence, not when the

hair of manhood grew on his chin,
  did Justice ever, even once,
  turn her eye on him or ever acknowledge him!
Nor does she now,
  now as he rapes his city, his parent
   land, in this violent, criminal assault!
For if she did, if Justice looked
  kindly on him, she would be justly misnamed
  for championing one who brings death on his city!

      Believing this,
I stand against him myself.
Who has a better right?
  Prince against prince,
  brother against brother,
  enemy against enemy!

     Bring my armor—
to ward off arrows and stones.

(During the following, six SOLDIERS enter with articles of armor.)
(Music.)

FIRST THEBAN WOMAN:
 Dearest son of Oedipus,
   dear son of this land,
 don't become like your brother who
  cursed us so violently.
 For Thebans to fight Argives is bad enough,
  and that blood can be purified.
 But for two blood-brothers to kill each other,
 for that there is no purification.

ETEOKLÊS:
 If a man must suffer evil,
  it must be without dishonor.
  That alone profits us in death.
 But evil and dishonor together bring no
       glory.

(A SOLDIER helps him buckle the greaves.)

FIRST THEBAN WOMAN: *(Chants.)*
    Dear son,
    why so eager?
    You must never resign yourself
    to the wild lust for
    battle.
    Cast it away!

ETEOKLÊS: *(Speaks.)*
    Winds of the gods that drive this on,
        let us set sail on the Sea of Death
        to Kokytos' stream,
    the end of all for the race of Oedipus
        so hated by Apollo!

(A SOLDIER helps him buckle the breastplate.)

FIRST THEBAN WOMAN: *(Chants.)*
    Hunger bites you,
    sharp hunger,
    and the banquet will be
    bitter!
    The flesh you tear
    is human flesh,
    the blood you spill is
    unlawful
    blood.

ETEOKLÊS: *(Speaks.)*
    My father's Curse appoints me to this ritual,
        tearing at me with tearless eyes,
            whispering:
    "First comes profit, then death!"

(A SOLDIER helps him buckle the sword.)

FIRST THEBAN WOMAN: *(Chants.)*
> Don't let it drive you on!
> Who will call you
> coward
> for a prosperous life?
> Avoid evil and
> honor the gods
> and the black-robed
> Fury
> will flee your house.

ETEOKLÊS: *(Speaks.)*
>   Gods?
> The gods have abandoned me by now.
> Only one gift would please them.
>   My death.
> Why cringe before death any longer?

(A SOLDIER helps him buckle the helmet.)

FIRST THEBAN WOMAN: *(Chants.)*
> No, no, stand
> fast!
> Now is the
> time, while death
> stands before you!
> In time the Spirit
> may cease to rage, and
> blow more kindly.
> But now she
> rages.

(A SOLDIER hands him the shield.)

ETEOKLÊS: *(Speaks.)*
>   Rages?
> Yes, rages, blown on by the
>   Curse of Oedipus!
>   My dreams,

the phantoms I see in nightly
visions, are true—my father's
heritage divided!

FIRST THEBAN WOMAN: *(Chants.)*
Let a woman persuade you for once.

ETEOKLÊS: *(Speaks.)*
Yes, if you speak to the point; be practical.

FIRST THEBAN WOMAN: *(Chants.)*
Don't go out to the seventh gate.

(A SOLDIER hands him the spear.)

ETEOKLÊS: *(Speaks.)*
Nothing you say will blunt my purpose.

FIRST THEBAN WOMAN: *(Chants.)*
The gods approve even cowardly victory.

ETEOKLÊS: *(Speaks.)*
Those are no words for a warrior's ears!

FIRST THEBAN WOMAN: *(Chants.)*
And yet you'd spill your brother's blood?

ETEOKLÊS: *(Speaks.)*
When god sends evil there's no escape.

*(Exit ETEOKLÊS after saluting the statues of the gods.
Exeunt the six SOLDIERS.)*

YOUNG THEBAN WOMEN: *(Sing.)*
I shudder,
shudder at the house-destroying god,
god unlike any other god,
infallible god that prophesies evil,
the Fury that Oedipus called upon,

Avenging Spirit,
to slay two brothers at each others' hands.
And now it happens,
now it comes true,
among us now,
Fury cried up by a father's curse,
wrathful Oedipus,
shouted in madness,
son-destroying Fury that spurs it to its end.

A stranger comes,
a stranger in a dream,
a stranger from Skythia,
savage-hearted Iron,
ruthless arbitrator of wealth,
keen-tempered Iron,
razor-sharp blade,
allottor of land,
but only so much as the dead require,
none of their vast plains and fields,
but only the space of a grave.

When they are dead,
when brother murders brother,
when their land's dust has
drunk down their blood,
black blood of slaughtered brothers,
who will come then,
who will give cleansing,
who will purify their hacked limbs,
wash them clean of evil pollution?
I weep for the miseries
old and new
that mingle in the history
of this house!

I tell of a crime of long ago,
one swift in retribution,
yet with us still,

to the third generation,
when Laïos defied Apollo
who three times told him at Delphi,
at Earth's navel,
if he chose to save his city,
he must live his life childless.
But Laïos listened to the folly of his own counsel
and sowed his own disaster,
Oedipus, son,
Oedipus, father-killer,
who sowed the field where he was sown,
and harvested a bloody crop;
Oedipus,
son of parents caught up in frenzy.

The sea rises,
waves of evil crash,
another rises,
rises high,
triple-crested,
crashes,
crashes hard on the city's hull,
a thin defense between us and doom,
the width of our walls.
I fear,
I tremble for our safety,
our city's and our princes'.

For ancient curses,
come home,
demand heavy payment,
and never depart.
Disaster knows poverty
and passes by.
But the rich grown fat
must pay their toll by
emptying out the
wealth of their hold.

Who was ever more honored
by man and god
than Oedipus
who purged our land
of the man-eating Sphinx?

But when at last
he knew the horror of his marriage,
overwhelmed with grief,
in misery,
he did two deeds,
two terrible deeds,
two deeds of evil.
First, with the hand that slew his father,
he ripped out his own eyes,
dearer to him than his sons.

And then when those sons disowned him,
he lashed them with wrathful curses,
saying the day would come
when with blades of iron
they would divide his property.
But now I tremble,
for now a Fury has come,
a swift-footed Fury,
to see it fulfilled!

(Enter the SCOUT running.)
(Music out.)

SCOUT:
Rest easy, daughters of Thebes!
Take courage!
Our city has escaped the yoke of
slavery!
The proud boasts of mighty warriors are
fallen, and our ship sails
again in calm waters.
For all that storm we shipped no water.

Our walls no less than our valiant
        warriors stood tight, and
all is well—at six of our seven
                        gates.
At the seventh,
        Apollo, Lord of Sevens, took
        charge, and brought down on the
                heads of the race of Oedipus
the ancient folly of Laïos.

FIRST THEBAN WOMAN:
    What new misery for Thebes do you have to tell me?

SCOUT:
    Thebes is saved; but the two royal princes—

FIRST THEBAN WOMAN:
    AIIII! My prophetic soul!

SCOUT:
    Dead—dead at each others' hands.
    They shared the Fury that haunted this house,
        and that Spirit of Vengeance
                now consumes them with it.
    My news is cause for happiness and
        tears. Happiness for our city
        saved from destruction; tears
                for our leaders, our two
        princes, tossed on the stormy
        sea of their father's
                Curse.
    They divided their lot with a sword of
        Skythian iron, and ended with a plot of
                earth to bury them.
        The city is escaped,
    and each brother has his inheritance:
        each his grave, and the
            earth to sop their
                        blood.

(Exit SCOUT.)
(Music. Song. Dance.)

FIRST THEBAN WOMAN: *(Chants.)*
    Great Zeus and Spirits
    that guard this
    city,
    the walls and towers
    of ancient Kadmos,
    shall I shout joyous
    hymns
    that Thebes has escaped
    unscathed; or
    weep
    the unhappy fate
    of our
    warlords,
    dead now, childless;
    who died true to their
    names:
    Man of True Glory
    and
    Bringer of Strife.

YOUNG THEBAN WOMEN: *(Sing.)*
        O dark and inevitable Curse
        of this race of Oedipus,
        my heart freezes in fear,
        I sing sorrow,
        sorrow,
        for the blood-drenched victims,
        the ill-fated brothers.
        I mourn,
        I mourn
        the song of the spears.

        The father's Curse has
        come to its end,
        and the folly of Laïos

is now fulfilled.
I fear for Thebes,
god's knife keeps its edge.
Brothers in blood,
brothers in sorrow,
you did the deed,
the unspeakable deed.
Disaster is here,
not prophecy only.

(Enter SOLDIERS with the bodies of ETEOKLÊS and POLYNEIKÊS.)

Here is our proof,
evidence of his words made visible.
I see twofold evil before me,
twofold grief,
twofold death,
death of brothers at each others' hands.
What words are there to mourn?
Double sorrows now fulfilled.
Sorrows born of sorrows,
sorrows of the home.

Come, friends,
come,
lament our loss,
let our wind of sighs blow,
beat,
beat your heads with your hands,
oars rowing the black-sailed ship,
holy vessel on the sad Acheron
to the unseen shore where Apollo never walks,
shore that knows no sun,
the dark land where all must come.

YOUNG THEBAN WOMAN 1: *(Sings.)*
IOOOO!
IOOOO!
Misguided men,

you never
                listened,
miserably you
fought to the
                end,
unafraid of disaster,
and struck,
                struck
down your father's
                house.

YOUNG THEBAN WOMEN: *(Sing.)*
                Men to be pitied,
                you won for yourselves
                a miserable death
                in the death of your house.

YOUNG THEBAN WOMAN 2: *(Sings.)*
IOOOO!
        IOOOO!

(To POLYNEIKÊS.)

You who struck down
your house and
                family,

(To ETEOKLÊS.)

you who possessed a
bitter
        sovereignty,
are united now, made
one by the
        sword.

YOUNG THEBAN WOMEN: *(Sing.)*
                The sovereign Fury of
                father Oedipus
                reaped a terrible fulfillment.

YOUNG THEBAN WOMAN 1: *(Sings.)*
> Pierced to the heart;
> both to the
> > heart.
>
> Sons of one
> > mother;
> pierced, cursed by a
> dread
> > Fury.

YOUNG THEBAN WOMEN: *(Sing.)*
> > Hearts pierced and house pierced.
> > Insane, the minds of men.
> > AIIII! AIIII!
> > Doomed to a double death,
> > death demanding death.

YOUNG THEBAN WOMAN 2: *(Sings.)*
> The sounds of
> > mourning
> spread through the city.
> Walls groan, and
> earth
> > groans,
> earth that loved them
> dearly groans.
> For whoever will
> > come
> their possessions remain,
> their inheritance
> > waits,
> the goods that
> brought them
> > doom,
> the goods that led them
> to battle, the goods
> that brought them
> > death.

YOUNG THEBAN WOMEN: *(Sing.)*
Sharp-hearted and with
Iron as their arbiter,
they divided their goods
in equal shares,
though the arbiter,
Arês,
Arês, wargod,
won no praise from their friends,
and no good came of their strife.

YOUNG THEBAN WOMAN 1: *(Sings.)*
Sword-struck they
lie before us,
            struck
down by the
            sword
they lie waiting—what?
Equal share in their
father's
            grave.

YOUNG THEBAN WOMAN 2: *(Sings.)*
Weep, let us
weep them to their
graves.
The pain we
            weep
is ours, ours,
the cry, o the
            cry,
terrible, terrible,
tears from the heart that
tear my
            heart,
weeping,
            weeping
for our dead
            princes.

YOUNG THEBAN WOMAN 1: *(Sings.)*
    We weep, we
           weep
    over the bodies of these
    two
        unhappy men,
    we weep for the death,
    the bloody, cruel
               death,
    they brought to our people,
    and to the
            enemy warrior
    destroyed in the field.

YOUNG THEBAN WOMAN 2: *(Sings.)*
    Wretched, most
    wretched of all
             women
    who have borne children,
    wretched is the
            mother
    of these two.
    She took her
          son
    as husband to her
            bed,
    then bore him these sons,
    brother-sons,
    who lie here in
    death, slain,
         slain
    by each others' hands,
    brothers of the same
            seed.

YOUNG THEBAN WOMAN 1: *(Sings.)*
    Of the same seed,
          yes,
    destroyed,

          destroyed,
no friendly parting,
parted in
          madness,
parted in rivalry,
and so in
          strife
their days are ended.

YOUNG THEBAN WOMAN 2: *(Sings.)*
And ended their
          hatred.
Now in the earth
their blood is mingled,
blood now truly
          one blood.
And Arês, arbiter,
bitter
     reconciler,
sped from far over the
Hostile Sea,
         Arês,
Arês,
     fire-forged Iron,
Arês, equal divider of
patrimony, impartial Arês,
sped on by the
         fatherly
Curse of
     Oedipus.

YOUNG THEBAN WOMAN 1: *(Sings.)*
Unhappy ones,
they have their share,
their lot of
         misery,
the gift of
     Zeus.

Beneath their bodies
lie the riches of
                    earth,
the limitless wealth
of the
        grave.

YOUNG THEBAN WOMAN 2: *(Sings.)*
    With how many wreaths
    of misery you have
                        crowned
    your house!
    With how many
                    flowers
    of destruction have you
    covered your family,
    a family now in
                    flight,
    in every direction,
    that the Curses take the day
    and shout
                victorious!
    At the gate where
    they perished,
                    these two,
    at each others' hands,
    stands only the
                    trophy
    to Ruin,
    to Disaster,
    to Destruction.
    The Daimon,
    the Spirit,
    the Fury
            triumphs over them,
    and the Curse has
    ceased to
            rage.

YOUNG THEBAN WOMAN 3: *(Sings.)*
You struck; you were struck.

YOUNG THEBAN WOMAN 4: *(Sings.)*
You killed; you were killed.

YOUNG THEBAN WOMAN 5: *(Sings.)*
You killed with the spear.

YOUNG THEBAN WOMAN 6: *(Sings.)*
With the spear you were killed.

YOUNG THEBAN WOMAN 7: *(Sings.)*
Terrible in doing.

YOUNG THEBAN WOMAN 8: *(Sings.)*
Terrible in suffering.

YOUNG THEBAN WOMAN 9: *(Sings.)*
Let the tears come.

YOUNG THEBAN WOMAN 10: *(Sings.)*
Let the tears flow.

YOUNG THEBAN WOMAN 11: *(Sings.)*
You lie there who were killed.

YOUNG THEBAN WOMAN 12: *(Sings.)*
You lie there who killed.

YOUNG THEBAN WOMAN 1: *(Sings.)*
É! É!

YOUNG THEBAN WOMAN 4: *(Sings.)*
É! É!

YOUNG THEBAN WOMAN 6: *(Sings.)*
Mind torn with grief.

YOUNG THEBAN WOMAN 3: *(Sings.)*
Heart torn with tears.

YOUNG THEBAN WOMAN 7: *(Sings.)*
Poor pitiful man.

YOUNG THEBAN WOMAN 2: *(Sings.)*
Brother of misery.

YOUNG THEBAN WOMAN 5: *(Sings.)*
Brother of pain.

YOUNG THEBAN WOMAN 8: *(Sings.)*
Killed by your brother.

YOUNG THEBAN WOMAN 11: *(Sings.)*
Your brother killed you.

YOUNG THEBAN WOMAN 9: *(Sings.)*
Two sorrows to tell.

YOUNG THEBAN WOMAN 10: *(Sings.)*
Two sorrows to see.

YOUNG THEBAN WOMAN 5: *(Sings.)*
Sorrow on sorrow.

YOUNG THEBAN WOMAN 8: *(Sings.)*
Brother by brother.

YOUNG THEBAN WOMEN: *(Sing.)*
IOOOO!
IOOOO!
O dreadful Fate,
great bringer of horror,
mighty, awesome
shade of Oedipus,
black Fury,
awful Vengeance,
how vast is your power!

YOUNG THEBAN WOMAN 2: *(Sings.)*
　É! É!

YOUNG THEBAN WOMAN 1: *(Sings.)*
　É! É!

YOUNG THEBAN WOMAN 6: *(Sings.)*
　Horrible, horrible.

YOUNG THEBAN WOMAN 3: *(Sings.)*
　The exile come home.

YOUNG THEBAN WOMAN 4: *(Sings.)*
　Not home; he killed.

YOUNG THEBAN WOMAN 9: *(Sings.)*
　And lost his life.

YOUNG THEBAN WOMAN 11: *(Sings.)*
　Lost, yes.

YOUNG THEBAN WOMAN 8: *(Sings.)*
　Killed his brother.

YOUNG THEBAN WOMAN 5: *(Sings.)*
　Dreadful to see.

YOUNG THEBAN WOMAN 7: *(Sings.)*
　Dreadful to tell.

YOUNG THEBAN WOMAN 10: *(Sings.)*
　Terrible tale of two brothers.

YOUNG THEBAN WOMAN 12: *(Sings.)*
　Triple sorrow, wave upon wave.

YOUNG THEBAN WOMEN: *(Sing.)*
　　　　IOOOO!
　　　　IOOOO!

O dreadful Fate,
great bringer of horror,
mighty, awesome
shade of Oedipus,
black Fury,
awful Vengeance,
how vast is your power!

YOUNG THEBAN WOMAN 1: *(Sings.)*
You knew her power, you felt it.

YOUNG THEBAN WOMAN 4: *(Sings.)*
You knew her, too; you suffered.

YOUNG THEBAN WOMAN 6: *(Sings.)*
Knew it when you came home.

YOUNG THEBAN WOMAN 5: *(Sings.)*
And raised your spear to your brother.

YOUNG THEBAN WOMAN 11: *(Sings.)*
House of misery.

YOUNG THEBAN WOMAN 10: *(Sings.)*
Miserable Fate.

YOUNG THEBAN WOMAN 7: *(Sings.)*
I weep for the pain.

YOUNG THEBAN WOMAN 3: *(Sings.)*
I mourn for the suffering.

YOUNG THEBAN WOMAN 2: *(Sings.)*
For the house.

YOUNG THEBAN WOMAN 9: *(Sings.)*
For the land.

YOUNG THEBAN WOMAN 8: *(Sings.)*
IOOOO! IOOOO!
Prince of grief!

YOUNG THEBAN WOMAN 12: *(Sings.)*
IOOOO! IOOOO!
Prince of miseries!

YOUNG THEBAN WOMAN 11: *(Sings.)*
IOOOO! IOOOO!
Most wretched of men!

YOUNG THEBAN WOMAN 7: *(Sings.)*
IOOOO! IOOOO!
By blindness possessed!

YOUNG THEBAN WOMAN 6: *(Sings.)*
IOOOO! IOOOO!
Where shall we lay them?

YOUNG THEBAN WOMAN 2: *(Sings.)*
IOOOO! IOOOO!
Where they have most honor!

YOUNG THEBAN WOMAN 1: *(Sings.)*
IOOOO! IOOOO!
By their father's side!

*(Exeunt SOLDIERS with the corpses of ETEOKLÊS and
POLYNEIKÊS, followed by the YOUNG THEBAN WOMEN.)*

SUPPLIANTS

(ΙΚΕΤΙΔΕΣ)

Cast of Characters

CHORUS OF DAUGHTERS OF DANAÖS *young women suppliants*

FIRST DAUGHTER OF DANAÖS *chorus leader*

DANAÖS *their father*

PELASGOS *king of Argos*

EGYPTIAN HERALD

CHORUS OF ARGIVE WOMEN

ARGIVE SOLDIERS

CHORUS OF EGYPTIAN SOLDIERS

SUPPLIANTS

An open space near the coast of Argos.
A large mound of stones serves as an altar sanctuary
   behind which twelve symbols of gods are placed,
   including those of Zeus, Apollo, Poseidon, and Hermês.
Enter from the shore the DAUGHTERS OF DANAÖS
led by DANAÖS.
Music. Song. Dance.

DAUGHTERS OF DANAÖS: *(Chant.)*
Zeus,
god,
Lord of Suppliants,
Zeus Protector,
hear me,
hear my cause,
and be favorable to me,
to me and these women,
sisters,
who set sail where Nile slips
languidly to the sea
through dunes of salt-washed sand.
We left behind a land Zeus loved,
sun-blest pastures that stretch to Syria,
left it exiles,
but not for blood-guilt,
but willing fugitives fleeing our pursuers,
sons of Aigyptos who
want us in marriage,
unholy marriage,
loathsome, detestable,
kinsmen,
cousins,
an unwanted marriage.

Danaös,
father, leader,

advised this rebellion
as the best of the evils that promise
sorrow.
And so we fled,
unchecked our flight,
across the tremulous salt sea,
to Argos,
her harbor,
here to these meadows,
where our race first saw
the light of day.
For we are Argive.
In flesh, in blood, in heart, in mind,
Argive.
Sprung from Io,
fly-maddened cow,
whose womb quickened with
the touch and breath of Zeus.

What shore, what land,
would receive us as kindly as this,
armed as we are with a suppliant's weapons:
olive branches twined with fillets of wool?

City and earth of Argos and your clear waters,
receive us!
Receive us, gods of the sky
and of the deep earth
who tend to vengeance in the tombs of the dead,
gods we honor!
And you,
Zeus Savior,
third and last,
who guard the houses of honest men,
receive us,
this suppliant band of women,
breathe on us the sweet winds of your breath,
breathe mercy, breathe pity,
a gentle breeze.

But on that swarm of Aigyptos' insolent sons
send death!
Death before they foul this marshy land!
Turn back to sea their swift-winged vessel!
Lash them with stormwinds,
sear them with lightning,
let thunder shake them and the sea rise
and swallow them in its
cascading mountains of foam!
Destroy them!
Kill!
Kill them before they make our beds unholy,
before they mount our beds of innocence,
seize us, cousins, kindred,
before they enter bodies,
brutally enter,
bodies that cannot be theirs!
Kill!

(Sing.)

I sing now,
I sing,
and call on the Zeus-calf
from across the sea,
child of Zeus,
by the breath of Zeus,
breath and touch that
ripened in her womb,
that brought forth a son
to our first mother,
a son,
Epaphos,
to our flower-grazing mother,
ancestress,
Io,
Epaphos,
Caress-child.
Epaphos,

Epaphos,
come,
be our defender.

I call him to come,
I call from these pastures
where once she grazed,
great mother of us all,
and in remembering her long-ago agonies,
the pain she suffered,
Argos will know,
her people will learn
from the tale I will tell,
the truth that time alone can prove,
that we are Argives
who come to these shores.

If anyone near,
any reader of bird cries,
hears my tears,
my sad lament,
he will think it the sorrow of Mêtis,
wife of Têreus,
hawk-hunted nightingale
denied her favorite haunt
along green-leafed rivers,
mourning,
singing her song of mourning
for the child her own hand killed
in a rage of unnatural
mother-fury.

Singing my wild Ionian dirges,
with my nails I tear
my sun-browned cheeks,
face darkened by Nile's bright summer.
My heart unused to tears,
I pluck from my heart
flowers of grief.

Is there a friend here,
is there a kinsman,
to stand in our cause,
to protect,
to defend us,
fugitives from that misty land?

Gods of our ancestors,
hear us!
Look kindly on justice.
Hate their pride.
Break their lust.
Let force not make my marriage bed,
but save me for a marriage in justice.
Even in war there is an altar,
a place secure,
a haven, a refuge,
for those who honor the gods.

May Zeus' will be done.
But who can know the will of Zeus?
His desire is dark and hard to see.
The paths of his mind
are a maze of thickets
in a winding wood
that I cannot make out.

What Zeus has willed
lands surefooted,
it cannot be shaken.
Its flames blaze
in the deepest dark,
and carry with it
black doom for man.

From towers of hope
he hurls men down,
from towers of heaven-
tempting hope

he hurls men down,
down to their ruin,
without strength,
without armor,
for his power, his force,
is all ease.
Unmoved mover,
he sits enthroned and
gives his thought being,
and it is done.

Let him look down,
let Zeus see them,
see these arrogant, insolent men,
new shoots on the old stem of Bêlos,
swelling, thrusting,
the rage of lust;
goaded by madness,
by frenzied desire,
delirium turns their mind
to folly.

Pain, pain,
tears and pain,
tears and pain my suffering tells,
my shrieks, my shouts,
shrill,
tears falling,
heavy tears
IOOO! IOOO!
keening wails,
lamentations,
I sing,
I sing my own lament,
my own despair,
my own death dirge.

Argos,
meadows and hills of Argos,

you know,
you understand,
my barbarous speech,
and Earth has seen me
tear and tear again
my fine-spun linen
Sidonian veil.

But when Death is absent,
when all is well,
then these rites run
stained to the gods.
IOOO! IOOO!
And then who knows what evils come!
Where will this wave,
this storm wave sweep me?

Argos,
meadows and hills of Argos,
you know,
you understand,
my barbarous speech,
and Earth has seen me
tear and tear again
my fine-spun linen
Sidonian veil.

Sturdy oars brought us homeward,
sturdy oars and fair winds,
and a shipboard shelter
to keep out the sea,
no tempest,
no stormwind threatening,
and I cannot complain.
But Father All-seeing,
give it a gracious ending.

Allow the brood
of a god-caressed mother

to flee the beds of unwanted men.
IOOO! IOOO!
Let us escape
unmarried,
unvanquished.

Virgin daughter of Zeus,
help us.
Give us protection.
As you guard the gates of your
hallowed shrine,
so guard ours with all your might.
Unconquered maid,
unbroken goddess of chastity,
guard our gates,
deliver us unconquered.

Allow the brood
of a god-caressed mother
to flee the beds of unwanted men.
IOOO! IOOO!
Let us escape
unmarried,
unvanquished.

If not,
if the sky gods scorn our petition,
then we,
we who are dark of skin
by the Nile-sun's rays,
will invoke the Zeus
of the world below,
Hades,
welcome host to many,
and hang ourselves with our
fillets of wool.

It is gods who plague us,
gods who pursue us;

revenge against Io,
undying revenge.

I know, Zeus,
the anger of your queen,
of her heaven-shaking wrath.
Rough winds come first
and then the storm.

And what of Zeus' guilt if we die?
He first disowned the child of the cow,
his own child,
of his making,
and now he turns his eyes from us,
turns away from our suppliants' prayers.
Hear us,
Zeus,
hear us on high!

I know, Zeus,
the anger of your queen,
of her heaven-shaking wrath.
Rough winds come first
and then the storm.

(Music out.)

DANAÖS:
                    Children.
This is a time for caution.
        Caution and cunning.
It was a cunning guide brought you here.
Your trusty father.
The crusty old man you see before you.
                    Me.
He was good at sea.
You know that.
And he'll be as good a
        father and guide on land.

So listen.
And write his words in your hearts,
        for I see dust there on the horizon.
        Dust rising in billows,
an army approaching, and needs no
        herald to tell it.
Soon we'll hear the sounds of
        axles hissing.
                Yes. I see them now.
                        There.
Swarms of men. Bodies
        wrapped in shields. Spears
                rattling. Horses
        pounding the earth, and
                curved chariots.

The land's rulers, I suspect.
                        Argive princes.
They've heard of our
        landing and have come to
        see what we're about.
It's wise to be
        cautious in any case.
Whether they come merely
                curious or hot for
        battle,
it's best you stay by this mound
        shared by the gods. An altar
        is stronger than any
fortress, a shield no man can
                                break.
Hurry.
        Now.
                Quick as you can.
Climb up.
        Sit.
                Arrange yourselves.
In your left hands your

branches crowned with white wool,
the emblem of Zeus who feels
pity.
Hold them solemnly.
Yes.

Now, when they ask you,
you must answer as is only
proper to suppliants.
With reverence.
With tearful voices.
Make it plain that you're fugitives,
but not for any crime, not for any
shedding of blood.
And show need.
As for boldness,
there will be none, and no
immodesty, your eyes will be
downcast at all times.
Speak when spoken to,
and don't delay
unduly in your responses.
People here are easy to take
offense.
You're foreigners and fugitives.
Remember that.
Bend with the wind.
Arrogance has no
part in weakness.

FIRST DAUGHTER:
Your words are wise, father,
and spoken to daughters who respect
wisdom.
We won't forget.
And may Father Zeus, our
first father,
look down upon us!

DANAÖS:
>   Yes, and with a gracious eye.

FIRST DAUGHTER:
>   If it is his will, all will be well.

DANAÖS:
>   Well, then. You know what to do.

FIRST DAUGHTER:
>   We'll sit here around you, father.
>   We'd like that.
>   Zeus, watch over us.
>   Keep us safe.

DANAÖS:
>   Pray to Zeus' eagle now.

FIRST DAUGHTER:
>   We pray that the sun will show us safety.

DANAÖS:
>   And Apollo, too, once exiled to earth.

FIRST DAUGHTER:
>   He shared our suffering; he'll understand.

DANAÖS:
>   He knows our sorrow; he'll show us mercy.

FIRST DAUGHTER:
>   What other gods should we ask for help?

DANAÖS:
>   This trident; look; a god's weapon.

FIRST DAUGHTER:
>   Poseidon gave us a good voyage.

DANAÖS:

And here is Hermês as the Greeks show him.

FIRST DAUGHTER:

Let him herald the news that we're free.

DANAÖS:

You must worship here at this
altar of all these gods.
Settle in this holy place like doves
swarming, seeking shelter from
ravening hawks:
blood cousins, but
enemies polluting the race.

Can a bird who eats birds be
pure?
Can a man who marries a
father's unwilling daughter,
equally against that father's own will,
be free of pollution?
Not even in death, in Hades,
can he who has done such outrage
escape his guilt.
It's said that even there
there is a Zeus,
another Zeus, who oversees
wrongdoing and pronounces final
judgment.

Remember, now.
Answer as I've advised and
you will win out in the end.

*(Enter KING PELASGOS with an escort of armed
ARGIVE SOLDIERS.)*

PELASGOS:

Who are these I see here

dressed in such luxury?
Surely not Greeks.
          Not in such splendid linen robes and
                    headdresses that no Argive or
          otherwise Greek woman wears.
Such barbaric wonder is
          unknown in these parts.

But where are you from?
And what brought you here?
          What daring,
          what fearlessness, to come here
unannounced, without
          patrons to stand for you?
I find this most wondrous.
                              It amazes me.
And yet I see suppliants' boughs
          near you here, before our assembled
          gods, surely a sign of those
seeking asylum, a custom that is clearly
                                        Greek.
As for the rest, I could guess,
          but choose not to.
I prefer to hear it from you.

FIRST DAUGHTER:
          As for our clothes,
                    you're quite right.
          But how do I address you?
          Private citizen?
          Spokesman?
                    The city's leader?

PELASGOS:
          You may address me in confidence.
                    I am Pelasgos, born of
          Ancient Earth, and this land's
                              ruler.
          The people who sow and reap this

country's harvests are known as
        Pelasgians, after me.
I hold as mine all the land
                west of the River Strymon
        in the direction of the setting sun.
My borders are the land of Paionia,
        the country beyond Pindos,
        near Perrhaibia, and the
                mountain districts of
Dodona, where the sea cuts
        short my kingdom.
I rule over all the land
        inside these boundaries.

This plain you see before you is
        known as Apia,
in honor of that ancient healing
        hero, Apis, the son of
                        Apollo.
He came here from Naupaktos long ago
        and purged the land of man-killing
        monsters, serpents that Earth had
spawned when polluted by the blood of
                ancient murders.
With a surgeon's skill he
        cut the pain from her womb and
saved not only Earth but the
                        Argives.
                Nor did he take payment.
But we paid him nonetheless.
From that day till this
        he is memorialized in Argive prayer.

                So much for that.
It's time now for you to tell me your lineage.
And be brief.
Argos is no friend to lengthy
                        speeches.

FIRST DAUGHTER:

    Our tale is as brief as it is clear.
    We're Argives by blood,
    descended from
        the child-blessed cow.
    My words will prove this true.

PELASGOS:
                Argive?
    But how can this be?
    Lydian, perhaps, but surely not
                  Greek.
    Or descendents of the Nile; or
        Kypris, where men stamp
        images such as yours on coins.
    Or India, where,
           or so I've heard,
        nomad women ride on saddled camels that
           move like horses,
        neighbors of the Aithiops.
    And then there are the Amazons,
        man-shunning women who feast on flesh.
    If you were armed with bows I'd
        liken you to them.
                But Argives?
    How is it possible?
    You must tell me.

FIRST DAUGHTER:

    There was an Argive
        priestess once,
           long ago,
    Hera's servant, they say,
        keeper of her temple keys—
               Io.

PELASGOS:

    Yes, they say so; a well-known tale.

FIRST DAUGHTER:

>   Do they also say Zeus made love to her?

PELASGOS:

>   Yes, and not unknown to Hera.

FIRST DAUGHTER:

>   And how did this war in heaven end?

PELASGOS:

>   She turned the woman into a cow.

FIRST DAUGHTER:

>   And even so the god pursued her?

PELASGOS:

>   He turned himself into a rutting bull.

FIRST DAUGHTER:

>   And what did his powerful wife do then?

PELASGOS:

>   She posted a watchman with a thousand eyes.

FIRST DAUGHTER:

>   For one cow? A thousand eyes?

PELASGOS:

>   Argos. Earth son. Hermês killed him.

FIRST DAUGHTER:

>   How else did Hera plague the poor creature?

PELASGOS:

>   She sent a winged cattle-goad—

FIRST DAUGHTER:

>   Gadfly is its Egyptian name.

PELASGOS:

—that drove her into a long wandering—

FIRST DAUGHTER:

Yes, our stories match exactly.

PELASGOS:

—to Kanobos and even to Memphis—

FIRST DAUGHTER:

Where Zeus caressed her and planted his seed.

PELASGOS:

And who claims to be this cow's Zeus-calf?

FIRST DAUGHTER:

Epaphos, named for Zeus' touch.

PELASGOS:

And who do they say is the child of Epaphos?

FIRST DAUGHTER:

Libyê, who harvests earth's largest land.

PELASGOS:

And Libyê's child was who? Name him.

FIRST DAUGHTER:

Bêlos; and my father is one of his sons.

PELASGOS:

This noble gentleman? Tell me his name.

FIRST DAUGHTER:

Danaös, whose brother has fifty sons.

PELASGOS:

And *his* name is? You mustn't hesitate.

FIRST DAUGHTER:
> > Aigyptos.
> Now you know.
> We are blood of your ancient
> > blood.
> I beg you,
> > defend us who are Argives.

PELASGOS:
> I acknowledge your ancient
> > claim on Argos.
> But why have you left
> > Egypt, the land of your fathers?
> What misfortune forced this on you?

FIRST DAUGHTER:
> > Lord Pelasgos,
> human sufferings come in various
> > colors, no two are the same.
> Who would have thought our
> > flight from hideous rape would
> > end us here among ancient
> blood relations?

PELASGOS:
> I see you here,
> > suppliants, wool wound
> > branches in your hands.
> What is it you want?
> What are you asking in the
> > name of these gods?

FIRST DAUGHTER:
> Not to be slaves to the race of Aigyptos.

PELASGOS:
> Because you hate them? Or because it's unlawful?

FIRST DAUGHTER:
> What woman would scorn a man she loves?

PELASGOS:
> Marriage gives power, even loveless marriage.

FIRST DAUGHTER:
> No, it breeds misery and easy divorce.

PELASGOS:
> As I reverence the gods, how can I help you?

FIRST DAUGHTER:
> Never surrender us to the sons of Aigyptos.

PELASGOS:
> A decision that will lead to war.

FIRST DAUGHTER:
> Justice protects those who fight for right.

PELASGOS:
> If Justice was with him from the start.

FIRST DAUGHTER:
> Respect your gods. They steer your state.

PELASGOS:
> I tremble before this shaded altar.

FIRST DAUGHTER:
> The wrath of Zeus Suppliant is great.

(Music. Song. Dance.)

FIRST DAUGHTER: *(Sings.)*
> Listen to me,
> hear me,
> son of Ancient Earth.

Listen with a kind
                         heart,
lord of
           Argos.
See me,
your suppliant,
an exile,
fugitive,
a wolf-hunted
                     calf
on jagged rocks,
trusting,
trusting the herdsman's
                          strength.
Be that
           herdsman.
Hear our cry.

PELASGOS: *(Speaks.)*
I see the gods nod in the
           shadow of your branches.
I see strangers who are citizens,
               our kin.
I pray to the gods they bring no
          disaster. Let them not bring
                     strife.
        Unwanted.
Unwanted strife
           Not war.

FIRST DAUGHTER: *(Sings.)*
I pray to
           Justice,
Justice,
daughter of Zeus,
to see my
             fugitive flight
and let it bring no
                 disaster.

You are wise, my lord,
there is wisdom in your
                                    years;
but now you must learn from me,
from the young.
Respect the
                    suppliant.
There is no greater
gift to the
                    gods.

PELASGOS: *(Speaks.)*
    If you were at *my* house,
            at my *private* hearth,
    seeking sanctuary,
            I would have no
                            fear.
    But whatever pollution
            comes with your plea, it is
            the city that would suffer, and
    the city that must find the cure.
    It is the people's risk.
            I must ask the people.
    Only then can I act
                            justly.

FIRST DAUGHTER: *(Sings.)*
    No, Lord!
    No, Majesty!
    You are the
                    people!
    You are the
                    state!
    No king can be judged!
    You rule the
                    altar,
    you rule the land's
                            hearth!
    Your will is one vote,

your will is
>   rule!
When you sit enthroned,
you speak for all!
Beware heaven's curse!
Beware
>   pollution!

PELASGOS: *(Speaks.)*
>   Pollution I wish on my enemies!
>   What do I do?
>>   If I protect you, I suffer
>>   harm. If I ignore you, I
>>>   suffer as well.
>   I see no solution.
>   To act or not to act is equally
>>>>>   fearful.
>   Or do I leave it to fate?

FIRST DAUGHTER: *(Sings.)*
>   Take care!
>   Look up and see him;
>   he's
>>   watching;
>   vigilant guardian of
>   suffering
>>   humanity
>   that seeks justice but is denied.
>   His wrath is great,
>   Zeus'
>>   wrath,
>   Lord of Suppliants,
>   on those who hear the
>>>   plea
>   but turn away.

PELASGOS: *(Speaks.)*
>   But what if the sons of
>>   Aigyptos are right, and as

next of kin they have
claim to rule you, as the
law of your land would have it?
How, then, could I oppose them?
You must plead in your own defense
that the laws of your land
give them *no* authority over you.

FIRST DAUGHTER: *(Sings.)*
Never,
I will never be
crushed
by the power of
those men!
My defense from this
loathed
marriage is flight,
under the stars, the
stars
as guides!
Choose Justice and heaven's
Law as
ally.
Side with the gods.

PELASGOS: *(Speaks.)*
This is no easy judgment,
so make me no judge.
I've told you.
I refuse to act without the people's
advice, king or no king.
If disaster should come of this,
I can hear them say:
"You honored strangers and
destroyed the city!"

FIRST DAUGHTER: *(Sings.)*
Zeus, who shares our
blood,

yours and mine,
impartial judge,
holds the
        balance.
The injustice of the
                wicked
he piles on one scale;
the justice of the
                good
on the other.
Why does it pain you
to do justice?

PELASGOS: *(Speaks.)*
    We must take counsel,
        deep counsel,
        to find salvation.
    Like a diver into the deep of the
                        sea,
    we must be clearsighted and
        sober, to find a way
        unharmful to the city,
            but also to me.
    War must not seize us,
        our lands,
        our goods.
    If we give you to them,
        you,
            here,
        in this holy place,
    we open our house to the
        burden of Vengeance, all-destroying
    god who even in Hades sets no man
                        free.
    We need deep counsel to
        find salvation.

DAUGHTERS OF DANAÖS: *(Sing.)*
            Then take deep counsel,

be our protector;
guard us with right;
don't desert us,
fugitives,
exiles,
driven out
by evil men.

Don't let them drag me
from this holy place,
you who are powerful,
who rule this land!
See their violence,
these insolent men,
and fear the anger of
god to come.

We're suppliants here,
don't let us be dragged
from these statues by our headbands,
like horses,
unjustly,
violent hands
grasping my robes.

Whatever you do,
Justice repays,
repays in your children,
repays in your house.
Think:
the rule of Zeus is
just.

PELASGOS: *(Speaks.)*
Think?
I have thought, and my thoughts have
run aground. A harsh
Necessity grips me.
I'm like a ship whose bolts are

fastened and whose hull is
    drawn by cables and winches
        down to the sea and a war
    whichever way I
               turn.
There is no harbor free of pain.

If a house's wealth is
    plundered, it may be that
Zeus Guard of Ownership will
        restore what was lost.
If the tongue aims its arrows unwisely
    other words can heal the wound.
But kindred blood must not be
            shed.

We must sacrifice, great
    offerings of sacrifice, many,
    many offerings to many gods, many
        victims must fall, many, to
ward off such ruin.

I'm withered by this dispute.
I would rather be ignorant than
        expert in evil.
But I hope against all hope that
    all will be well.

(Music out.)

FIRST DAUGHTER:
    I have one more plea.

PELASGOS:
    I'm listening.

FIRST DAUGHTER:
    I have bands and cords to fasten my dress.

PELASGOS:
>   Proper articles for women.

FIRST DAUGHTER:
>   An excellent means—

PELASGOS:
>   I don't understand.

FIRST DAUGHTER:
>   —if you don't promise—

PELASGOS:
>   To do what?

FIRST DAUGHTER:
>   New offerings for these gods.

PELASGOS:
>   You speak in riddles. What?

FIRST DAUGHTER:
>   We'll hang ourselves from them. Now!

PELASGOS:
>   Your words lash at my heart.

FIRST DAUGHTER:
>   Now you understand. Now you see.

PELASGOS:
>   See?
>   Yes.
>   I see that I am outwrestled.
>   I see that I am caught in a
>   floodtide of evils, an unfathomable
>   sea of disaster that cannot be
>   crossed,
>   and there is no harbor, no

rescue from distress.
If I fail to help you,
    I must meet head-on your threat of
        pollution with no chance of escape.
And if I stand at the city walls and
    fight the sons of Aigyptos,
        my kinsmen and yours,
what can the outcome be but a
                bitter one?
Men's blood staining the ground for the
    sake of women!

              And yet,
    what choice do I have but to
bow to the wrath of Zeus Protector of
    Suppliants, the most feared power of
    all among mortals?

        Old man,
           old Danaös,
    father of these girls,
you must at once take up these
    boughs and place them on other
        altars in Argos.
It will be seen that you come as
    suppliants and the people will not
    take me to task.
They're quick to criticize their leaders,
    these people.
Do this and it's likely they will take
    pity and turn against the insolent men
    pursuing you.
People are often better disposed
    toward the weak.

DANAÖS:
    We thank you for championing our cause,
        and for the respect you show toward
           strangers.

But now you must send me with
        attendants to guide me to the altars and
        temples of the city's gods.
My looks are not like yours—
        the Nile breeds a different
                stock from the Inachos—
and I may need some advice to get about safely.
My boldness in appearing alone
        might cause fear, and
friends have at times killed friends
        through mere ignorance.

PELASGOS:
                        He's right.
You men will go with him.
Lead him to the city's altars and
        seats of the gods.
And don't gossip overlong.
        You're escorting this sailor
                to the hearths of the gods.

*(Exit DANAÖS carrying a number of suppliants' boughs, accompanied by
the ARGIVE SOLDIERS.)*

FIRST DAUGHTER:
You've instructed my father,
        but what am I to do?
How do I act?

PELASGOS:
Leave your branches there.
Signs of your need.

FIRST DAUGHTER:
Yes, I do as you ask.

(They place their branches on the altar.)

PELASGOS:
> Now come down here to level ground.

FIRST DAUGHTER:
> Leave the altar? Is that safe?

PELASGOS:
> We won't let winged monsters molest you.

FIRST DAUGHTER:
> And those more heartless than snakes?

PELASGOS:
> As I've been kind, so should you be.

FIRST DAUGHTER:
> I'm sorry. I'm unreasonable. I'm frightened.

PELASGOS:
> There's nothing to fear.

FIRST DAUGHTER:
> Then cheer me with your own words.

PELASGOS:
> All right,
> you have nothing to worry about.
> You won't be fatherless
>   long; he'll be back shortly.
> But first I'll go call the people to assembly.
>   I'll win them over for you and will
>   teach your father what to say when he
>   addresses them.
> Stay here for now.
> Use the time well. Pray the gods to
>   grant what you most desire.
>   I'll see to the rest.
> Persuasion be with me,
>   and Good Fortune.

(Exeunt PELASGOS and the remaining ARGIVE SOLDIERS.)
(Music. Song. Dance.)

DAUGHTERS OF DANAÖS: *(Sing.)*
Lord of lords,
most blest of the blest,
most perfect power of perfect powers,
mighty Zeus!
Hear me, lord!
Kinsman, hear!
Save us,
save us from the insolence of men,
hated by you,
hated men,
save us from the lust of men,
save us from outrage!
Turn back their ship,
their black-benched ship,
hurl it to the depths of the purple sea!

Look on us,
look down,
smile,
show us your kindness,
women descended,
as legend tells,
from the woman you loved.
Remember her!
Remember!
Io,
mother,
mother by your touch,
ancient mother,
mother of us all.
Remember.
Remember, Father.
We are your children,
descended from this land.

I have found again the ancient traces,
age-old tracks made by my mother
who browsed these meadows,
was watched, was stung,
stung to madness by the cruel gadfly.
She fled,
fled frenzied,
through many lands,
through many, many tribes of men,
and by swimming the waves
of the storm-tossed strait,
as Fate required,
as Fate demanded,
she marked out a boundary
for the land opposite
and the waters were named:
Bosporos,
Cow-ford.

Headlong she rushed,
headlong, headlong,
stung by the gadfly through Asia's plains,
through the sheeplands of Phrygia,
the city of Teuthras among the Mysians,
the valleys of Lydia,
and the mountains of Kilikia,
across the broad land of the Pamphylians,
to rivers never dry and
deep, dark soil,
and onward to Aphroditê's wheat-rich land.

To Egypt then,
gadfly goaded,
driven, driven,
to Zeus' garden,
fertile fields where all things grow,
meadows snow-fed by flooding Nile,
Nile that knows no disease
but only the lash of whirlwinds.

And so she ran,
the sting-goaded maid,
Hera's maddened maenad.

And all who lived there
trembled at the sight,
shook in terror,
the color of corpses,
fearful sight,
part woman, part cow,
monster most horrible.
Who was it then healed her,
who was it healed Io,
relieved the wandering wearied sufferer
of her unrelenting goad?

Zeus.
Zeus who rules forever.
Zeus caressed her with painless might.
Zeus breathed gently and
freed her from pain,
and she wept, and weeping
washed out her shame.
And Zeus' caress,
and Zeus' breath
gave her the perfect child she bore.

And he lived long,
and he lived happily.
And now all the earth shouts aloud
that this is the race that Zeus gave life to,
this the race that the Life-giver made.
Who but Zeus could have
stopped the sufferings
cruel Hera laid on?
Who but Zeus?
And when you say we are
sprung from Epaphos,
you speak the truth.

Which god could I more justly summon
than the Father,
the maker,
the great artificer,
founder,
planter of our race's seed,
Zeus who made all things,
god of fair breezes?

Than Zeus there is no greater power;
he bows to none;
his might unbeatable.
His deed is in the thought and it is done.

(Enter DANAÖS.)
(Music out.)

DANAÖS:
Children,
good news,
be joyful!
They've voted, the people,
in assembly!
We have their support!

FIRST DAUGHTER:
Dear old man,
what wonderful news!
But tell me how it happened,
how they came to their
decision, how great a majority
of hands.

DANAÖS:
O my dear,
it was a sight to make me
young again.
The air bristled with their
hands. Not a voice

dissenting. Not a doubt among them all.
They decreed that we would
        settle in this country, that we would be
        free and subject to no one, safe from
seizure and certain of protection.
                No one,
        citizen or foreigner,
        may take us captive; and
if we are done violence against, any
        Argive citizen who
        fails to come to our aid
                will lose his civic rights and be
exiled by popular vote.

These words King Pelasgos used
        to persuade his people, warning them
not to feed the wrath of Zeus of Suppliants.
                For if they did,
        the city would suffer double
        pollution from us who are
                Argive citizens as well as
suppliant guests, a plague so
        great it has no cure.

Hearing these words,
        they raised their hands to a
                man, without even
        a herald's proclamation to do so.
These citizens of Pelasgos
        accepted what he said,
        persuaded by him, and Zeus
added his final ratification.

(Music. Song. Dance.)

FIRST DAUGHTER: *(Chants.)*
        Sisters,
        let us sing in praise of
        Argos,

prayers of good
for good received.
And may
Zeus Lord of Suppliants
guide a stranger's prayers
to blameless fulfillment
for our hosts.

DAUGHTERS OF DANAÖS: *(Sing.)*
                    Gods,
              children of Zeus,
               Zeus-born gods,
      listen as we pour libations of praise
            to our Argive hosts,
                  our kin,
                our defenders.
        May Argos never fall to fire,
       never be destroyed by willful Arês,
        whose warcry is not fit for dance,
      who reaps men like wheat in the fields.
   Great Argos pitied us and cast a kind vote,
      honored suppliants that no one envies.

       They did not cast their votes for men,
        they did not dishonor women's rights,
         but watched the eye of Zeus Avenger,
                that none can battle,
                  no house endure,
          too heavy a defiling burden on the roof.
              They honor their kin,
                Zeus' suppliants,
        and their altars will offer pure sacrifice
               and the gods be pleased.

     Let eager prayers take wing from my mouth,
            prayers to honor their goodness,
              prayers to keep plague at bay
           and not empty their city of men.
           Let no man strike down his brother

and stain the land with its children's blood.
Let the flower of Argive youth grow ungathered,
and man-slaying Arês,
Aphroditê's bedmate,
not shear off its tenderest blooms.

And let altars tended by elders blaze high,
for where Zeus gets his due a state is well governed,
Zeus Lord of Strangers whose law upholds destiny.
We pray for this land a host of new heroes,
and Artemis-Hekate to guard women in birth.

Let civil strife not cleave it apart,
rend it asunder,
slaughter its men,
arming Arês, god of no music,
no master of dance, but father of tears,
Arês maker of havoc.
Let sickness settle its joyless swarms
far from their heads,
and Wolfgod Apollo show mercy to the young.

Grant them fertile fields, great Zeus,
heavy harvests and perfect fruits,
in every season.
And herds of cattle and countless calves,
and endless blessings that flow from the gods.
Let hymns of thanksgiving rise round altars
and harpists raise their voices in song
from lips burnt pure by awe.

Keep safe the people's rule,
keep safe wise counsels,
great prerogatives;
and offer to strangers
justice,
fair hearing,
not war,
not Arês' unsheathed sword.

And honor the country's gods,
gods who keep the land;
honor them with laurel,
with oxen.
Make sacrifice,
sing them praise,
as your fathers did.
Honor parents,
the third great law of mighty
Justice.

(Music out.)

DANAÖS:
I approve your prayers, my children.
They're prudent as well as
wise. But I have news.
Unwelcome and unexpected news,
so be brave.
Here from this sanctuary, this
high rock, I see the ship.
There can be no doubt.
I see it clearly.
Every detail.
Egyptian sails, wide side-guards, and
eyes painted on the prow
searching out its course, all too obedient
to the hand on the tiller.
And I see men onboard,
black limbs, white clothes,
behind them an entire armada
loaded with troops, meaning us no
good.
There's the lead ship furling its sails,
oars clattering to bring it
ashore.

Again I tell you, be brave.
Prudence and calm are

all-important.
And don't forget the gods.

I'm going now to bring help,
    men ready to defend you with
    steel if necessary.
Whoever comes from the enemy,
    a herald or a company of
        soldiers, and tries to
    seize you as booty and lead you off,
don't be afraid,
    it will never happen.
Not one of them will touch you.

But if help is slow in coming,
    if something delays us, never forget the
            gods.
This is where their help resides.
This is your altar of defense, your
    strength!
And be brave.
Time will bring just payment to
    those who scorn the gods.

(Music. Song. Dance.)

FIRST DAUGHTER: *(Speaks.)*
    Father, I'm afraid!
    The swift-winged ships!
        They're here!
            No time!
        There's no time!

DAUGHTERS OF DANAÖS: *(Sing.)*
            Father, I'm terrified!
            Why did we run?
            What good,
        what good has it done us?
            Father!

DANAÖS: *(Speaks.)*
>Children, be calm.
>The Argive vote is certain.
>>They'll defend us.
>I know.

FIRST DAUGHTER: *(Speaks.)*
>Abominable race of Aigyptos!
>>Maddened by lust!
>Starved for battle!

DAUGHTERS OF DANAÖS: *(Sing.)*
>>Wooden hulls
>>pierced the sea,
>>dark-eyed prows
>>in wrathful haste,
>>>sped on,
>>>sped on,
>>a huge black host.

DANAÖS: *(Speaks.)*
>And the men they'll find here
>>are sun-toughened warriors.

FIRST DAUGHTER: *(Speaks.)*
>Don't leave me, father!
>Don't leave me alone!
>Alone a woman is
>>nothing!
>Nothing!

DAUGHTERS OF DANAÖS: *(Sing.)*
>>>Evil,
>>evil-minded,
>>treacherous,
>>lecherous,
>>ravens defiling
>>sacred altars!

DANAÖS: *(Speaks.)*
> It's to our advantage
> if the gods hate them, too.

FIRST DAUGHTER: *(Speaks.)*
> Nothing, father, nothing,
>> not this trident,
> not any image of the gods,
> will keep their hands off of us!

DAUGHTERS OF DANAÖS: *(Sing.)*
>>>> Arrogance,
>>>> rage,
>>>> unholy rage,
>>>> they're dogs,
>>>> shameless,
>>>> they scorn the gods!

DANAÖS: *(Speaks.)*
> There's a proverb that wolves are
>> stronger than dogs;
> that papyrus fruit cannot
>> master corn.

FIRST DAUGHTER: *(Speaks.)*
> They're animals, beasts,
>> easy to anger;
> we must avoid their mastery.

DANAÖS: *(Speaks.)*
> It takes time to get a fleet under way,
>> and time to get it moored.
> No captain is going to
> leap ashore first thing on a
>> coast with no harbor and the
>>> sun about to set.
> Even an experienced seaman takes
>> extra precautions at night.
> And no army can disembark

properly before the ships are
        secure at their moorings.

I know that you're
        frightened, so just be careful.
And remember the gods.
I'll return with help as soon as I can.
Argos won't find fault with an old man;
        not as long as his mind and
            heart are young.

(Exit DANAÖS.)

DAUGHTERS OF DANAÖS: *(Sing.)*
          O hills,
        o land,
      o earth of Argos,
       so dearly loved,
    what must we suffer?
Where in Argos can we hide?
     What hollow,
   what dark crevice?
      I wish,
    like my dark skin,
I were black smoke that could
      rise, rise,
to join with god's clouds,
  wingless dust that could
    vanish to nothing!

    There is no escape!
    My heart trembles!
Trapped in the net of my father's watching,
    I quiver with terror!
Rather death by the noose
  than their hated hands!
   Death for our master,
    Death's caress!

Is there a place in the blue sky,
where misty rain clouds turn to snow,
where no one can see,
a crag,
slippery,
where goats fear to climb,
vulture's eyrie,
lonely-minded,
beetling height,
to see,
to witness
my fall,
my plunge
to the depths before my heart is pierced
by a murderous marriage!

No,
let death come from ravening dogs,
tearing my flesh,
from birds of prey sailing the skies;
the dead are free of life's cruel pains.
Come, Death, come!
Come before marriage!
What road,
what path,
can I cut to deliverance?

Shriek,
howl,
grief,
prayers!
Hear us, heaven!
Hear us, gods!
Hear and help us!
Find us release!
Father!
Zeus!
With eyes of justice look and deliver me!
See their violence,

see and destroy them!
Almighty Zeus of Suppliants,
save us!

Hear them!
The sons of Aigyptos!
Hunting me,
hunting the fugitive,
violent,
unbearable,
ruthless,
swaggering,
bellowing lust,
to force me,
to take me!
Yours,
Great Father,
yours is the balance,
you hold the scales,
the decision is yours!

(Enter the EGYPTIAN HERALD and a CHORUS OF EGYPTIAN
SOLDIERS. The DAUGHTERS scramble in wild confusion to the
symbols of the gods.)

Ó! Ó! Ó!
Á! Á! Á!
They're here!
AIIII!
Here!
From the shore!
From the ship!
AIIII!
Rapists!
AIIII!
On land!
Die!
Die!
Drown in the sea!

EGYPTIAN SOLDIERS: *(Sing.)*

> Down!
> Come down!
> Down!
> Now!
> To the ship!
> Now!

DAUGHTERS OF DANAÖS: *(Sing.)*

> AIIII! AIIII!
> It begins!
> The suffering!
> AIIII!
> The violence!
> Hurry! Hurry!
> Our refuge!
> The sanctuary!
> AIIII!
> Savages!
> Hurting!
> Pain!
> Escape!
> AIIII!
> Savages!
> Evil lust!
> Lord of Earth,
> Earth-god,
> protect us!
> Defend!

EGYPTIAN SOLDIERS: *(Sing.)*

> Now!
> To the ships!
> To the ships!
> Hurry!
> Now!
> On your feet!
> Quick!
> I'll tear you!

Tear!
Hair!
Clothes!
Heads!
Bloody!
Blood will flow!
Blood gushing!
Now!
Damn you!
Now!
To the ships!
Damn you!
Come down!

DAUGHTERS OF DANAÖS: *(Sing.)*
You should have drowned
in the salt sea waves!
In the dark deeps
of the salty road!
You,
your ship,
your bolt-bound
ship!
You,
your violence,
your slaveholder's
arrogance!

EGYPTIAN SOLDIERS: *(Sing.)*
Down from there!
Down!
Down to the ships!
Violence!
You haven't begun to see violence!
I'll drag you,
screaming,
bleeding,
drag you!
You have no rights!

Insane,
insane your screaming,
howling!
Away from the altar!
Now!
Down!
Come down!
This city gives you no honor,
no rights!

DAUGHTERS OF DANAÖS: *(Sing.)*
May you never,
never,
never see again
the great wide Nile,
gentle waters where cattle drink,
nourisher of life-giving blood!
I am an Argive!
This is my land!

EGYPTIAN SOLDIERS: *(Sing.)*
No, *my* land is your land!
Egypt!
Now get to the ship!
Like it or not!
I'll drag you by the hair,
by force,
now!

DAUGHTERS OF DANAÖS: *(Sing.)*
AIIIII!
AIIIII! AIIIII!
I hope you die,
die,
in the salty waves,
driven,
driven by violent winds
on a roaring sea,
and run aground on the sandy
banks of Sarpêdon.

(The EGYPTIAN HERALD begins to approach the sanctuary.)

EGYPTIAN HERALD: *(Speaks.)*
 Listen to me and listen carefully!
 You can shriek and howl all you like,
  and call on your
    gods,
 you won't be leaping overboard
  from Aigyptos' ship!

DAUGHTERS OF DANAÖS: *(Sing.)*
              AIIIII! AIIIII!
              Arrogance!
                AIIIII!
               Outrage!
             Lecherous beast
           swelling with pride!
            May great Nile
            witness your evil
            and swallow you,
               swallow,
         drown your insolence!

EGYPTIAN HERALD: *(Speaks.)*
 I'll say it again!
  Get to the ship!
              Now!
 We're headed seaward!
     Get aboard!
 Or I'll drag you by the hair!
          Go!

DAUGHTERS OF DANAÖS: *(Sing.)*
            Father! Father!
          Your altar is no help!
              A spider,
             like a spider
            he closes me in,
              traps me,

                    drags me to the sea,
                    step by step,
                    dream,
                    a dream,
                    black dream!
                    OTOTOTOTOI!

                    Mother Earth!
                    Mother Earth!
                    Save me, save me!
                    He frightens me!
                    His terrible cries!
                    Father!
                    Son of Earth!
                    O Zeus!

EGYPTIAN HERALD: *(Speaks.)*
        They don't frighten me,
            your local gods!
        They didn't raise me;
        they won't feed my old age!

DAUGHTERS OF DANAÖS: *(Sing.)*
                    He writhes!
                    Near me!
                    Snake with two legs!
                    Lust-mad serpent!
                    Lunges!
                    Viper!
                    Hideous!
                    Horrible!
                    His prey!
                    AIIII!
                    OTOTOTOTOI!

                    Mother Earth!
                    Mother Earth!
                    Save me, save me!
                    He frightens me!

His terrible cries!
Father!
Son of Earth!
O Zeus!

EGYPTIAN HERALD: *(Speaks.)*
    To the ship!
            Get going!
    Or you'll see those finespun
        clothes of yours ripped!
    Soon there will be no mercy!

(The EGYPTIAN SOLDIERS grab at the DAUGHTERS.)

DAUGHTERS OF DANAÖS: *(Sing.)*
                Help us, princes of Argos!
                    I'm breaking!
                    Breaking!

EGYPTIAN HERALD: *(Speaks.)*
    You either come now
    or be dragged by the hair!

DAUGHTERS OF DANAÖS: *(Sing.)*
                Lord Pelasgos!
                    King!
                They're destroying us!
                    The pain!

EGYPTIAN HERALD: *(Speaks.)*
    You'll soon have all the lords you want!
    The sons of Aigyptos!
    You won't be short of men!

(Enter PELASGOS with ARGIVE SOLDIERS.)
(Music out.)

PELASGOS:
            You!

What's the meaning of this?
How dare you insult the men of
                              Argos?
What do you think we are, a city of women?
For someone who's a stranger you
        play insolent games with Greeks.
This time I'd say you've
                    overshot your mark.

EGYPTIAN HERALD:
    And what exactly have I done to do that?

PELASGOS:
    Failed to realize how strangers are meant to act.

EGYPTIAN HERALD:
    I see. Well, I'm recovering lost property.

PELASGOS:
    And what authorities did you notify in Argos?

EGYPTIAN HERALD:
    The greatest. Hermês the Searcher. None higher.

PELASGOS:
    Notify the gods, but show them no reverence?

EGYPTIAN HERALD:
    I reverence the gods along the Nile.

PELASGOS:
    The gods of Argos mean nothing to you it seems.

EGYPTIAN HERALD:
    I'll take these women. I won't be robbed of my property.

PELASGOS:
    Lay one hand on them and you'll suffer for it.

EGYPTIAN HERALD:
What a splendid welcome you offer to strangers.

PELASGOS:
I have little respect for strangers who steal from the gods.

EGYPTIAN HERALD:
Shall I go back and tell this to the sons of Aigyptos?

PELASGOS:
Do whatever you like, it doesn't concern me.

EGYPTIAN HERALD:
                         Well, then,
    may I ask, since I'm
            required—a herald, you see, must
            relay precise information—
    who shall I say to the sons of
            Aigyptos has relieved me of their
                    female cousins?
    Arês needs no witnesses in such cases,
            nor can it be settled with a fine.
    But many, many men will
            fall and kick off their lives
            before this is
                         ended.

PELASGOS:
    Tell you my name?
            I don't see why.
    You and your cohorts will
            learn it in due
                    time.
    As for these girls,
            by all means, take them back.
    But be certain you have their
            consent by means of proper
                             persuasion.
            You see,

the people have voted
unanimously never to give them up
to force.
A decree not written on
tablets or on sealed papyrus, but kept
alive and vital on the lips of free men.
A bolt driven through a ship's
hull to hold it fast.

Get out.
Out of my sight.
Now.

EGYPTIAN HERALD:
I see we stand on the verge of a new war.
Victory and power to the men!

PELASGOS:
Our men drink a stronger brew than barley-beer.

(Exeunt EGYPTIAN HERALD and the EGYPTIAN SOLDIERS.)

Take courage!
All of you!
And together enter our fortified city
with its ring of
towers.
We have many houses there,
dwellings of the people as well as my
own rich palace.
Choose as you will:
to live, to share lodgings with others,
or, if you prefer,
alone, if that pleases you.
The choice is yours;
whatever is best for you.
You are under the protection now of
me and my people, the same whose vote
carried this decree.
What higher authority could you want?

FIRST DAUGHTER:

> For your blessings, great king,
> > we wish you a treasure-house of
> > > blessings.
> But we ask you one more favor.
> Send our brave-hearted father to advise us.
> He's wise and we listen to his
> > counsel. He'll know best
> > where we should live.
> Even though you now
> > welcome us with kindness,
> people are apt to criticize
> > > foreigners.
> But still I hope for the best,
> > and no harm to our reputation.

(Exeunt PELASGOS and the ARGIVE SOLDIERS. Enter DANAÖS escorted by ARGIVE SOLDIERS and a CHORUS OF ARGIVE WOMEN.)

DANAÖS:

> > > Children,
> we must pray and make
> > sacrifice of burnt offerings and pour
> > libations to the people of
> Argos as if they were Olympian
> > gods, for they have
> > stood by us and been our
> > > > saviors.

> When I had told them what we had
> > suffered, they showed
> > > kindness to you as kin, and
> > bitter hatred toward your cousins.
> To me they assigned this bodyguard of
> > spearsmen, both as an honor and to
> > guard against my death by
> ambush, a death that would be
> > an eternal pollution to this land.

For such gifts we must thank them
        with all our hearts.

Listen to me again now;
        and to the other wisdom I have
        given you, write these words in your
                memory.

Time is the only test,
        the foreigner's only proving-ground,
                and we are foreigners here.
We all have sharp tongues to use against
        foreigners like us, and it's
        easy to let slip a slanderous word;
we must guard against inviting
                                criticism.
So you must bring no disgrace on me with your
        youth that turns men's heads.
Summer fruit is not easily guarded.
Animals, beasts, birds come to
        plunder it, as well as men.
                                What else?
And in matters of love,
Aphrodite spreads her feast in
        gardens of desire, and men when
passing the charming beauty of
        girls, conquered by the sight,
send out bolts of seductive glances to
        enchant them.

Never forget the seas we
        fled across to escape this lust of men,
and the pain we suffered in doing so.
Let us not fall to it again.
Let us not shame ourselves, only to
        delight our enemies.
A new life awaits, my dears,
        and the choice is yours.
To live alone or in company with others,

as the king has offered.
                    And what's more,
            at the city's expense.
    That much is easy.
                    But remember to value
    modesty even more than life itself.

FIRST DAUGHTER:
    I pray the great gods to rain down good
                    fortune upon us!
    As for my summer fruit, father,
            unless the gods have laid new
                                    plans,
            my path is set.

    (Music. Song. Dance.)

DAUGHTERS OF DANAÖS: (Sing.)
                    Sing glory,
                    sing honor
            to the gods of Argos!
        Sing glory and honor
            to the lords who guard it,
        and to all who dwell beside
                ancient Erasinos!
            Hear us, women,
                hear our song,
        for now we praise Argos,
                city of Pelasgians,
            and no longer honor
            the Nile in our hymns.
        For now we praise rivers
            that rise on our plains,
                gentle, life-giving,
                    radiant waters
        that flow through the land and
            give us rich offspring.
                Virgin Artemis,
                    see us,

pity us.
Spare us marriage that
comes by force,
for that way is death.

ARGIVE WOMEN: *(Sing.)*
Never ignore Aphroditê.
With Hera she stands next to Zeus.
And that cunning goddess of love
is greatly praised for her solemn rites.
Dear to their mother are
Passion and seductive Persuasion,
to whom nothing is denied.
And to Harmony is given love's
whispers and cries
and the gentle touching of flesh.

But it is for you I fear,
fugitives fleeing love's hot breath.
Stormwinds rise,
cruelty, suffering,
bloody war threatens the future.
Why was their pursuit so fast,
your kin, your cousins,
the fair crossing?
What Fate has ordained
Fate will see through.
The mind of Zeus cannot be crossed.
May this strife end in marriage.
For many women
marriage is destiny.

DAUGHTERS OF DANAÖS: *(Sing.)*
Zeus,
great Zeus,
protect us!
Not marriage with
Aigyptos' sons!

ARGIVE WOMEN: *(Sing.)*
>
> And yet that might be best.

DAUGHTERS OF DANAÖS: *(Sing.)*
>
> You will never charm me,
> never!

ARGIVE WOMEN: *(Sing.)*
>
> But you know
> nothing of the future!

DAUGHTERS OF DANAÖS: *(Sing.)*
>
> How could I see into
> Zeus' mind?

ARGIVE WOMEN: *(Sing.)*
>
> Then pray a more
> moderate prayer.

DAUGHTERS OF DANAÖS: *(Sing.)*
>
> With what limits?

ARGIVE WOMEN: *(Sing.)*
>
> Make no undue demands
> on heaven.

DAUGHTERS OF DANAÖS: *(Sing.)*
>
> Spare us, Zeus,
> from a hateful marriage
> to men who are loathsome enemies.
> In mercy once
> you saved Io from evil,
> with a healing hand you eased her pain,
> curing her with gentle might.
>
> Zeus, give power,
> give victory
> to the women.
> I am content

with the better share of evil,
content if good
outweighs the bad.
I pray that Justice see justice done,
for my cause is just.
I pray for freedom,
I pray for innocence,
in Justice's name!

(Exeunt DANAÖS and ARGIVE SOLDIERS in procession; after them the DAUGHTERS OF DANAÖS and the ARGIVE WOMEN.)

Prometheus Bound

(ΠΡΟΜΗΘΕΥΣ ΔΕΣΜΩΤΗΣ)

CAST OF CHARACTERS

POWER

VIOLENCE

HÊPHAISTOS *god of fire and the forge*

PROMÊTHEUS

CHORUS OF THE DAUGHTERS OF OCEANOS

FIRST DAUGHTER OF OCEANOS *chorus leader*

OCEANOS

IO

HERMÊS *messenger god*

PROMÊTHEUS BOUND

Skythia.
A desolate mountain crag at the edge of the world.
Enter POWER and VIOLENCE leading PROMÊTHEUS as captive;
    after them HEPHAISTOS.

POWER:
    This is it.
        Skythia.
            Wasteland.
                The world's edge.
    No man sets foot here.
            You!
    Hêphaistos!
            Get busy!
    You know what to do.
    You have orders.
    Straight from the Father.
                    Get on with it!
    Spike this bastard to the crags.
    Iron, iron and steel,
            nothing to break or shatter.
    It was your flower he stole,
                your pride,
            your flaming fire!
    The power that makes all things that
                hands make!
        Yours!
                And gave it to mortals!
        That's his crime.
    That's his offense to the gods.
    And the gods demand payment.
                    He'll learn.
    He'll learn to bow to Zeus' tyranny,
            and like it!
    He'll learn that the gods have no great
            love for man.

HÊPHAISTOS:

Power and Violence,
you've carried out your orders,
Zeus' orders, your duty,
you brought us here,
so what's keeping you?
It's for me to do what comes
next, and I haven't the
heart.
How do I chain a brother-god to this
wintry ravine to be pounded by merciless
storms and cruel weather?
I have to.
I have no choice.
Have to find the heart.
Not even a god turns his back on
Zeus.

Your heart is too good, Promêtheus,
your mind too high,
too proud, too ambitious.
You might have learned good
judgment from your mother Themis,
but you'd have done this deed at any rate.

I'm not the one doing this, I want you to know.
This is no more my will than it is yours.
So I nail you to this man-deserted crag
where no human voice will reach you,
or your eyes see human form.
The sun's bright rays will
scorch you black with his
fire so that you will cry out for
night with her mantle of stars;
and then again for dawn and the sun that
scatters the frost and renews your terrible
pain.
Your burden of torture will never leave.
Every minute of every day and every

night it will bear upon you.
The one who will be your deliverer has
        yet to be born.

And it's your own fault.
        You chose it.
Chose your reward for loving
                                    mankind.

You're a god, Promêtheus,
and you defied the gods,
        refused to tremble before their anger.
You insisted on giving to man gifts
        that no man should possess.
You acted beyond right and justice.
So now you will hang here,
        erect in place,
                never again to move,
        to bend your knee, never know
                rest or sleep—here,
here on this cruel rock, a sentinel
        who will keep eternal watch.
You will cry and scream out your pain.
You will curse and groan.
        But for what?
                For nothing. The mind of
Zeus will never be softened.
All new rulers are harsh.

POWER:
    Get on with it, damn you!
        Don't waste time! Your pity
        makes me sick!
    Learn to hate the god the other gods hate!
    What's the problem?
        He was a traitor!
        He betrayed you!
    Gave your greatest power to human beings!

HÊPHAISTOS:
> And kinship?
> And what about friendship?
>> There's power there, too!

POWER:
>> True.
> But Zeus's orders?
>> You ignore that? Don't they
>> frighten you even more?

HÊPHAISTOS:
> You have a heart of stone.
> You have no pity.

POWER:
> Pity for him cures nothing.
>> Back to work.
> Don't waste time on a lost cause.

HÊPHAISTOS:
> I damn these hands of mine,
>> hate their skill!

POWER:
>> Why?
> Was it your skill that brought him here?

HÊPHAISTOS:
> If only I weren't the one who has to—

POWER:
>> Who else?
> We're all slaves, we all know pain.
> All except the god at the top
>> who rules us all.
> Only Zeus is free.

HÊPHAISTOS:

      I know.
I have only to look at him there to know that.

POWER:

 Begin!
  Now!
   Chain him!
Before Zeus sees you dawdling.

HÊPHAISTOS:

     All right!
 The chains are there!
 Can't you see them?
  Are you blind?

POWER:

 Then chain him! Put his
  hands through. And strike,
 strike hard! With everything you've got.
  Spike him,
   rivet him to the rock!

HÊPHAISTOS:

 All right, all right!
  I'm working.
 It's coming.

POWER:

    Harder!
 Another wedge.
Leave nothing loose. He's a sly one.
He could work his way out of anything.

HÊPHAISTOS:

 This arm won't come loose.

POWER:

 Now the other! That'll teach this
 sophist that he's stupider than Zeus.

HÊPHAISTOS:

                         There.

               Done.

Only this man himself could blame me.

POWER:

     Now the chest.

     Spike his chest to the rock!

                         Harder!

                         Hammer!

     Pin his flesh to the rock!

                         Harder!

                               Hammer harder!

HÊPHAISTOS:

     I groan for you, Promêtheus!

     I groan for your agony!

POWER:

                    Pity again?

     Moaning and groaning for Zeus'
               enemies?

     Take care. You could be next.

(HEPHAISTOS drives in the spike.)

HÊPHAISTOS:

                         Done!

     Here is a sight to tear out the eyes!

POWER:

     I see a bastard getting his due.

     The ribs now.

               Clamp them tight.

HÊPHAISTOS:

     I know what I have to do.

               Don't push me!

POWER:

    O I'll push you all right!

    And hound you!

    Get down there!

        Now!

            The legs!

(HÊPHAISTOS fastens the legs.)

HÊPHAISTOS:

    There.

        Done.

            It didn't take long.

POWER:

    The shackles now!

        Hammer!

        I want them tight!

            Hit hard!

    We have a harsh Overseer.

HÊPHAISTOS:

    You're hard.

            Hard!

    Looks. Voice.

        Hard!

POWER:

    Be as soft as you want,

        just don't harp at me for my strength!

    I know what I want and I do it!

HÊPHAISTOS:

    His legs are shackled.

        Let's go.

(Exit HEPHAISTOS. POWER addresses PROMÊTHEUS.)

POWER:
                              Bastard!
    Let's see your defiance now!
          Plunder the gods privileges!
          Squander them on
                    mortals!
    What can mortals do for you!
⌐ Ease your pain, your
          agony?
                              Ha!
    And that name of yours:
                "Forethought"!
    Let's see a little of that
          forethought get you out of
                                   this!

(Exeunt POWER and VIOLENCE.)
(Music.)

PROMÊTHEUS: *(Speaks.)*
    O Light,
          Light,
                    blessèd Light,
          bright Light of
          day, gleaming sky,
    swift-winged winds, and
          rivers, springing, fed by
                    Ocean, countless, uncountable
    laughing ocean waves, and
          Earth, our mother, mother of us
                all, and Sun, great
          Sun that sees over all,
                all-seeing round,
    I call on you to see what a god may
          suffer at the hands of gods!

(Chants.)

Here is my agony,

here is my torment,
these I will battle
through ten thousand years.
Here,
here is the torture
the new Tyrant of the Blest
has made for me,
bondage,
shameful,
unspeakable!
AIIII!
AIIII!
I groan in pain present,
and groan for pain to be!
When will it end?
Where has he set
the limit?
Where?

(Speaks.)

But what am I saying?
I know the future.
I know what will come.
Forethought they named me, the gods.
No pain will be unexpected,
and it will come. I'll bear it,
my fate, as best I can,
for I know one thing for certain:
Necessity cannot be wrestled down.
To speak, not to speak,
both are hard, for both I am
punished.
I gave our privilege,
the gods' great privilege,
to man, to mortals, and for
that I am yoked to
Necessity,
to this.

From the secret stores of
    heaven I searched out fire,
      the fount of fire,
       where it begins, its
    source, and stashed it, a spark,
in a fennel stalk, and gave it to
               man:
fire that gives every skill,
    every craft, every art,
    fire that fulfils every
      need.
This is my crime, and for this
    I am punished, for this I
      pay, naked, nailed to this
    rock, staked, chained beneath this
      enormity of sky.

(A distant rushing sound as if of wings approaches.)

(Sings.)

Á! Á!
    ÉA! ÉA!
What? What
      sound,
what smell, what
perfume floats by me
on the
    air?
I can't see it,
what it is!
Divine?
    Human?
A demigod?
    What?
What comes to this
rock at the world's
      edge
to see my
    sufferings?

(Chants.)

Behold me,
here,
you I cannot see,
I, a god,
a prisoner chained,
an enemy of Zeus and
all who throng his palace halls!
I who loved man
too much!

This rustle of wings!
I hear it again!
Near!
Nearer!
Wings of birds?
The air whispers
with wings!
I'm afraid!

(Enter the CHORUS OF THE DAUGHTERS OF OCEANOS.)
(Song. Dance.)

DAUGHTERS OF OCEANOS: *(Sing.)*
> Don't be afraid.
> We come in love,
> come because we're friends,
> come in a rivalry of wings
> on the wind's chariot.
> Our father growled,
> father grumbled,
> Father Oceanos,
> but let us come,
> he let us.
> The sound of hammers,
> pounding, pounding,
> iron on iron,
> iron on stone,

echoed in our cavern and we
trembled in terror.
All shyness fled,
all girlish modesty,
and on the wind's swift car we sped here,
in haste, in haste,
on unsandaled feet.

PROMÊTHEUS: *(Speaks.)*
AIIII!
AIIII!
Children of fertile Têthys,
offspring of Oceanos who
circles Earth with never-resting
waters,
behold me here,
pinned to this precipice,
in chains, above this
abyss, keeping eternal
watch that none would
envy!

DAUGHTERS OF OCEANOS: *(Sing.)*
I see,
Promêtheus,
I see,
I see in fear and with tears in my eyes,
I see you, see you
withering on this rock,
your body in pain,
shamefully bound by unbreakable bonds.
A new master steers Olympos.
Zeus lords it over all.
New king,
new laws,
laws that trample Right.
Past glory and mighty powers,
swept away.

PROMÊTHEUS: *(Speaks.)*
>   He should have hurled me
>> down to Tartaros, to Tartaros
>>> beneath even Hades' dismal
>> kingdom, the land of
>> corpses, and bound me in
>> unbreakable
>>>> bonds.
>   Who would see me there,
>> who would shame me with
>   joy at my agony, what
>> god, what man?
>>> No one, none,
> to triumph over me!
>>> But here I hang,
> a toy for winds to
>> play with, a source of
> joy to my
>> enemies.

DAUGHTERS OF OCEANOS: *(Sing.)*
>>> Who could be so hard-hearted,
>>> what god, what enemy,
>>> as to take joy in your misery?
>>> Who but Zeus?
>>> Zeus whose will will never bend;
>>> whose will will crush the children of Father Sky;
>>> who will not end till his heart is glutted,
>>> or someone comes with force or cunning
>>> to toss him from his throne.

PROMÊTHEUS: *(Speaks.)*
>   I'll have my day.
>   It will come, that day,
>> when this Immortal King of the Blest
>> will come to me,
>> will call for me,
>   who suffer here in chains,
>>> in agony,

for I will know what he *must* know,
how his throne and scepter will be
stripped from him.
He will not charm me with
honeyed words of sweet
Persuasion, nor will I bend to the
hammer-blows of his
threats, not till he
sets me free from these cruel chains and
pays me satisfaction for my
outrage.

DAUGHTERS OF OCEANOS: *(Sing.)*
You're bold, Promêtheus,
and brave;
you refuse to give in to pain;
but you speak much too freely.
Fear pierces my heart
for where you will end,
how your ship will sail the sea of pain
and come to a safe harbor.
This son of Kronos,
Zeus,
will never relent,
his heart is fixed,
it can never be moved.

PROMÊTHEUS: *(Speaks.)*
Zeus is hard,
his mind savage, and Justice
he sees as his only.
But the time will come when he will
melt, when that glacier of his
heart will dissolve, when what I
know will come has
crushed him.
Then he'll come,
mild and gentle,
with smiles,

a friend,
and I will have my friend again.

(Music out.)

FIRST DAUGHTER OF OCEANOS:
                    Tell us,
          tell us everything,
      why Zeus took you captive,
          why he tortures,
          humiliates you so
                         bitterly?
          Tell us, please.
      Unless it's too dangerous to
                    speak.

PROMÊTHEUS:
      To tell it is painful,
          and painful not to tell.
      There's misery every way.

      Civil war broke out on Olympos
          when the gods split on whether
              Kronos was to stay in
          power.
      One faction supported Zeus and
              pressed hard to topple
          Kronos and take his
          throne; the other strove that
      Zeus would never rule the gods.
      It was then I appealed with good advice
          to the Titans, those children of
              Earth and Sky.
      But they scorned my cunning strategy.
      In their obstinate self-confidence
          they were certain they would
              win with sheer brute force and
          power of muscle.

Our mother Themis, I told them,
Themis who is also Earth, many names
        but one form, our mother told me
        how the future would turn out.
The war would be won, she said,
                not by force or
        violence, but by cunning,
                as Fate would have it.

I told them all this, but I
        might as well have been talking to stone.
                        And so,
        together with my mother,
we went with what we knew and
        freely offered our services to Zeus.
Thanks to me and my strategy,
        dismal Tartaros is now the dwelling place
                        of ancient Kronos,
        the Titans,
                and all his allies.

Zeus now sits on his throne
        as king of the
                gods—because of me;
        and this is how he repays me:
        with pain and humiliation.
There is a disease shared by tyrants:
        they cannot trust their friends.

But you asked me why he tortures me,
        what is my guilt, and why he
        treats me with such
                        outrage.
I'll tell you.

The war no sooner over,
and he now seated on his father's
        throne, he began dispensing
                privileges to each of the gods,

a different power to each.
But to man he gave
    nothing, nothing for mortal
    humans—except loathing—loathing and the
        resolve to stamp them out,
to start again,
    a whole new race.

And who stood in their
    defense, this race of humans?
No one.
    Only I.
    Only I dared.
And because I dared the race of
    humans was saved from being thrust into
Hades,
    destroyed utterly.
And for that, you see me now,
    wracked,
            tormented,
                    tortured,
        pitiable to behold.
I who pitied humans am shown no
                            pity.
You see here a sight that does
    dishonor to Zeus.

FIRST DAUGHTER OF OCEANOS:
    The heart must be made of
        stone, Promêtheus, that
        feels no pity for your suffering.
    Little as I would have wished to
        see this, now that I see,
            my heart is torn with
        anguish.

PROMÊTHEUS:
    Yes, and what a pitiable sight for my friends.

FIRST DAUGHTER OF OCEANOS:
Was there anything more you did to add to your guilt?

PROMÊTHEUS:
Humans could once foresee their death. I ended that.

FIRST DAUGHTER OF OCEANOS:
What cure could you have found for such a disease?

PROMÊTHEUS:
Blind hope. I sowed blind hope in their hearts to free them.

FIRST DAUGHTER OF OCEANOS:
This is a great gift you gave to mortals.

PROMÊTHEUS:
Yes, but there's more still. I gave them fire.

FIRST DAUGHTER OF OCEANOS:
Those creatures of a day have bright-eyed fire?

PROMÊTHEUS:
And from that they will learn many arts.

FIRST DAUGHTER OF OCEANOS:
I see. And this is the crime for which lord Zeus—

PROMÊTHEUS:
Torments me and will never send relief!

FIRST DAUGHTER OF OCEANOS:
But surely there's a time when this horror will end?

PROMÊTHEUS:
No. None. Not till he sees fit.

FIRST DAUGHTER OF OCEANOS:
When he sees fit?
What kind of hope is that?

Don't you see how you went wrong?
What else can I call it but wrong?
Believe me, this is no pleasure for me,
        and for you it can only be pain.
But enough of that. It's time to find
            some way to free you of your

                                    agony.

PROMÊTHEUS:
It's easy for an outsider to
advise and criticize when he's
        free of the sufferer's
                        pain.
But I knew what I was doing.
        I knew I was doing wrong.
I needed no one to tell me,
            and I don't deny it.
I willed it.
        I did it.
            Of my own free will I did it.
By helping mortal man
        I condemned myself to misery.
But I never dreamed of such a punishment,
to be chained to a desolate crag in midair,
            left to rot—and the loneliness.

But enough of tears and
        wailing over my torment.
Come,
        step down,
                down to Earth,
and let me tell you what's to come,
        my story from end to end.
        Do as I beg you.
            Please. Do as I beg you.
Share with me the misery of one who's
        suffering, for all of us suffer, each in
                            turn.
Sorrow wanders the world
        settling first here, then there.

(Music. Song. Dance.)

DAUGHTERS OF OCEANOS: *(Sing.)*
                    We hear you,
                    Promêtheus,
                 and we answer you.
                    See us now,
                    light of foot,
                step from our chariot,
            down from Sky and Sacred Air,
                  where birds fly,
                    down, down
                 to stony ground.
                    Tell us,
                tell us all of your
                    sorrows.

(Enter OCEANOS on a winged monster.)

OCEANOS: *(Chants.)*
    I left my home, Promêtheus,
    in the depths of Ocean-stream,
    only to see you,
    and a long journey it was.
    I needed no bridle or reins
    to steer this swift-winged monster,
    but did so by the power of mind alone.

    I see your pain, Promêtheus,
    and I feel sorrow for your
    misfortune.
    Not only out of kinship,
    but because we're friends
    and there's nothing I wouldn't
    do for you.
    But you know me.
    I don't deal in flattery.
    Empty, high-sounding words
    are not my style.

So, to the point, dear friend.
How can I help you?
What must I do?
Anything.
You'll never say you have a
faster friend than Oceanos.

(Music out.)

PROMÊTHEUS:
                        Ah, my friend!
What is this?
        Why have you come?
Are you here, too, to see my
               suffering? To see your friend
               Promêtheus in his pain?
How could you bring yourself to
        leave the waters
               named for you, and the
        caves the sea itself carved out,
        and come, here,
             to this iron land,
        to see my misery?
                     Then look.
Look and take your fill of my
               pain.
I, the friend of Zeus,
        I, who set him on his
throne and put
        power in his grip,
             and this is my reward.

OCEANOS:
    I see you, Promêtheus.
        Indeed I see you.
    And I want you, for all your
        cunning and cleverness, your
            intelligence—I want you to
        hear some good advice I have for you—

no, in fact, the best advice,
the best I have to give.

Know yourself.
        That's it.
     It's that simple.
Know yourself, adapt yourself.
These are new times, and new
     times have new ways. And
         this new time has a new tyrant, a new
     ruler of the gods.
You must change, my friend,
     change to suit the
        times, to fit in.
If you continue in the way you're going,
     hard, harsh words with every breath,
Zeus can't help but hear you,
     far off as he is, up there in the sky.
And when he does,
     when he hears you, your
        present suffering will seem like
     child's play.
Give it up, my friend,
       give up this attitude, this
     anger of yours.
            You're in pain,
so learn control and find a way
     free of your misery.

O I know what you're thinking.
You've heard it all before.
       Old advice.
Old, maybe, but none
     better.

I presume you know what put you here.
An excess of arrogance and a braggart's
     tongue. A little humility
would help; but you won't

have that. You refuse to yield,
    to turn with the time.
You prefer to pile pain on pain until you're
        buried.

      Let me teach you.
      Let me try.
First of all, don't kick the goad.
He's a hard master, our new
    leader, accountable to no one.

All right, I'm going.
I'll try working on him
    to get you out of this.
In the meantime, control yourself
    and keep that razor tongue of yours
        in check.

The only thing, I think, you've never
    learned is that foolish words never escape
        punishment.

PROMÊTHEUS:
How lucky you are!
    You dared with me,
    you shared with me.
        Everything.
And yet you're free of blame and
        punishment.
I envy you.
    Stay out of it.
    You're only heading for trouble.
He won't change.
    His mind is set.
Persuasion will get you nowhere.

OCEANOS:
You're better at advising others than yourself.
I take my cue not from what you say,

but what you do.
No, my mind is made up.
    I'm going, and don't try to
        stop me.
I know he'll listen,
    I'm certain.
Zeus *will* do me this favor,
        and set you free.

PROMÊTHEUS:
    Thank you, my friend,
    thank you for your loyalty, your
        eagerness.
            I'm grateful.
    But you mustn't trouble yourself on my
        account. I mean, well,
        if that's what you intend.
                You'll fail.
    All that effort, and you'll
                fail.
    My advice is to do nothing.
    Stay clear of it all, for your
        own sake. Steer clear of
            harm. Keep your silence.
    Over my head in misfortune myself,
        why should I want to drag my
        friends in after me?
    I have enough anguish as it is
        with my brother Titan,
            Atlas,
        who stands at the world's western edge
    supporting the twin pillars of Heaven and Earth,
        no easy burden for any
                shoulders.

    Pity struck me, too, for Typhos,
        that hundred-headed, Earthborn
            monster who dwelt in the caves of
    Cilicia and was put down by
        violence.

He challenged the gods,
 hissing terror from his horrid
 jaws, his eyes glaring like gorgon
glances, thinking that with violence he could
  topple the tyranny of Zeus.
But Zeus' lightning bolt that never
 sleeps hurled its deadly flaming
 breath at him, blasting his
boasting tongue and scorching his
 heart, his strength sent packing.
      He lies there now,
 helpless, limp,
an unrecognizable sprawl at the
sea's narrows, clenched tight
 in the clawing roots of mighty
Aetna that rises above him.
On its summit sits limping Hêphaistos,
  the eternal smithy,
 hammering out iron
 from the molten ore.
One day rivers of fire will
 leap from that peak, and flowing
  devour Sicily's fruitful plains.
This will be Typhos,
 Typhos burnt to ashes by Zeus' thunderbolt,
  but his rage will spew out
 mountains of glowing
 rock and fiery spray.

    You're no fool.
You've been around.
Be warned. Save yourself
 however you can.
I'll bear it, my fate,
 stick it out, drain it to the
      dregs.
Until the time when Zeus thinks differently.

OCEANOS:
>Surely you know, Promêtheus,
>>that words are a cure for the sick mind?

PROMÊTHEUS:
>If the time is right, yes.
>If the heart is soft.
>But you can't reduce the swelling
>>of a mind still hard.

OCEANOS:
>I'm over-eager, then?
>Is that what you're saying?
>What's the harm there?
>>Tell me.

PROMÊTHEUS:
>You're wasting your time.
>>It's nonsense.

OCEANOS:
>Then let it be. Allow me this
>>illness. Let me seem a
>>>fool but be wise underneath.

PROMÊTHEUS:
>That would seem to be my condition, not yours.

OCEANOS:
>It's obvious you're saying: Go home.

PROMÊTHEUS:
>Pity for me will get you hatred.

OCEANOS:
>From our new Almighty Master, you mean?

PROMÊTHEUS:
>Beware of rousing his heart against you.

OCEANOS:
>Yes, I learn quickly. From the sight of you.

PROMÊTHEUS:
>Then leave. Now. Before you forget.

OCEANOS:
>No need to say it twice.
>>I'm on my way.
>My swift-winged monster
>>is eager to get back home to his
>>>own stall.

(Exit OCEANOS on his winged monster.)
(Music. Song. Dance.)

DAUGHTERS OF OCEANOS: *(Sing.)*
>I weep for you,
>Promêtheus,
>I mourn for you,
>for your bitter fate.
>Tears flood my eyes like streaming brooks,
>my gentle eyes,
>stain my soft cheeks.
>Zeus rules by oppression and tyranny,
>new laws of his own making,
>trampling the ancient gods of old.

>All the Earth cries out its grief,
>loud laments for your once great power,
>mighty, honored power,
>you and your brothers,
>glorious Titans.
>Men of Asia's sacred land,
>ancient plains,
>howl,
>howl with you in your pain.

>And so in Kolchis,

Amazons,
who know no fear in battle,
and Skythians,
who live at the world's edge by
Lake Maiotis;
and the warlike flower of Arabia,
mountain warriors
who guard the high citadel near
Kaukasos,
warriors bristling for battle
with clashing spears.

I know of only one other
so savagely punished:
Atlas,
powerful Atlas,
god of great strength,
who heaves up Earth and Heaven
on his shoulders
and groans.

All things moan for Promêtheus.
Waves roll and crash and cry as they fall,
the deeps lament and dismal Hades
rumbles in its depths,
and rivers, streams,
all, all,
cry your terrible,
piteous torment.

(Music out.)

PROMÊTHEUS:
You think me stubborn, do you?
Stiff-necked, proud, arrogant?
Because I am silent,
because I say nothing?
No.
Not true.

My heart is eaten away with
painful brooding at the outrage
I'm made to suffer,
the brutality, the humiliation.
                    Who but I
assigned their privileges and powers
among these upstart gods?
But why speak of that? Why tell
what you already know?
Listen at least to this.
Listen to how men's minds were empty,
how they were helpless as babies,
and how I brought them thought,
the power to reason,
I brought them intelligence.
I say this not to shame them, but to
show how great-hearted, how kind were the
gifts I gave them.

They had eyes,
but did not see,
ears, but did not hear.
They dragged their way through their
long burden of days like figures in
dreams, confused,
                    directionless.
What did they know of building houses of
bricks to bask in the
warm rays of the sun?
                    Nothing.
And nothing of working in wood.
Like ants they lived in swarms beneath the Earth,
in caves and caverns never lighted by the sun.
Nor did they know the seasons by their signs:
winter, flowering spring, and
summer heavy with harvests of fruit and crops.
Life had no reason behind it,
                    no order.

I showed them how the stars moved through the sky,
    their risings and their settings; no easy
        text to decipher.
I gave them numbers then,
    my own invention,
    of all skills the most useful,
                mathematics.
And letters,
    the servant of memory,
    eternal storehouse of knowledge,
        mother of arts.
I yoked wild beasts, the first to do so,
    tamed them to bearing man's weightiest burdens.
I broke horses, too, and harnessed them
    beneath the chariot, made them love the reins,
      the playthings of the wealthy.
                And then ships.
I gave them ships,
    ships, my own invention,
      mine alone,
linen-winged chariots for sailors to ride the seas.

These were the gifts I gave to man—I who have no
    cleverness to escape this agony of my own.

FIRST DAUGHTER OF OCEANOS:
    You've suffered pain and humiliation.
    Your mind wanders into distraction,
      like a bad doctor taken ill and
        unable to find the cure.

PROMÊTHEUS:
    Hear the rest and be even more
            amazed.
    I'll tell you of the crafts and
      methods I found for them.
            The greatest,
    the way to health.
Before, they had nothing.

They grew ill, they shriveled and
    died, no cure, neither to eat or drink
    or rub into the skin,
                nothing.
I showed them then how to mix
    herbs into remedies to soothe ills,
    but also to avoid all disease.
           And then prophecy.
I gave them many ways to see the
    future. The first to see what in
    dreams would come true, how to
        unravel oracles, chance phrases caught in
passing, omens met on the
    road, and the lore of birds.
Crook-clawed birds in flight,
    which bring luck, which not,
how they live, their likes, their
    hates, what others they
        cohabit with.
I taught them of the smoothness of
    entrails; what color bile would be
    pleasing to the gods; and the speckled
    symmetry of liver-lobes.
I wrapped thigh bones in fat,
      and long, graceful backbones,
    and burned them, showing mortals
      the path to this difficult
            art.
I instructed them in the reading of signs in
    flames, which before they could not
        see.

              But enough of these.
What of the riches hidden beneath the Earth?
Who before me could
    claim to have discovered them?
Bronze and iron and silver and gold!
Every one of them a benefit to man!
           Who?

Who but a babbling fool?

One word sums it up.
All human skill and science was
    the gift of Promêtheus.

FIRST DAUGHTER OF OCEANOS:
    Yes, but you gave more than you should,
        more than was right,
            and forgot your own self in the bargain.
    But I know that one day you'll be freed and
        rival Zeus in power.

PROMÊTHEUS:
    No; not yet; that's not yet
        written in destiny.
    There's no escape till I'm bent by
        ten thousand torments.
            Necessity is greater than skill.

FIRST DAUGHTER OF OCEANOS:
    And who is the helmsman of Necessity?

PROMÊTHEUS:
    The threefold Fates and the watchful Furies.

FIRST DAUGHTER OF OCEANOS:
    And Zeus has less power than they?

PROMÊTHEUS:
    Not even Zeus escapes what destiny holds.

FIRST DAUGHTER OF OCEANOS:
    And what is that destiny? Eternal rule?

PROMÊTHEUS:
    Don't ask. You'll never learn that. Not yet.

FIRST DAUGHTER OF OCEANOS:
What is this solemn secret you're hiding?

PROMÊTHEUS:
Ask whatever you like, not that.
You'll never drag that from me.
The time is not right.
Not yet.
The secret must be kept.
That knowledge is my only escape
from these chains and humiliation.

(Music. Song. Dance.)

DAUGHTERS OF OCEANOS: *(Sing.)*
May Zeus never,
never,
never may Zeus,
All-powerful Zeus,
impose his power against my will.
Let me never fail,
never fail,
to make holy offerings to gods,
feasts made holy with the blood of bulls,
blood drenching the altars
by Ocean's unending stream.
And may I never offend in any
word.
I pray that these pillars of piety
support me beyond collapse.

How sweet,
how sweet is the life of
length of days,
life lived in hope and joy,
a soul that feeds on
radiant happiness.
But I tremble,
tremble to see you,

Promêtheus,
see you like this,
wracked with pain,
tortured with ten thousand torments.
You refused to cower to Zeus;
you gave to man too much,
Promêtheus.

You gave,
gave all,
and what did you receive?
What but nothing?
What good did it do you?
What help can impotent man
who lives for a day give?
What?
You must have seen their infirmity,
their blindness,
their weakness,
feeble as a dream phantom,
shackled to darkness.
No plan of men will ever outstrip
the order of Zeus'
law.

This song I sing today,
Promêtheus,
this song,
this song of pain,
I learned from seeing your dizzying
anguish.
How far from the song I
sang for your wedding,
your wedding bath,
your wedding bed,
when you wooed and won
my sister Hesione,
a song for you to bring her
home.

(Enter IO, a young woman with the horns of a heifer.)

IO: *(Chants.)*
What land is this?
What people?
What creature
beaten by storms
is yoked by this
rock?
What have you done
to suffer so terrible
a punishment?
Tell me.
Where have I come to?

(Sings in frenzy.)

Á!
   Á!
É!
   É!

again
     again
stinging
      stinging
it bites me
my body
bites
   bites
phantom demon
ghost of Argos
Earthborn
      Argos
gadfly Argos
keep him away
keep him
     AIIII!
away

AIIIII!
thousand-eyed herdsman
                              Argos
his eyes scaring me
terror
        AIIII!
even in death he
wanders the
                    Earth
to hunt me
                stalk me
from the dark of the
                          dead
he comes
he comes to hound me
drive me
starving down to the
                          sandy
shore

(Less frenzied.)

The reed-pipe
                  drones
its monotonous hum,
the drowsy hum
that invites to
                  sleep.
IOOOO!
                IOOOO!
Where have I wandered?
Where am I wandering?
What did I do,
                Zeus
son of Kronos, what,
to be yoked with such
suffering,
to be driven mad,
tormented,

           terrorized,
by this stinging gadfly?
É!
   É!
Burn me,
bury me,
feed me to the
             sea,
to monsters of the
              deep,
but hear me,
          hear,
hear me, lord Zeus,
I've suffered enough,
wandered too far,
stripped naked by
pain, by
        anguish,
agony.
How, how do I
flee this
       misery?
Lord, do you hear this
cow-horned girl?

PROMÊTHEUS: *(Speaks.)*
    The voice of Io,
        daughter of Inachos!
    How could I not know it?
    You fired the heart of
        Zeus with passion, and now,
          gadfly-stung,
    you run through the world
        pursued by Hera's
          hate.

IO: *(Sings.)*
    How do you know me,
    my name,

how?
Io, daughter of Inachos.
You know my
                god-sent
pain, my agony, my
wandering that
                    wastes me
away, the sting that
drives me mad with
suffering.
Who are you, you who
suffer the same as I,
you who know the
                        truth of me?
É!
    É!
Tormented I come here,
starving I come here,
high leaping I come here,
prodded,
            prodded
by Hera's
            hate!
Hera broke me,
Hera,
        my spirit,
broke me!
Who in all the company
of the
        unfortunate
endures such pain
as mine?
Tell me, o tell me
the pain I have yet
to suffer,
                what fate lies
ahead, what
                remedy,
what cure to

                    end this horror?
Tell me, o tell me
if you
        know.
Tell me,
tell the wandering
                    girl.

(Music out.)

PROMÊTHEUS:
    Yes, I'll tell you.
    I'll tell you all.
        No riddles.
        Clearly.
    As a friend should to a friend.
    You see here the man who gave
    fire to mankind:
        Promêtheus.

IO:
    Promêtheus!
    What a beacon to humanity you have been!
    But what was your crime?
    Why are you suffering?
        Tell me.

PROMÊTHEUS:
    I've only now told my tale of tears.

IO:
    But not to me. Won't you give me this gift?

PROMÊTHEUS:
    Ask whatever you wish.

IO:
    Who nailed you to this ravine?

PROMÊTHEUS:

The will of Zeus, the hands of Hêphaistos.

IO:

What crime could earn such punishment?

PROMÊTHEUS:

No, it's enough I've said what I've said.

IO:

Then tell me the end of my wandering.

PROMÊTHEUS:

It's better not to know.

IO:

Tell me what must I endure.

PROMÊTHEUS:

I don't begrudge you this favor.

IO:

Then why not tell me everything?

PROMÊTHEUS:

I don't want to break your spirit.

IO:

I want to hear the worst.

PROMÊTHEUS:

Yes, if you insist. I can't refuse.

FIRST DAUGHTER OF OCEANOS:

                Not yet.
Let me, too, have a share of this
                        gift.
Let her tell us first what caused her
     disease, her great misfortune,

and then she can learn from you
            the suffering still to come.

PROMÊTHEUS:
     It's your turn now to grant a favor, Io,
     especially since these are your father's
           sisters. Besides,
     a sympathetic ear for a sad tale
           makes it easier to bear.

IO:

               I can hardly refuse.
I'll tell you all you ask.
       Even so,
it shames me to speak of the
           storm the god let loose upon me,
           my lovely body deformed
               as you see.

Visions would come to my bed at night,
           dream-phantoms with
               soft, seductive voices,
           whispering, whispering: "Why so
selfish, Io? Still a virgin,
           and Zeus longing to
       hold you in his embrace.
How lovely you are,
           and lovely, too, in the eye of Zeus
whose heart is stung with passion for you.
               What a match you could make.
     The highest power.
       Zeus himself to
               love you.
       Now, girl, now.
Out to Lerna's grassy meadows with you,
           where your father's sheep and cattle graze,
           and ease the great lord's passion."

Such dreams plagued me night after night,

till one day I went to my father, and
he sent to Delphi and Dodona
messengers to learn what word or deed
            would appease the gods.
But they brought back only riddling, muddled
                            oracles.
Then one day it came,
      an oracle,
            clear,
      to my father,
            from Apollo:
"Banish her,
banish the girl,
from your house,
from your country,
let her wander the wide Earth to its
very ends.
Refuse and Zeus' fiery thunderbolt will
dash to perdition
you, your house, and your
                        race!"

Hearing the words of Apollo,
      my father yielded,
tears in his eyes, as in mine,
      and banished me from my
            home and country.
Zeus' bridle-bit dug deep in his mouth.
Suddenly I was changed,
      deformed,
            my mind,
            my body,
            these horns,
      as you see!
Stung by the savage-toothed
      gadfly, I bucked and ran, my
            mind maddened, for the sweet
      waters of Kerchneia and Lerna's
                        spring.

And there was Argos,
    Earthborn Argos,
        Argos of the fierce temper,
    herding me, staring, his
hundred eyes, spying on my
            every step.
At once then Fate stole his life
    when he least expected.
But still the gadfly goads me,
    drives me to the ends of the Earth.

        You have my story.
Now tell me what lies ahead,
    what sorrows will come.
Don't pity me and cover me with lies.
False words are the foulest plague.

(Music. Song. Dance.)

DAUGHTERS OF OCEANOS: *(Sing.)*
        ÉA!
        ÉA!
        APECHE!
        FÉU!
      I can't listen!
      Can't listen!
      Terrible!
     Terrible words
I never thought to hear!
Horrible story, horrible!
      Suffering!
       Terror!
      Outrage!
    I can't watch,
      can't see it!
My soul is pierced!
    I can't endure!
     I shudder,
      shudder,

                              at your fate,
                              poor Io!

(Music out.)

PROMÊTHEUS:
    You cry out too soon.
    Hold off your moans and fears
        till you hear what's to come.

FIRST DAUGHTER OF OCEANOS:
    Tell her then. It helps when ill
    to know beforehand what's to come.

PROMÊTHEUS:
    Your first request was easy for me to grant;
    you wanted her to tell of her own
                            troubles.
        I'll now tell you the rest,
    the agony still to come for this child
            so hated by Hera.

    Io, daughter of Inachos, listen to me,
        take my words to heart, and you'll
        know when your journey has reached its
                            end.

                    When you leave here,
    turn in the direction of the rising sun and
        proceed across plains and meadows
                never plowed.
    You will arrive at the site of the
            Skythian nomads who live in the air in
            wicker huts on ox-carts with
                sturdy wheels. Beware,
    these people are archers who kill from
                great distances.
    Make your way through their land,
            but don't come near them; keep your
            feet to the rugged shore of the

sea where the surf breaks with a
                              roar,
      and so pass on.

At your left you'll come upon the Chalybes,
      iron workers. Stay clear of them,
            they're savages, and
      death to strangers.
The Hybristes is next, a river as
      violent as its name. Don't cross it,
it's almost impossible, but
      follow it to its source, upward,
                        upward,
to the highest pinnacle of mighty
Kaukasos, where it gushes downward in a raging
      torrent. It is there,
            at the world's ceiling,
      scraping the stars, that you will
      cross the crest and head south.

You will come by that route to the
      land of the Amazons, women warriors
who hate men, and whose home will
      one day be Themiskyra on the
      banks of the River Thermodon.
It is here the rocky sea-jaws of Salmydessos,
      cruel stepmother of ships,
            welcomes sailors to their death.
They'll help you, those man-hating Amazons,
      help you on your way,
            and gladly, too.

Next you will reach the Crimea,
      the isthmus, the narrow gateway
      leading to the lake.
Leaving it behind, you must be
      brave and cross the Maiotic Strait.
                  Having done so,
for all time the world will speak of your

crossing, and call it Bosporos:
    the Cow-crossing.

Europe now behind you,
    the continent of Asia lies before.

Do the Daughters of Oceanos now
    see how this tyrant of the gods is
equally violent to all without discrimination?
Io, the mortal, had imposed upon her
    the agony of these wanderings
only because he lusted for her.

Dear Io, yours was a savage seducer.
                    And yet,
    not all I've said is even
    prologue to your pain.

IO:
    IO MOI MOI! É! É!

PROMÊTHEUS:
    Yes, moan your mournful wail!
    How will you take it when you
        hear of the terrors to come?

FIRST DAUGHTER OF OCEANOS:
    More? More suffering to tell?

PROMÊTHEUS:
    A storm, a winter sea of troubles.

IO:
              Why live then?
    Why not hurl myself from this rock and
    end it all, smashed on the earth
                    below?
    Better to die than to
        live out my days in agony.

PROMÊTHEUS:

                And me?
    How would you endure my pain?
    I who will never know death,
          never know the relief that
          death can bring, the freedom from
                pain.
    There's no end to my suffering
          till Zeus is hurled from his tyrant's throne.

IO:

    Zeus? Fall from power?

PROMÊTHEUS:

    You'd welcome that, I know.

IO:

    I would. It's at his hand I suffer.

PROMÊTHEUS:

    Rejoice, then, for it will happen.

IO:

    Who will strip him of his scepter?

PROMÊTHEUS:

    Himself. Himself and his mindless strategy.

IO:

    How? Tell me, if it's no hurt to you.

PROMÊTHEUS:

    He'll make a marriage that will harm him one day.

IO:

    With a goddess or a mortal? Tell me.

PROMÊTHEUS:

    You mustn't ask. I can't tell you.

IO:

And his wife will hurl him from the throne?

PROMÊTHEUS:

She'll give a son mightier than his father.

IO:

And from that there's no escape?

PROMÊTHEUS:

Only me—if I were freed of these chains.

IO:

But who's to free you? Zeus forbids it.

PROMÊTHEUS:

As fate has it, a descendant of yours.

IO:

A son of mine—will free you?

PROMÊTHEUS:

A descendant in the thirteenth generation.

IO:

This is a riddling prophecy I don't understand.

PROMÊTHEUS:

Then ask me no more questions about your own sufferings.

IO:

Don't first make promises and then break them.

PROMÊTHEUS:

I have two stories to tell. You can have one.

IO:

What are they? Tell me. Let me choose.

PROMÊTHEUS:
                    Yes.
I'll either tell you what more you'll
    suffer, or who will free me.

FIRST DAUGHTER OF OCEANOS:
                    No,
give one to her and one to me.
Don't begrudge me my share.
Tell her first about her wanderings,
        and then me about your rescuer.
It's what I want.

PROMÊTHEUS:
Eager as you are,
    I won't refuse.
First, I'll tell you, Io, of your
    wanderings. Write them,
        inscribe them in your mind, and
                    remember.

Once you have crossed the
        channel between Europe and
        Asia, turn toward the flaring eye of the
            rising sun, and wander across
the waves of the surgeless
        sea till you come to the Gorgonian
            plains of Kisthênê.
Here you will find the daughters of Phorkeus,
        three ancient virgins who
share one eye and one tooth, and whose
            hair is white as a swan.
Neither sun nor moon has ever
                        seen them.

Near them their three sisters abide,
        Gorgons,
man-hating winged women with

snakes for hair, whom no one
looks on and survives.
Such is the danger I warn you of.

But now there comes another horrible sight.

Beware of Zeus' silent, unbarking
hounds with sharp beaks,
the Griffins.
Stay clear of them, but also of the
one-eyed Arimaspians,
horse warriors who live beside Pluto's stream
that flows with gold.
Stay away.

You will then come to a distant land,
to the edge of the world opposite to me,
where the men are black,
the land of the Sun's source,
and the River Aithiop.
Follow along its banks to the Great Cataract
where sacred Nile with its pure, sweet waters
bursts from the Papyros Mountains.
And he,
that great river,
will lead you down to the Delta where
you, Io, you and your descendants,
will found your distant and long-enduring
colony.

If anything I've said has not been clear,
ask and I'll explain.
I have the time,
and more than I would like.

FIRST DAUGHTER OF OCEANOS:
If there's more to tell her of her
ruinous wanderings, or you've left
anything out, tell her.

Otherwise move on to what you promised me.
    I know you remember.

PROMÊTHEUS:
    She's heard everything now,
        everything up to the end of her
                wanderings.
    But to prove to her the truth of my words,
        I'll now tell of her sufferings
      before she came here.

    I'll speak only of these last days,
        the events that led to your
                arrival.

    You came to the plains of Molossos,
        to the sheer ridges that tower above
        Dodona, where Thesprotian Zeus
           has his throne and oracle.
  It was there the oracular
      oaks miraculously spoke, and
      not in riddles, but told you clearly
  that your destiny was to be the bride of
                Zeus.

    Does this make you smile, Io?

        Then, goaded by the gadfly,
  you fled to the shore of the Gulf of Rhea,
  where you were turned back by a storm and
      again fled inland into Skythia.
              But know this,
  that sea will be named after you,
      the Ionian, and men
        for all time will know that you once
      passed here.

    This will be a sign to you
        that I see more than may be
           seen.

As for the rest,
   resuming where I left off my tale,
I'll tell both you and her together.

There is a city,
        Kanobos,
at the utmost edge of the land of
        Egypt, at the Nile's mouth where
               silt clogs the sea.
There, finally, Zeus will
        restore your reason, with a hand's
touch, no more, and you will
        know no fear.
That will be enough to implant you with a
        dark-skinned son,
Epaphos, born by touch,
        son of Zeus, and he will harvest
               all the land that great Nile
                          waters.

Danaös, his descendant in the fifth
        generation, will return from there to
Argos with his fifty daughters,
               not of their own will,
               but to save them from
        marriage with their own cousins.
In heated, lustful pursuit, like
        hawks for doves, these cousins will
               descend on their prey;
        but the gods will forbid the
marriage and their possession of the
               girls' bodies.
The Argive earth will accept these
        sons of Egypt in
death when through the daring cunning
        of the girls their throats are
               slit in the dark of night and the
earth drinks up their blood.

I wish such love for my enemies as well!

But one of those girl will fall
        prey to passion and rescue her
        lover from death,
                preferring to be called
coward rather than murderer.
                        It is she,
your descendant, who will
found the royal line of Argive
                                kings.

To tell it all to you would be
        a long tale, but one of her
descendants, a man of bravery and
        famed for archery, will
free me from my agonies.

This is the prophecy given me by Themis,
        my ancient Titan mother.
How it will happen and when is too
        long a tale to tell you,
and would be of no use to you.

IO:

                ELELEÚ!
        ELELEÚ!
                spasm
                        again again
        madness
                burning
        burning my brain
                                        AIIII!

                fire fire
        stings gadfly
                spear speadhead
        not by fire
    forged
                        sticks

AIII!
sticks fear-struck
heart kicks
    ribs
        roll
            eyes roll
madness madness
spin spin round
               AII!
where is my
      course
blasts blow me
         madness
whirlwind
        tongue run wild
        wild words
      words muddy words
dash against waves of
                doom

(Exit IO.)
(Music. Song. Dance.)

DAUGHTERS OF OCEANOS: *(Sing.)*
      He was wise,
      that man,
      wise who said,
    who weighed in his mind,
that to marry in your class is best,
    like to like is best.
      Never, never
    should the poor aspire,
those who work with their hands,
  to marry men puffed with
      wealth or mighty in
      pride of birth.

      Never, o never,
  majestic goddesses of Fate,

never may you see me
come to the bed of Zeus,
to Zeus' bed as mistress,
nor be the bride of any god.
I tremble to see the loveless virginity of Io,
maiden Io who shuns her would-be mate,
Io,
wandering Io,
Io sorely wounded by
Hera's hate.

But for me,
the marriage of equals brings no fear.
I do not dread it.
My fear is the eye of some
mighty god
casting his irresistible light on me.
That is a fight not to be fought,
not to be won.
What I would do,
I can't say.
How do I flee
Zeus' design?

(Music out.)

PROMÊTHEUS:
Hear me all who can hear.
Zeus in his willful, arrogant
   mind will be humbled yet and brought
   low, for at this moment he is
planning a marriage that will
      hurl him from his tyrant's
   throne and into
            oblivion.
His father Kronos
      once fell from his ancient throne
            and in falling uttered a curse, which
      Zeus now brings to

consummation.

      Except for me,
there is no god who can show him the
  means to escape destruction,
   so great are his troubles.
I alone know the when and the how.
So let him sit on his throne
  deluding himself in his
    safety. Let him
trust in his rumbling thunder down the skies,
his rattling fistful of fire-spewing lightning.
     Nothing,
    nothing,
   not even these, can
save him from ruin, being
  wrestled to earth in dishonor and
   ignominy, for now, even now he is
planting the seed of that hero who will
     lay him low with a triple fall,
himself against himself,
     a prodigy,
a wonder of irresistible might—this giant
  who will find fire to outface Zeus'
    lightning, and roaring that will
  confound his petty thunder.
Poseidon's trident that makes the sea to
    heave, the land to
   shiver, will be shattered, and
Zeus in his plunge from power will
    learn the difference between
  sovereignty and
      slavery.

FIRST DAUGHTER OF OCEANOS:
These threats you hurl at Zeus are only wished.

PROMÊTHEUS:
Wishes, perhaps, but they will happen.

FIRST DAUGHTER OF OCEANOS:

And you say there's a power that will conquer Zeus?

PROMÊTHEUS:

His punishment will be harder on the neck than mine.

FIRST DAUGHTER OF OCEANOS:

How can you hurl such threats and not be afraid?

PROMÊTHEUS:

Afraid? What's to be afraid of? I'm immortal!

FIRST DAUGHTER OF OCEANOS:

He can make you suffer worse than any death.

PROMÊTHEUS:

Then let him! I'm ready. He has no surprises for me.

FIRST DAUGHTER OF OCEANOS:

Wise men bow down to Necessity.

PROMÊTHEUS:

Bow down, grovel, kiss the ground under
        Zeus' feet! But to me he's
                nothing, less than the
        dust he walks on! Let him
        lord it over the little time left him!

(HERMÊS appears.)

But no, wait,
        what have we here?
Zeus' private errand-boy?
Kowtowing ass-wipe of the
        latest Tyrant?
Surely he's come with
                        news.

HERMÊS:

You!

You there!

Yes, you who think you're so smart!

Cleverer than clever,

bitterer than

bitter! You who have

angered the gods by honoring those

creatures of a day with the gods'

privileges!

You,

you who stole fire from the

gods, I'm talking to you!

You boast of a marriage that will

topple him from power.

The Father demands to know what you

know.

These are his orders. And he'll

have no riddling speeches from you.

The truth and nothing but,

all of it, you hear?

And I warn you,

I won't be called back

a second time, Promêtheus.

Zeus knows what he

wants, and he gets it.

PROMÊTHEUS:

Ah, what a grand speech, Hermês,

little god that you are.

Pompous and puffed with

pride, as befits a puppet of the

gods.

Little man, you're new,

new as your gods, and deceive yourselves

that your battlements are free of

threats.

But I have seen two tyrants
    hurled from those heights,
and a third, this latest installment of
    divinity,
is about to follow them in their
    downward plunge.
It will be swift, and will not be
    lacking in shame.

Do you think these upstart gods make me
    tremble and cringe?
                     No.
    Not a chance.
Now, get on back to where you came from,
    scamper off home, and tell your
    fledgling tyrant I have
nothing to say.

HERMÊS:
    Outrageous behavior like this is what
    moored you here in this harbor of calamity.

PROMÊTHEUS:
    Make no mistake:
    nothing could make me trade my
        misery for your servility.

HERMÊS:
    Yes, well, undoubtedly it's better being a
    slave to this rock than Zeus' personal,
        trusted messenger god.

PROMÊTHEUS:
    You seem to know the language of the insolent.

HERMÊS:
    You seem to revel in your present misery.

PROMÊTHEUS:

    Revel? I wish my enemies such
        reveling, and you among them!

HERMÊS:

    What are you saying? You blame me for this?

PROMÊTHEUS:

    You? No. I hate all the gods.
    I put them in power and they do this to me!

HERMÊS:

    I say you're out of your mind. What you say is sick.

PROMÊTHEUS:

    If it's sick to hate your enemies, then welcome sickness.

HERMÊS:

    If you were well and prosperous, you'd be insufferable.

PROMÊTHEUS:

    AIIIIIIIII!

HERMÊS:

    Cry out in pain all you like. Zeus is deaf.

PROMÊTHEUS:

    Then time will unstop his ears.

HERMÊS:

    Has time taught you good sense?

PROMÊTHEUS:

    No, or I wouldn't be talking to a slave.

HERMÊS:

    You'll say nothing the Father demands?

PROMÊTHEUS:
    Yes, despite all I owe him.

HERMÊS:
    You treat me like a child.

PROMÊTHEUS:
    But you are a child, aren't you?
        No, sillier than a child.
    You expect me to tell you
            everything.
    Zeus can do nothing.
        Zeus is helpless. Nothing will
        pry from me what he needs to
                        know.
    Not till I'm freed from these shameful chains.
    So let him hurl his lightning fire!
    Let him send blizzards to confound the world,
        and rolling thunder deep in the belly of Earth!
    I will not be bent!
    I will not stoop to tell him whose
        hands will topple him from his
                        sovereignty!

HERMÊS:
    Think what this foolish, stubborn pride will get you?

PROMÊTHEUS:
    I thought it out long ago and my mind is resolved.

HERMÊS:
                        Fool!
    Change your mind!
        Force yourself!
            Think!
    Think of the pain!
        While there's still time!

PROMÊTHEUS:

  Why hound me like this?
  Go lecture the tides of the sea.
  Zeus is no terror to me.
  Zeus and his will
      will never turn me womanish,
          palms up in prayer,
  begging release from my chains.
                              Never!

HERMÊS:

  Why waste more words?
  I've done what I can.
  Begged you and still you refuse to
                          relent.
  You're like a young colt, new-harnessed,
      straining at the bit,
      struggling, bucking,
          fighting the reins.
  But what use is it, this tactic of yours?
  This rabid, confident belief in your
      cleverness is your downfall.
  Stubborn-headedness gets you
      nowhere when you're wrong.
                  It's useless.
  Either my words persuade you or you can
      look for a storm of such force to come down on you
      like a triple sea of troubles that will
                              destroy you.
      There's no escape.
  First, the Father's thunder and lightning will
  shatter this craggy cliff and enfold your
  chained body in a rocky womb in the earth.
                  After eons
      you will return to the light of the sun,
      and Zeus' winged hound,
          the ravening eagle,
  will invite himself to your banquet,
  tearing your flesh to ragged bits,

and all day long feast on your liver till it's
    black with his gnawing.

Expect no term to your agony, until, of course,
some god appears to take on your suffering and
    descends into the farthest reaches of Hades,
the dead dark depths where River Tartaros
                      flows.

There it is.
    I've said it.
It's for you to decide.
This is no idle fiction I've spun,
    no boast, but truth.
The mouth of Zeus speaks no lies.
And what he speaks is accomplished.

Look around you.
              Consider.
Which is better?
Stubbornness?
Or common sense?

(Music. Song. Dance.)

FIRST DAUGHTER OF OCEANOS:
    His advice is good, Promêtheus.
    Give up this stubbornness.
        Listen to him and learn.
    To be wise and wrong is a shameful thing.

PROMÊTHEUS: *(Chants.)*
    I knew!
    Knew it before he
    bellowed out his advice!
    Knew what he'd say!
    This is war!
    Where's the shame
    when an enemy's hurt
    by an enemy?

Now let it come,
let it come now,
now!
Now let forked lightning-fire
swirl down and strike me,
and thunders rattle and
shake the skies, and hurricanoes
tear up Earth by its
roots!
Now let seas surge and moan
their turmoil and rise and overwhelm
the stars in their wanderings,
and lift me,
lift me high, and toss me
down, down to the depths of
dark Tartaros, to the harsh and swirling
whirlpool of Necessity!
Do what he likes,
he can never kill me!

HERMÊS: *(Chants.)*
These are the ramblings and
fantasies of lunatics!
Every word he
trumpets is insane!

You! You girls who
sympathize with him!
Leave here now or be
shocked into madness
by the thunder's
roar!

FIRST DAUGHTER OF OCEANOS: *(Chants.)*
Try other words.
These words are foul.
Give us advice we'll listen to.
Your words are shameless.
How dare you tell me to be a

coward?
I'll suffer with him,
I'll be at his side,
no matter what comes.
I've learned hate,
hate for traitors.
There is no more filthy
disease that I can spit at you!

HERMÊS: *(Chants.)*
Remember this!
And don't say when
doom comes searching you out that I
didn't warn you, that Zeus
cast you into calamity you
could not foresee!
No!
No, it's you,
you yourselves who'll have done it—you in your
stupidity who'll have brought this on yourselves!
You saw, and you
knew, and yet you jumped
headlong into the
boundless, inescapable
net of disaster!

(HERMÊS disappears. Thunder. Wind. Storm.)

PROMÊTHEUS: *(Chants.)*
no more words
deeds

IT IS!

earth staggers and writhes in agony
thunder bellows from the hollow deeps resounding
lightning's fiery tendrils flash and coil
winds whirl and dust in columns
dance a deadly dance on the wide world

sky and sea are one
all this is Zeus
Zeus this terror
Zeus this storm
down down on me this storm of Zeus

(Exeunt screaming in terror the DAUGHTERS OF OCEANOS.)

PROMÊTHEUS: *(Chants.)*

O MOTHER EARTH
my
MOTHER
and SKY
great SKY
whose glorious eye
sees all and
lights our way
behold me now
see how unjust
my

suffering

(Pandemonium. The mountain collapses.)

GLOSSARY

ACHAIANS: another name for the Greeks.

ACHERON: river in the underworld.

ACHILLEUS: one of the central heroes of Greek myth; son of King Peleus and the nereid Thetis; father of Neoptolemos; commander of the Myrmidons on the side of the Greeks.

ADRASTOS: king of Argos in *Seven Against Thebes,* and leader of the Argive army.

AETNA: volcano in northeast Sicily.

AGBATANA: the capital of Media; summer home of the Persian kings.

AGENOR: descendent of Io in the third generation; father of Kadmos, who founded Thebes.

AIAS: one of the strongest and bravest of the Greek warriors at Troy; killed himself when not awarded the armor of Achilleus; son of Telemon; known as Telemonian or Greater Aias; commander of the Greek forces from Salamis.

AIGYPTOS: eponymous king of Aigyptos (modern Egypt); twin brother to Danaös.

AITHIOPIA: territory south of Egypt.

AKTAION: Theban prince turned by Artemis into a stag when he boasted he could hunt better than she; savaged and torn apart by his own dogs on Mount Kithairon near Delphi.

AKTOR: a defender of Thebes.

AMAZONS: tribe of female warriors; they were known to cut off one breast to facilitate their aim as archers.

AMPHIARAÖS: one of the Seven against Thebes; also a prophet.

AMPHION: Theban ruler who is said to have built the walls of Thebes by leading the stones to their proper place with the music of his lyre; husband of Niobê; took his life after the death of all their children.

ANCIENT EARTH: Pelasgos' father; sprung from the earth; first human being to live in Argos; means, literally, ancient land

ANDROS: island in the Aegean Sea.

ANTIGONÊ: daughter of Oedipus and Iokastê; sister to Ismenê, Polyneikês and Eteoklês; niece to Kreon.

APHRODITÊ: goddess of love, beauty and fertility; wife of Hephaistos; said to have been born out of the seafoam; also known as Kypris after the island that was the seat of her cult.

APIS: son of Apollo; a healer.

APOLLO: born on Delos; one of the twelve Olympian gods; symbol of light, youth, beauty; synonymous with music, poetry, medicine, and prophecy; his temple of oracular prophecy at Delphi in central Greece was the most famous in the ancient world; twin brother of Artemis; archer known for his unfailing aim.

ARABIA: believed by Greeks to lie in the area now known as Saudi Arabia; in the text, though, Aeschylus places some Arabians in the region of the Kaukasos.

ARÊS: god of war unpopular among the Greeks; son of Zeus and Hera; lover of Aphroditê and probably father of Eros.

ARGOS: ancient city in southeastern Greece in the northeastern Peloponnesos; in general terms mainland Greece.

ARIOMARDOS: governor of Egyptian Thebes in Aeschylus.

ARSAMÊS: a son of Dareios; ruler of Memphis.

ARTEMIS: daughter of Zeus and Hera; twin sister of Apollo born on the island of Delos; virgin huntress associated with wild places and animals; primitive birth goddess; known as an archer.

ASOPOS: river in Boiotia.

ASTAKOS: father of Melanippos.

ATÊ: the goddess personifying criminal folly or reckless ambition in man, bringing on him punishment by Nemesis.

ATHÊNA: daughter of Zeus who sprang fully armed from his head; goddess of wisdom, skills, and warfare; chief defender of the Greeks at Troy; particular defender of Odysseus; in competition with Poseidon, who produced the horse, she won the favor of the Greeks by producing the olive tree, considered the more valuable, for which she was made patron of Athens, her namesake.

ATLAS: Titan and brother of Promêtheus; condemned by Zeus to support the weight of the heavens on his shoulders for his participation in the war between the Titans and the Olympian gods.

ATOSSA: powerful and influential queen mother of Persia; wife of Dareios and mother of Xerxês.

AXIOS: river in Makedonia that flows into the Aegean Sea.

BAAL: descendant of Io in the third generation; brother of Agenor.

BABYLON: principal city of Mesopotamia; third capital of Persia after its conquest by Kyros in 538 B.C.E.

BAKTRIA: Persian territory east of the Caspian Sea.

BÊLOS: son of Libyê and Poseidon; father of Aigyptos and Danaös.

BEREKYNTHIA: area of Phrygia ruled by Tantalos.

BOIOTIA: province of east central Greece northwest of Attica; dominated by Thebes.

BOLBE: lake in Makedonia.

BOREAS: the North Wind.

BOSPOROS: the strait between the Sea of Marmara and the Black Sea.

CHALKIS: chief city of the island of Euboia.

CHALYBES: an eastern tribe associated by the Greeks with being the first to forge iron.

CHIOS: large Aegean island off the coast of Lydia.

CHRYSA: coastal city near Troy.

CURSES: personified prayers for justice.

CYRUS: founder of the Persian Empire.

DANAË: daughter of Acrisios, king of Argos; locked in a bronze tower by her father upon learning that a male child of hers would kill him; Zeus visits her in the tower as a rain of gold, which gives birth to Perseus who accidentally kills Acrisios while throwing a discus.

DANAÖS: twin brother to Aigyptos; ruler of Libye who fled with his fifty daughters to Argos.

DAREIOS: king of Persia; husband of Atossa; father of Xerxês; brought Persia to the climax of its empire.

DELPHI: Greek city on the southern slopes of Mount Parnassos; site of the most famous oracle of Apollo.

DÊMÊTER: goddess of agricultural fertility; protector of marriage and women; sister of Zeus; mother of Persephonê.

DIKÊ: personification of natural order and the laws that govern it.

DIONYSOS: god of divine inspiration and the release of mass emotion; associated with wine, fruitfulness, and vegetation; son of Zeus and Semelê; leader of the Bakkhai; bestower of ecstasy; worshipped in a cult centered around orgiastic rites and veiled in great mystery; also known as Iakkhos and Bakkhos.

DIRKÊ: river near Thebes.

DODONA: Greek town in Epiros in northwestern Greece; site of an ancient sanctuary and oracle of Zeus.

DORIS: small, mountainous area in northwest Greece.

EARTH: the wife of Ouranos, also known as Sky, who together first ruled the universe; in Aeschylus, the mother of Promêtheus; also identified with the goddess Themis.

EPAPHOS: son of Zeus and Io; founder of Egypt's royal line; his name means "touch," from the touch Io received from Zeus, thus impregnating her with Epaphos.

ERASINOS: river on the Argive plain.

ETEOKLÊS: son of Oedipus and Iokastê; brother of Antigonê and Ismenê; killed his brother Polyneikês in a battle at Thebes over right to the Theban throne; killed by Polyneikês in the same encounter.

ETEOKLOS: one of the seven against Thebes.

EUBOIA: island in the western Aegean Sea; second largest island in the Greek archipelago.

FATES: three who control the destinies of humans.

FURIES: snake-haired goddesses of vengeance; usually three in number, named Alekto, Tisiphone, and Megera.

GERYON: a three-bodied giant from the island of Erythia in the far west of the ancient world; in late legend Spain.

GLAUKOS: a fisherman from Boiotia who ate a magic grass that turned him into a sea-god who foretold the future.

GORGONIAN PLAINS: a geographical coinage of Aeschylus; he situates them in the Far East.

GORGONS: three snake-haired sisters, monsters who live in the Far East; daughters of Phorkys and Keto; of the three Medusa is the best known.

GRIFFINS: winged beasts with an eagle's beak, otherwise like lions.

GULF OF MÊLIA: an inlet at the border between Greece and Thessaly.

HADES: underworld abode of the souls of the dead; lord of the kingdom bearing his name; also known as Pluto; son of Kronos and Rhea; brother of Zeus, Dêmêter and Poseidon; husband of Persephonê.

HALYS: the main river of Asia Minor, emptying into the Black Sea

HARMONIA: daughter of Arês and Aphroditê; wife of Kadmos.

HEKATE: a primitive goddess of the underworld later associated with Artemis; connected with sorcery and black magic.

HÊKTOR: eldest son of King Priam of Troy; supreme commander of Troy's forces in the Trojan War; killed by Achilleus.

HELEN: daughter of Zeus and Lêda; half-sister of Klytaimnêstra; wife of Menelaos whose defection to Troy caused the Trojan War.

HELLAS: classical Greek name for Greece.

HELLESPONT: strait connecting the Sea of Marmara with the Aegean Sea; boundary between Europe and Asia.

HÊPHAISTOS: god of fire; son of Zeus and Hera; husband of Aphroditê.

HERA: goddess; daughter of Kronos and Rhea; sister and wife of Zeus; associated with women and marriage.

HERAKLÊS: son of Zeus and Alkmênê; of outstanding strength, size, and courage; known for the performance of twelve immense labors imposed upon him.

HERMÊS: god; son of Zeus and Maia; messenger and herald of the gods; associated with commerce, cunning, theft, travelers, and rascals.

HESPERIDES: nymphs who guarded a garden of golden apples in the Far West in the vicinity of Atlas.

HIPPOMEDON: one of the seven against Thebes.

HYPERBIOS: brother of Aktor; one of the seven against Thebes.

IDA: mountain in Phrygia, near to Troy.

IKARIA: island in the Aegean Sea,

INACHOS: an Argive and father of Io; gave his name to the main Argive river.

IO: daughter of Inachos and founder of the first royal house of Argos. Zeus' desire for her caused Hera to turn her into a cow.

IONIA: west coast of Asia Minor and neighboring islands; an early Greek colony.

IONIAN SEA: the expanse of sea between Greece and Sicily; in Aeschylus, the entire Adriatic.

ISMENÊ: daughter of Oedipus and Iokastê; sister of Antigonê, Polyncikês, and Eteoklês.

ISMÊNOS: 1) river near Thebes; 2) worshipped as a son of Apollo by a Theban cult in a temple southeast of Thebes.

ISTHMIAN GAMES: one of the four major panhellenic festivals held every second and fourth years in Korinth.

KADMOS: son of King Agenor who killed a dragon, planted its teeth, from which sprang a host of warriors who fought each other until only five remained, who joined Kadmos in founding Thebes.

KANOBOS: city east of Alexandria on the coast of Egypt.

KAPANEUS: one of the seven against Thebes.

KARIA: territory in southwestern Asia Minor.

KAUKASOS: mountain range east of the Black Sea where Aeschylus places Promêtheus' punishment.

KERCHNE: a village in the vicinity of Argos.

KILIKIA: on the southwest coast of Asia Minor.

KISSIA: a district of central Persia in which Susa is located; Aeschylus thinks of it as a separate walled city.

KNIDOS: an island-port linked to Karia by a causeway.

KOKYTOS: river in the underworld; its name means wailing.

KOLCHIS: land of the Amazons in Aeschylus; north of the Black Sea.

KRONOS: Titan; son of Ouranos and Gaia; father of Zeus who dethroned him.

KYPRIS: goddess of love, beauty, and fertility; wife of Hêphaistos and lover of Arês; said to have been born out of the seafoam; also known as Aphroditê.

KYPROS: island off the southern coast of Asia Minor.

LAÏOS: king of Thebes; father of Oedipus; husband of Iokastê; failed to keep the terms of Apollo's oracle that he should not have children, leading to the final destruction of the royal house in the deaths of Eteoklês and Polyneikês.

LASTHENES: one of the seven defenders of Thebes.

LEMNOS: island in the northeastern Aegean Sea; famous for its medicinal earth; place of Philoktêtês' exile.

LESBOS: large Aegean island off the coast of Asia Minor.

LETO: mother of Apollo and Artemis.

LIBYA: granddaughter of Zeus and Hera; the mother of Agenor and Baal by Poseidon.

LIBYÊ: daughter of Epaphos, son of Zeus and Io.

LOXIAS: a cult title of Apollo; possibly as one who speaks riddles, indirectly, through his oracle.

LYDIA: region on the coast of western Asia Minor.

MAIOTIS: a lake north of the Black Sea.

MAKEDONIA: area north of Greece where the rivers Lydia, Axios, and Strymon flow into the Aegean.

MARATHON: plain on the east coast of Attica where Dareios was defeated by the Athenians in 490 B.C.E.

MARDOS: usurper of the Persian throne between the reigns of Kambyses and Dareios.

MARIANDYNIAN: pertaining to the tribe of Mariandynoi on the northern coast of Asia Minor; known for their funeral dirges.

MEDES: a kingdom north of Persis, which after incorporation into the Persian Empire, was synonymous with the term *Persians.*

MEGABATES: cousin of Dareios.

MEGAREUS: one of the seven defenders of Thebes; a son of Kreon; a descendant of the Sown Men.

MELANIPPOS: one of the seven defenders of Thebes.

MEMPHIS: a major ancient Egyptian city on the west bank of the Nile.

MENELAOS: son of Atreus; king of Sparta; husband of Helen; brother of Agamemnon.

MESSAPION: mountain on the Boiotian coast, opposite Euboia.

METIS: usually Proknê; named so in *Suppliants;* kills her son Itys to revenge her husband Tereus for the rape of her sister Philomela; became a nightingale to escape pursuit by Tereus; her nightingale's song is her lament for Itys.

MINOS: king of Krete; son of Zeus and Europa; in death he became a judge in Hades.

MYKONOS: a central island in the Aegean Sea.

MYRMIDONS: inhabitants of Phythia ruled by Achilleus.

MYSIA: northwestern corner of Asia Minor.

NAUPAKTOS: a small town in Lokris.

NAXOS: a central island in the Aegean Sea.

NEMESIS: goddess of anger and divine retribution.

NIOBÊ: queen of Phrygia whose six sons and six daughters (in some versions seven) were killed by the gods Apollo and Artemis because she boasted they were more beautiful than the two gods.

OCEANOS: Titan; lord of the waters that surround the continents.

ODYSSEUS: son of Laërtês; father of Telemachos; leader of the Ithicans at Troy.

OEDIPUS: son of Laïos; son and husband of Iokastê; father and brother of

Antigonê, Ismenê, Polyneikês, and Eteoklês; rid Thebes of the Sphinx and unknowingly married his mother.

OIKLEOS: father of Amphiaraös.

OINOPS: father of Hippomedon and Aktor.

OÏTA: mountain in southern Thessaly.

OLYMPOS: mountain in northeastern Thessaly; seat of the Olympian gods.

OURANOS: first of the gods; name means sky or heaven.

PALLAS: name for Athêna; of unknown origin.

PAN: Arkadian god; son of Hermês; a man with goat's legs, horns, and ears; god of fields, woods, shepherds, and flocks.

PAPHOS: two towns, old and new, on the west coast of Kypros.

PARIS: son of Priam and Hêkabê; also called Alexander; his abduction of Helen began the Trojan War.

PAROS: an Aegean island.

PARTHENOPAIOS: means maiden-faced; son of Atalanta.

PELASGOS: son of Palaichthon; king of Argos in *Suppliants*.

PERRHAIBOI: inhabitants of the region to the west of Mount Pindos and in the vicinity of Dodona.

PERSEUS: son of Danaë by Zeus; killed the Gorgon, Medusa.

PHASIS: river flowing into the eastern end of the Black Sea, near Korinth.

PHILOKTÊTÊS: hero in the Trojan War in which he killed Paris with the bow and arrows given him by Heraklês; exiled from the Greek encampment at Troy and marooned on the island of Lemnos because of a noxious and festering snake-bite wound on his leg; returned to Troy by Odysseus when it was learned that without the magic arrows given him by Heraklês Troy could not be taken.

PHOIBOS: cult title of Apollo; means bright.

PHOKIS: territory in northern Greece, northwest of Boiotia.

PHRYGIA: region in northwestern Asia Minor near Troy.

PINDOS: mountain range in northwestern Greece.

POLYNEIKÊS: son of Oedipus and Iokastê; brother of Antigonê, Ismenê, and Eteoklês; invaded Thebes at its seven gates to wrest the throne from his brother Eteoklês.

POLYPHONTES: one of the seven defenders of Thebes.

POSEIDON: god of the sea; son of Kronos and Rhea; brother of Zeus.

PRIAM: king of Troy.

PROMÊTHEUS: Titan; helped the human race by the gift of fire that he stole from the gods; his name means "forethought."

RHADAMANTHOS: son of Zeus and Europa; fled Krete in fear of his brother Minos; known for his justice and became a judge in the underworld.

RHEA: daughter of Ouranos and Gaia; wife of Kronos; mother of Zeus and other gods.

RHODOS: large island in the southeastern Aegean Sea.

SALAMIS: Greek island in the Saronic Gulf off the coast of Athens; home of the Greater Aias.

SALMYDESSOS: city on the southwest coat of the Black Sea, west of the Bosporos.

SAMOS: island off the coast of Ionia.

SARDIS: capital of Lydia.

SILÊNOS: father of the satyrs; tutor of Dionysos; inspired prophet.

SKY: see OURANOS above.

SKYTHIA: a large country of unknown limits; generally speaking European Russia.

SOLOI: town on the island of Kypros.

SOWN MEN: also known as Spartoi; ancestors of the Thebans; sprung from the earth from dragon's teeth.

SPARTA: principal city of the Peloponnesos; a powerful military force.

SPERCHEIOS: river in southern Thessaly.

SPHINX: a female-headed monster with the body of a lioness and eagle wings; held Thebes in thrall till Oedipus solved her riddle.

STRYMON: river in northeastern Greece between Makedonia and Thrace.

STYX: main river of the underworld.

SUSA: winter capital of kings of Persia.

TANTALOS: son of Zeus; father of Pelops and Niobê.

TARTAROS: river and territory in the lowest region of the underworld; below Hades; the place where Zeus imprisoned the Titans; a place reserved for evildoers.

TEIRESIAS: blind Theban prophet; called up from the underworld by Odysseus during his wanderings following the Trojan War.

TELAMON: king of Salamis; father of the Greater Aias.

THEBES: main city of Boiotia.

THEMIS: goddess of established law or custom; Right or Tradition; the Titan daughter of Earth whose function is to see that crime is punished; first dispenser of oracles at Delphi.

THESSALY: region of east-central Greece on the Aegean Sea; extensive fertile plain ringed with mountains.

THETIS: sea nymph; wife of Peleus and mother of Achilleus.

THRACE: tribal lands north of the Aegean Sea and the Hellespont.

THRACE: tribal lands north of the Aegean Sea and the Hellespont.

TITANS: children, male and female, of Ouranos and Earth; overthrown by Zeus in the battle of the Titans.

TMOLOS: mountain in Lydia.

TYDEUS: one of the seven against Thebes.

TYPHOS: hundred-headed monster who breathed fire; challenged Zeus after the defeat of the Titans and was blasted by Zeus' thunder; buried beneath Aetna.

XERXÊS: son of Dareios and Atossa; king of Persia after Dareios' death.

ZEUS: king of the Olympian gods; son of Kronos and Rhea; brother and husband of Hera; brother of Poseidon; father of many of the gods and mortals as well; has many epithets arising from his host of functions.

SELECT BIBLIOGRAPHY

Adkins, A. W. H. *Merit and Responsibility: A Study in Greek Values.* Oxford: Oxford University Press, 1960.

Arnott, Peter. *Public and Performance in the Greek Theatre.* London: Routledge, 1989.

Arnott, Peter. *Greek Scenic Conventions in the Fifth Century B.C.* Oxford: Oxford University Press, 1962.

Barker, Ernest. *The Politics of Aristotle.* Oxford: Oxford University Press, 1946.

Bieber, Margarete. *The History of the Greek and Roman Theater.* 2nd ed. Revised. Princeton: Princeton University Press, 1961.

Boesche, Roger. *The Theories of Tyranny from Plato to Arendt.* University Park: The Pennsylvania Press, 1996.

Broadhead, H. D. *Persians.* Cambridge: Cambridge University Press, 1960.

Burkert, Walter. *Greek Religion.* Cambridge: Harvard University Press, 1985.

Buxton, R. G. *Persuasion in Greek Tragedy.* Cambridge: Cambridge University Press, 1982.

Cameron, H. D. *Studies on the Seven against Thebes of Aeschylus.* The Hague, 1971.

Conacher, D. J. *Aeschylus' Prometheus Bound: A Literary Commentary.* Toronto: The University of Toronto Press, 1980.

Else, Gerald F. *The Origin and Early Form of Greek Tragedy.* Martin Classical Lectures, Vol. 20. Cambridge: Harvard University Press, 1965.

Ewans, Michael. *Wagner and Aeschylus: The Ring and the Oresteia.* New York: Cambridge University Press, 1982.

Fergusson, Francis. *The Idea of Theater: A Study of Ten Plays, The Art of Drama in Changing Perspective.* Princeton: Princeton University Press; London: Oxford University Press, 1949.

Finley, M. I. *The Ancient Greeks: An Introduction to Their Life and Thought.* New York: The Viking Press, 1964.

Forrest, W. G. *The Emergence of Greek Democracy.* New York: McGraw-Hill, 1966.

Gagarin, M. *Aeschylean Drama.* Berkeley and Los Angeles: The University of California Press, 1976.

Goldhill, Simon. *Reading Greek Tragedy.* Cambridge: Cambridge University Press, 1986.

Green, J. R. *Theatre in Ancient Greek Society.* London: Routledge, 1994.

Green, J. R. and Handley, E. *Images of the Greek Theatre.* Austin: University of Texas Press, 1995

Griffith, M. *Prometheus Bound.* Cambridge: Cambridge University Press, 1983.

Hall, Edith. *Persians.* Warminster: Aris and Phillips, Ltd., 1996.

Hall, Edith. *Inventing the Barbarian: Greek Self-definition through Tragedy.* Oxford: Oxford University Press, 1989.

Herington, J. C. *Aeschylus.* New Haven: Yale University Press, 1986.

Herington, J. C. *Poetry into Drama: Early Tragedy and the Greek Poetic Tradition.* Berkeley and Los Angeles: The University of California Press, 1985.

Hogan, James C. *Commentary on the Complete Greek Tragedies: Aeschylus.* Chicago: The University of Chicago Press, 1984.

Hornblower, Simon and Spawforth, Antony, eds. *The Oxford Classical Dictionary.* 3rd ed. Oxford: Oxford University Press, 1996.

Hornby, Richard. *Script into Performance.* Austin: University of Texas Press, 1977.

Hutchinson, G. O. *Seven Against Thebes.* Oxford: Oxford University Press, 1985.

Jaeger, Werner. *Paideia: The Ideals of Greek Culture.* New York: Oxford University Press, 1945.

Jones, John. *On Aristotle and Greek Tragedy.* Stanford: Stanford University Press, 1980.

Kitto, H. D. F. *Word and Action: Essays on the Ancient Theater.* Baltimore and London: The Johns Hopkins University Press, 1979.

Kitto, H. D. F. *Form and Meaning in Drama: A Study of Six Greek Plays and of Hamlet.* 2nd ed. London: Methuen, 1964; New York: Barnes and Noble, 1968.

Kitto, H. D. F. *Greek Tragedy: A Literary Study.* 2nd ed. New York: Doubleday, 1964; 3rd ed. London: Methuen, 1966.

Kitto, H. D. F. *Poiesis: Structure and Thought.* Berkeley and Los Angeles: The University of California Press, 1966.

Kott, Jan. *The Eating of the Gods: An Interpretation of Greek Tragedy.* New York: Random House, 1973.

Lattimore, Richmond. *The Story-Patterns in Greek Tragedy.* Ann Arbor: The University of Michigan Press, 1964.

Lattimore, Richmond. *The Poetry of Greek Tragedy.* Baltimore: The Johns Hopkins University Press, 1958.

Ley, G. *A Short Introduction to the Ancient Greek Theater.* Chicago: The University of Chicago Press, 1991.

Lloyd-Jones, Hugh. *The Justice of Zeus.* Sather Gate Lectures, Vol. 41. Berkeley and Los Angeles: The University of California Press, 1971.

Mastronarde, D. *Contact and Disunity: Some Conventions of Speech and Action on the Greek Tragic Stage.* Berkeley and Los Angeles: The University of California Press, 1979.

Michelini, A. M. *Tradition and Dramatic Form in the Persians of Aeschylus.* Leiden: 1982.

Murray, Gilbert. *Aeschylus: The Creator of Tragedy.* Oxford: Oxford University Press, 1940.

Neils, Jenifer. *Goddess and Polis: The Panathenaic Festival in Ancient Athens.* Princeton: Princeton University Press, 1992.

Neuberg, M. *An Aeschylean Universe.* Ann Arbor: The University of Michigan Press, 1981.

Pickard-Cambridge, A. W. *The Dramatic Festivals of Athens,* 2nd edition. Oxford: The Clarendon Press, 1968.

Pickard-Cambridge, A. W. *The Theatre of Dionysus in Athens.* Oxford: The Clarendon Press, 1946.

Podlecki, Anthony J. *The Political Background of Aeschylean Tragedy.* Ann Arbor: The University of Michigan Press, 1966.

Rehm, Rush. *The Greek Tragic Theatre.* London and New York: Routledge, 1992.

Scott, William C. *Musical Design in Aeschylean Theatre.* Hanover: The University Press of New England, 1984.

Seaford, Richard. *Reciprocity and Ritual; Homer and Tragedy in the Developing City State.* Oxford: Oxford University Press, 1994.

Smyth, Herbert Weir. *Aeschylus.* Vol. 1. Cambridge: Harvard University Press, 1988.

Steiner, George. *The Death of Tragedy.* New York: Alfred A. Knopf; London: Faber and Faber, 1961.

Taplin, Oliver. *Greek Tragedy in Action.* Berkeley and Los Angeles: The University of California Press; London: Methuen, 1978.

Taplin, Oliver. *The Stagecraft of Aeschylus.* Oxford: The Clarendon Press, 1977.

Thalmann, W. *Dramatic Art in Aeschylus' Seven against Thebes.* New Haven: Yale University Press, 1978.

Vernant, Jean-Pierre. *Myth and Society in Ancient Greece.* New York: Zone Books, 1990.

Vernant, Jean-Pierre and Vidal-Naquet, Pierre, eds. *Myth and Tragedy in Ancient Greece.* New York: Zone Books, 1990.

Vickers, Brian. *Towards Greek Tragedy.* London: Longman, 1973.

Walcot, Peter. *Greek Drama in Its Theatrical and Social Context.* Cardiff: The University of Wales Press, 1976.

Walton, J. Michael. *The Greek Sense of Theatre: Tragedy Reviewed.* London and New York: Methuen, 1984.

Walton, J. Michael. *Greek Theatre Practice.* Westport and London: Greenwood Press, 1980.

Wiles, David. *Tragedy in Athens.* Cambridge and New York: Cambridge University Press, 1997.

Winkler, John, and Zeitlin, Froma I., eds. *Nothing to Do with Dionysus.* Princeton: Princeton University Press, 1990.

Winnington-Ingram, R. P. *Studies in Aeschylus.* Cambridge: Cambridge University Press, 1983.

CARL R. MUELLER has since 1967 been professor in the Department of Theater at the University of California, Los Angeles, where he has taught theater history, criticism, dramatic literature, and playwriting, as well as having directed. He was educated at Northwestern University, where he received a B.S. in English. After work in graduate English at the University of California, Berkeley, he received his M.A. in Playwriting at UCLA, where he also completed his Ph.D. in Theater History and Criticism. In addition, he was a Fulbright Scholar in Berlin in 1960–61. A translator for more than forty years, he has translated and published works by Büchner, Brecht, Wedekind, Hauptmann, Hofmannsthal, and Hebbel, to name a few. His recently published translation of von Horváth's *Tales from the Vienna Woods* was given its London West End premiere in July, 1999. For Smith and Kraus he has published volumes of plays by Wedekind, Schnitzler, Strindberg, Pirandello, Kleist; and he has also co-translated the complete plays of Sophokles. Forthcoming are a translation of Goethe's *Faust* and the complete plays of Euripides. His translations have been performed in every English-speaking country and have appeared on BBC-TV.

HUGH DENARD lectures in Theatre Studies at the University of Warwick (UK). He has published articles on ancient drama and its reception and on the use of Virtual Reality in studying places of performance. He is Editor of Didaskalia: www.didaskalia.net. Currently he is working on a co-authored book on Roman wall paintings and Roman theater for Yale University Press with Richard Beacham (Warwick). He is also co-director of major research grants from the Leverhulme Foundation and the Joint Information Systems Committee (UK). His theater work includes a devised production called *Dionysos,* co-directed with Carl Mueller in August 2000 at the Warwick Arts Centre, and he is Resident Director for Two Hats Theatre Company.